SEA EAGLES
OF EMPIRE

About the Author

Dr Simon Elliott is an award-winning and best-selling histo-rian, archaeologist and broadcaster. He has published fifteen books to date on themes related to the classical world, is widely published in the historical and archaeological media, and frequently appears as a presenter and expert on broad-cast media around the world. He is a trustee of the Council for British Archaeology, ambassador for Museum of London Archaeology, guide lecturer for Andante Travels and Hidden History Travel, and president of the Society of Ancients. Simon is also a PRWeek Award-winning, highly experienced com-munications practitioner who began his career as a defence journalist.

Also by Simon Elliott

Alexander the Great vs Julius Caesar: Who Was the Greatest Commander in the Ancient World
Ancient Greeks at War
Empire State: How the Roman Military Built an Empire
Julius Caesar: Rome Greatest Warlord
Old Testament Warriors
Pertinax: The Son of a Slave Who Became Roman Emperor
Ragstone to Riches
Roman Britain's Lost Legion: Whatever Happened to legio IX Hispana
Roman Britain's Pirate King
Roman Conquests: Britain
Roman Legionaries
Romans at War
Septimius Severus in Scotland

SEA EAGLES
OF EMPIRE

THE CLASSIS BRITANNICA
AND THE BATTLES
FOR BRITAIN

SIMON ELLIOTT

FOREWORD BY ANDREW LAMBERT

To my mum and dad for encouraging a love of all things Roman, and to Sara, Alex and Lizzie for their love and patience!

Front cover illustrations: Simon Elliott, Martin Latham and iStockphoto.

First published 2016
This paperback edition first published 2022

The History Press
97 St George's Place, Cheltenham,
Gloucestershire, GL50 3QB
www.thehistorypress.co.uk

British Library Cataloguing in Publication Data.
A catalogue record for this book is available from the British Library.

ISBN 978 1 80399 158 0

Typesetting and origination by The History Press
Printed and bound in Great Britain by TJ Books Limited, Padstow, Cornwall.

Trees for L♀fe

CONTENTS

FOREWORD

For Imperial Rome, the greatest empire of them all, the sea was an essential connecting medium. The grain supply from Egypt and North Africa, the strategic mobility that enabled the legions to deploy quickly to meet new threats and the trade that funded the Universal Monarchy of the Ancient Mediterranean all depended on sea communications. And yet the Romans remained profoundly Continental by culture, so fearful of the sea crossing to Britain that they needed religious sites at both ends of the short passage. Their navies reflected this reality.

Rome won much of the empire with powerful naval forces, focused on combat and control, using great fleets of polyremes to demolish the rival maritime empires of Carthage and the Hellenistic world. Then the Romans abandoned their fleet and left the seas to traders and pirates. A brief resurgence of naval warfare culminating in the decisive victory at Actium saw the establishment of standing fleets, reconfigured for support roles, small cruisers and transports replacing specialised battle galleys. Imperial Roman sea power was responsive, and reflected a Continental world view: naval forces would move, support and sustain the legions, develop large-scale economic activities and secure trade routes.

As the outermost element in Roman power, the force that circumnavigated the British Isles, and helped pacify the Highlands, the *Classis Britannica*, has long stood in need of a dedicated history. In this book Simon Elliott provides the essential combination of ancient scholarship, archaeology and sea power theory to recover and interpret the First British Navy – extending the reach of Roman power and the antiquity of British maritime exceptionalism.

Andrew Lambert
Laughton Professor of Naval History and War Studies
King's College London
2016

INTRODUCTION

The Roman war machine comprised both land and naval forces. In the case of the former one can look to the well-known and famous legions and their auxiliaries, and later in the Empire *comitatenses*, *palatina*, *limitanei* and *foederates*. Much less understood though are the naval forces, particularly the regional navies that participated actively in most military operations and policed the seas and rivers for much of the history of the Empire. Until the middle of the third century, in a British context this navy was the *Classis Britannica*, a fighting force in its own right. This book will tell the story of this illustrious naval force in their iron- and bronze-beaked galleys and laden transport ships, and specifically detail their exploits in defeating the Emperor's enemies while keeping his peace around the islands of Britain.

A reasonable question to ask would be, 'Why is it relevant now to write a history of Britain's first navy?' The answer lies not with classical but with modern history. For the first time in two generations naval power is coming to the fore again in the context of the overall capability of the UK armed forces. After 'boots on the ground' deployments in both Iraq and Afghanistan in the 1990s and 2000s, which ultimately lacked public support (though not to the detriment of support for the armed forces), and in an increasingly uncertain world geopolitically, priorities in regard to the UK's defence and foreign policy have turned full circle. Now, instead of deploying the British Army in major operations abroad, attention is focusing again on the Royal Navy and RAF as the means of executing expeditionary foreign policy. To my mind it is the former that is set to benefit most from this new level of attention, with two new aircraft carriers set to enter service in the next few years, a new fleet of frigates in the same time scale, and a new generation of nuclear-powered submarines to carry the nuclear deterrent on the cards. In short, naval power and thus naval history in the UK are back in vogue, and in that context it seems only right to look at the beginnings of naval power in the islands of Britain.

A second and equally valid question might be, 'Why is there a need for a new appreciation of the *Classis Britannica*?' In the first instance, while there is a plethora of excellent works on the market aimed at both academic and popular audiences regarding Roman military power, such works tend to be dominated by a focus on land-based warfare. Sitting here in my office researching and writing this work surrounded by piles of such publications, I know this first hand! There are, of course, some excellent works on Roman naval military capability, both old and new. Further, in some of the general works on the Roman military, naval warfare is well referenced, though usually as an addition to the much wider appreciation of land forces and with a focus on maritime conflict in the later Republic. Yet even within this limited canon regarding Roman naval power, after extensive research I have yet to find a work specifically focusing on the *Classis Britannica*. I hope that this book addresses this omission!

With this work I have decided to take a different approach to the usual narrative history format for books of this type, playing to the strengths of my own background. These include being the former naval writer at *Jane's Defence Weekly* having a Masters degree in war studies from King's College London (KCL, where I studied British naval history under Professor Andrew Lambert, and where my dissertation was on post-war British naval power), having a Masters degree in archaeology from the Institute of Archaeology at University College London (UCL, where my dissertation looked at the role of the *Classis Britannica* in occupied Britain), and now with my PhD at the University of Kent where, again, the *Classis Britannica* is a major part of my research. This background has allowed me to review the *Classis Britannica* not just through the eyes of a historian, but also from the perspective of the application of naval power (both in the past and now).

Therefore the flow of this work will feature a background section (examining among other things the various issues that had an impact on the maritime activities of the *Classis Britannica* around Britain), a review of Roman naval power (including an appreciation of Roman naval activity to the advent of the Principate, an examination of Roman naval technology and a look at the manpower aspects of the Roman navy), an analysis of the Roman military presence in Britain within which the *Classis Britannica* sat, a review of the military roles of the *Classis Britannica* (through the prism of the modern academic appreciation of naval power), a similar review of the civilian roles of the *Classis Britannica*, then three chronologically sequential chapters looking at the early, mid- and late history of this key regional fleet (broadly fitting into the first, second and third centuries AD), they being followed by a discussion of the potential reasons for the end of the *Classis Britannica* and what followed. The book then finishes with a conclusion reviewing in context the high points of the *Classis Britannica*'s existence, a chronological timeline covering the major events in occupied Britain and finally a detailed list of references (the latter incorporating the bibliography).

My interpretation of the story of the *Classis Britannica* set out in this book is based as far as possible on hard data. In the first instance this means the archaeological record that has provided a great deal of insight into the narrative of Britain's first fleet. Next I have used the historical record to best advantage, including epigraphy from the time of the Roman occupation and wherever possible primary sources, the latter to make my own interpretations on the events of 1,800 years ago (and noting that where the sources used are ambiguous or contradictory I have used common sense to determine what I believe to be the truth). Other data has also been derived from scientific observation, and finally here I have also made extensive use of analogy. To add to these various kinds of data I have also used, where appropriate, anecdote.

In terms of classical and modern names I have been pragmatic in the narrative to ensure that the work is as accessible as possible for the reader. By way of example, where there is a classical version of a modern name for a given city I have used the current name, referencing the occupation-period name at the point of its first use. However, with common and well-understood classical names for a given role, for example *legate* (general), I use that throughout the work, providing the modern name in brackets at the first point of use as illustrated here.

Where the term province is mentioned in the text, until the Severan-Caracallan reforms of Britain in AD 211–212 (originally planned in AD 197) this references the original single province of *Britannia*. After the reforms it references either *Britannia Superior* or *Britannia Inferior* dependent on the context (for example in the case of the *Classis Britannica* the former, see Chapter 8 for discussion, and in the case of the northern frontier the latter), or indeed where appropriate both. Following the Diocletianic reformation and the establishment of the *diocese* with its four and perhaps later five provinces (see Chapter 9 for detail), given the complexity the full name of a given province is detailed for clarity.

In terms of the military activities of the *Classis Britannica* I have deliberately stripped down my description of the various marine environments in which such activity would have taken place into two, namely the oceanic zone (for blue water naval activity) and the littoral zone (for littoral military combat activity along the coast). There are a number of definitions available for both, particularly the latter, but I have decided yet again to ensure that this work is as accessible as possible to the general reader (while retaining enough specific detail for the specialist). The same goes for all other technical terms – where the option has been available to simplify things, I have done so with the reader in mind.

Finally, I would like to thank all those who have made this work possible. Firstly, Professor Andrew Lambert of the War Studies Department at KCL for his constant encouragement. Secondly, Dr Andrew Gardner at UCL's Institute of Archaeology for his similar support. Thirdly, Dr Steve Willis at the University of Kent for his guidance regarding my PhD, which features the *Classis Britannica* so significantly. And, of course, my publisher Chrissy McMorris of The History Press for believing in this work. Others also deserve a specific thank you, for example Dr Paul Wilkinson of the Kent Archaeological Field School, Dr Gustav Milne at UCL, Jeremy Hodgkinson of the Wealden Iron Working Group, Sam Moorhead at the British Museum, Dr Ian Betts at Museum of London Archaeology, Meriel Jeater at the Museum of London, Professor Sir Barry Cunliffe of the School of Archaeology at Oxford University, Professor Martin Millett at the Faculty of Classics, Cambridge University, Ray Chitty of the Medway River Users Association, and lastly here my patient proof reader and lovely wife. All have contributed freely and greatly to my wider research, enabling this work on the *Classis Britannica* to reach fruition. Finally, of course, I would like to thank my family, in the first instance my mum and dad, Eileen and John Elliott, for instilling a love of all things Roman at an early age, and last but not least my always supportive and tolerant wife, Sara (again!) and children, Alex and Lizzie. Thank you all.

Simon Elliott,
August 2016

Land Campaigns Supported by the Sea Eagles

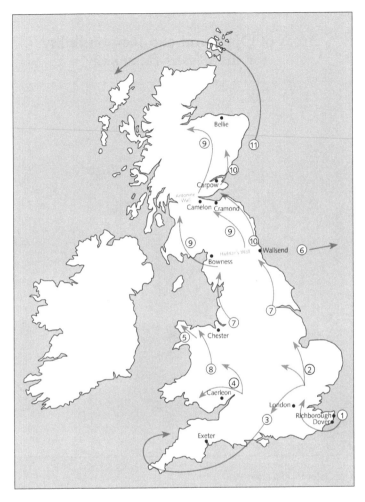

① The Claudian Invasion, AD 43

② The Claudian Breakout, AD 44–47

③ Campaigns of Vespasian, AD 44–47

④ Campaigns of Scapula and Gallus, AD 47–57

⑤ Campaigns of Paullinus, AD 60

⑥ *Classis Britannica* transports troops to help suppress Batavian Revolt in Germany, AD 70

⑦ Campaigns of Cerialis, AD 71–74

⑧ Campaigns of Frontinus, AD 75–77

⑨ Campaigns of Agricola, AD 78–84

⑩ Campaigns of Septimius Severus AD 209–211

⑪ Circumnavigation of Britain by Agricola

Areas of Operation and Responsibility for the *Classis Britannica*

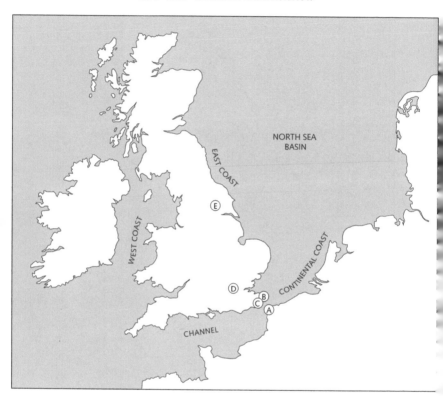

(A) Boulogne, Fleet Headquarters

(B) Richborough

(C) Dover

(D) London

(E) York

1

BACKGROUND

The *Classis Britannica* officially came into being in the Flavian period towards the end of the first century AD, being first mentioned by Tacitus in the context of the Batavian uprising in Germania Inferior in AD 70 (*Histories*, 4, 79, 3), though the fleet owes its origins to the Claudian invasion of AD 43. It is therefore firmly rooted in the Imperial period of Roman history and, given it is last referenced between AD 244 and AD 249, in the Principate originally established by Augustus.

A major fighting force in its own right, and also a resource used by the province for many other purposes, the *Classis Britannica* acts as a unique cypher to enable us to view the Roman experience in Britain and elsewhere on multiple levels. In the first instance it was one of the major regional fleets of the Principate, fulfilling a wide variety of military roles around the islands of Britain and along the North Sea Continental coast. It therefore played a major part in all of the great campaigns in Britain through to the mid-third century, while patrolling the littoral around the province and at the same time securing the eastern coastal flank of the *limes Germanicus*. Thus we can see from the primary sources a Roman fleet (pre-eminent among the regional fleets according to Pitassi in his wide review of Roman naval power, 2012, 50) in action on the open ocean and in the littoral zone, providing insight that is relevant to research not just for occupied Britain but for Roman naval activity across the Empire.

Through these campaigns and the fleet's regular intelligence gathering and patrolling activities we also get insight into the nature of the province of Britain, the wild west of the Empire with its northern and western borders ever a militarised border zone.

Throughout Britain's incorporation in the Roman Empire the province had an existentially large military presence. Because of this, and also because it was farthest geographically from Rome in the western part of the Empire, the province was a regular hotbed for usurpations and revolts. In these the *Classis Britannica* played a major role, again providing insight for the historian and archaeologist, though this involvement may ultimately have cost the fleet its existence.

Finally, in an age before the advent of the modern civil service, state-owned industries or a free market able to facilitate major capital infrastructure projects, those running a Roman province would have used any asset available to provide administration, transport, construction and engineering services, and to run the Imperial estates through which the major industrial enterprises were managed. In Britain, through to its demise, this asset was the *Classis Britannica*. The regional navy was therefore the very lifeblood by which the province maintained its existence. All of these themes above are discussed in depth in the following work.

This first chapter of our investigation into the British regional fleet is designed to provide all of the background information needed to appreciate the in-depth review of the *Classis Britannica* that follows. In the first instance I appraise

how Britain was perceived in the classical world, before looking more specifically at Britain's place in the Roman Empire.
I then detail specifically the sources of the data used in my
research, before finally looking at some of the practicalities
that had an impact on those carrying out maritime activities
around the islands of Britain and along the north-western
Continental coast during the Roman period. These include
tidal and weather patterns at the time, the differential in sea
level compared to today, and a review of some of the models
available to help us understand maritime activity around the
islands of Britain during the occupation.

Britain in the Classical World

Even before its separation from the Eurasian landmass around
6,100 BC, Britain's maritime context was shaping its destiny. Prior
to this date it was a promontory stabbing out into the Atlantic at
the north-western tip of Europe, and ever since its island nature
has shaped its relationship with the rest of the Continent.

Britain was well known prior to the Roman occupation,
though as a place of mystery at the very edge of the known
world. The earliest reference to its existence appears in the
sixth century BC *Massaliot Periplus* merchants' handbook, now
lost but referenced in the *Ora Maritime* by fourth-century
Roman poet Avienus. Designed for use by those trading
along the sea routes to northern Europe, this work shows that
even at the earliest dates maritime activity around the islands
of Britain was a key focus of regional attention. The original
sixth-century work is also the first to attribute a name for the
inhabitants of Britain, namely the Albiones for the British and
Iverni for the Irish.

Herodotus is the next to reference islands in north-western
Europe in the fifth century BC, he describing the Cassiterides
in his *Histories*. These have often been associated with Britain

given that the name translates as 'tin islands', the metal being a key export from Britain in the prehistoric let alone classical world. More clarity then comes in the form of the fourth-century BC Greek geographer Pytheas. Originating from Marseille (the Greek colony of *Massalia*, also home of the *Massaliot Periplus* detailed above), his definitive work is similarly lost to us, but key sections have been preserved by ancient authors including Strabo, Pliny the Elder and Diodorus.

Pytheas was the first person to record a circumnavigation of Britain during his maritime exploration of north-western Europe, which took in a visit to modern Denmark and seemingly an extraordinary visit to Iceland. His reports on the British Isles set a template for most of what followed in the classical world, highlighting their triangular shape and describing Kent, Land's End in Cornwall and the Orkneys. He also notes for the first time the name from which our current 'Britain' is derived, reporting that the natives were called the Pretani (painted ones, referencing the prevalence of tattooing among the natives he encountered). Both Strabo and Pliny made extensive use of Pytheas in their much later descriptions of Britain, the latter going into an immense amount of detail, for instance describing the forty islands of the Orkneys, the seven of the Shetlands, the thirty of the Hebrides and also describing the island of Anglesey. Pytheas' work is also evident in the physical descriptions of Britain by others, for example Caesar (who of course visited himself twice) and Agrippa.

The definitive classical map of Britain though is derived from Claudius Ptolemy's mid-second-century *Geography*. This extensive gazetteer of the peoples and places of the Empire crucially included latitude and longitude, allowing for the first time a representation of the province to be created that appears vaguely recognisable to modern eyes. By the time his work appeared, however, Britain had been part of the Empire for more than a century, the *Classis Britannica* was in its prime and the islands had long since ceased to be the subject of mystery and awe.

Britain in the Roman Empire

Rome had designs on Britain well before the Claudian invasion in AD 43. Caesar famously made two incursions in 55 BC and 54 BC, though these might best be regarded as armed reconnaissances in the context of his conquest of Gaul (given the assistance provided to his Gallic enemies by some of the tribes of Britain). Augustus himself, founder of the Principate, planned at least three invasions in 34 BC, 27 BC and 25 BC (the first and last cancelled because of issues elsewhere in the ancient world, and the second abandoned after successful diplomacy). These false starts were certainly viewed negatively at the time, with the first century BC poet Horace (*Odes*, III.v) reflecting that, 'Augustus will be deemed a God on Earth when the Britons and the deadly Parthians [also targets for Early Imperial Roman expansion] have been added to our Empire.'

Although Augustus' plans to invade Britain came to naught, naval activity is definitely evident in the North Sea and along the north-western European coast during his reign. For example, in 12 BC his stepson, Drusus, deployed a fleet in the Ems Estuary while campaigning in Germania to subdue the Sicambri, while Drusus' brother, Tiberius, also used naval forces to protect the North Sea flank of his similar campaigning along the German *limes* in AD 5. Drusus' son, Germanicus, also used substantial naval forces while campaigning in Germany in AD 14 and AD 15, including an amphibious operation in the latter campaign to transport several legions.

Next, and bringing the focus back to Britain, in AD 40 Caligula famously abandoned his invasion of Britain from the beaches of northern Gaul (see Chapter 2 for full details), before finally Claudius went ahead with his invasion three years later.

The reality was that, from the moment of Caesar's conquest of Gaul in the mid-first century BC, let alone the first of his two journeys across the English Channel, the proximity of the new superpower had begun to radically change the political, economic and social nature of Late Iron Age (LIA) society in Britain. This was particularly the case in the south and the east, where a case can be made that there was at the very least a Roman mercantile presence prior to Claudius' invasion. Closest to Gaul was Kent (pre-Roman Cantion), populated by the Cantiaci. Kent may well have had a unique place in occupied Britain (discussed in depth in Chapter 4) and many have argued it long had a closer association with northern Gaul than it had with its neighbours in Britain, dating from the Mesolithic through to the early Medieval period (post-Roman burials in the county, for example, have a particularly Frankish feel). These neighbours included the Trinovantes to the north, the Catuvellauni to the north-west and the Atrebates and Regnii to the west.

Spreading out around Britain, one then has the Durotriges and Dumnonii along the south coast heading west, the Belgae, Dubonni and Cornovii heading northwards into the Welsh Marches, the Silures, Demetae, Ordovices and Deceangli ranging south to north in Wales proper, the Brigantes and Carvetti in the north country heading into the Scottish Borders, the Parissi north of the Humber, Caritani south of the Humber and Iceni in modern Norfolk. The impact of the presence of Rome prior to the occupation diminished as one headed north and west, and even after the province came into being and began to flourish this division remained in place, with the dividing line being roughly on a line from the Severn running north-eastwards to the Humber. If you lived south of that line during the occupation you were in a fully functioning part of the Empire, with all the economic benefits that this entailed. Caesar (V.135) himself famously describes Britain at the time of his 55 BC sortie as being densely populated and heavily cultivated, and it is clearly the south and the east that he is describing here. If, however, you lived north of the Severn–Humber line, you were in a military border zone where the

whole local economy was bent towards maintaining the barrier between the *Romanitas* of the Empire and the darkness of
barbaricum to the north and west beyond.

The Claudian invasion, prompted by opportunities presented when the Catuvellauni displaced the Trinovantes as
the leading kingdom in the south-east (see Chapter 6 for full
details), marked a huge watershed in the story of the islands
of Britain. The most likely landing areas would have been the
coast of eastern Kent, with the then shelter of the Wantsum
Channel and the broad expanses of beach from Sandwich to
Deal being particularly inviting to the invaders, adding to the
relatively safe harbourage of Pegwell Bay. The landing place
in this part of Kent was later marked in monumental fashion
by the construction of a fine *quadiphons* triumphal 25m-high
arch at Richborough that became the official gateway to the
new province.

It should be noted here, of course, that despite the success
of the Claudian invasion, which survived the significant threat
of failure in the early 60s AD with the Boudican Revolt, the
whole of mainland Britain was never fully conquered (with
no attempt at all evidently being made to conquer modern
Ireland). This story will be told in detail in Chapters 6 to 9
through the experiences of the *Classis Britannica*. For the purposes of this background chapter, however, one should note
that it was not until the later first century when a claim could
be made that Britain was fully part of the Roman Empire. For
the period of activity of the regional navy the border in the
north ran either along the Solway Firth–Tyne line (once built,
Hadrian's Wall) or the Clyde–Forth line (the Antonine Wall),
except in periods of intense campaigning north of the border
during the failed attempts to finally conquer the whole main
island. It was this northern border (in either of its locations,
by far the most northerly of the entire Empire) that proved
so troublesome, with Irish raiding in the west later joining
it in problematic intensity to create the militaristic frontier

zone described above. Truly, if you were a Roman aristocrat wanting to make your name as a military leader, it was to the wilds of northern Britain that you would come, a fact much reflected in modern fiction!

As to why the whole archipelago were never conquered, James (2011, 144) makes the case that this was the result of a failure of the 'open hand alongside sword' strategy that had underwritten much of Rome's early Imperial growth. He says that this required an elite sophisticated enough in newly conquered territories to buy into the Imperial project once conquest had taken place, adding that despite repeated attempts to conquer the north of the islands, such an elite appears to have been singularly lacking in what is now Scotland. In short, and to be blunt, the conquest of the extreme north and Ireland were simply not economically viable during the Principate, though interestingly contact with Rome in the border zone did create the conditions through which such an elite as described by James did begin to emerge in the later second century among the Maeatae north of Hadrian's Wall and the Caledonians to the north of them (see Chapters 6 and 7). Such coalescence of power was later to evolve into the Pictish Kingdom, which caused major problems for the *dioceses* of Britain in the fourth century.

In terms of being a political entity, Britain became the province of *Britannia* shortly after the Claudian invasion. This lasted from the mid-first century through to the early third century, when the province was divided in two in AD 211–212 by Septimius Severus or his son, Caracalla, the new components being *Britannia Superior* and *Britannia Inferior* (Mattingly, 2006, 229). Following Diocletian's reformation when the Empire was divided into twelve *dioceses* controlled by a *vicarius*, the Verona List of AD 303–314 details Britain from that point being comprised of four provinces in the new *diocese* of Britain, these being *Maxima Caesariensis*, *Flavia Caesariensis*, *Britannia Prima* and *Britannia Secunda*. The same provinces are

listed a century later in the *Notitia Dignitatum* with the addition of the problematic *Valentia*. This continued sub-division
of occupied Britain should be viewed in the context of the
comments regarding Britain being particularly vulnerable
to usurpation attempts given the large military presence and
distance from Rome. Simply put, smaller political units were
expected to present less of a threat (though in reality this actually proved not to be the case given the usurpation attempts
actually gathered in pace).

Determining the exact size of the population of Roman
Britain is problematic, though both David Mattingly and Martin
Millett have usefully attempted such a calculation, breaking
down the occupiers into three broad communities as below:

Community Type	Sub-unit	Millett 1990	Mattingly 2nd C	Mattingly 4th C
Military	Army	10,000–20,000	45,000–55,000	20,000–25,000
	Garrison settlement (*vici* and similar)	50,000–200,000	100,000	50,000
Urban	Major towns	183,971–290,057 (both major and small towns)	120,000	100,000
	Small towns		25,000	50,000
Rural	Villa dwellers	Mid-point average of 3.3 million, both villa and non-villa.	5,000	60,000
	Non-villa settlement		1,700,000	2,215,000
Total		3,665,000	2,000,000	2,500,000

(After Mattingly, 2011, 219.)

Taking Millett's figure of 3,665,500, this would have been up from a maximum of 2 million in the LIA, it then falling back to below 2 million after the occupation, then beginning a steady climb and reaching up to 8 million before the Black Death in the fourth century (Cunliffe, 2013, 97).

A final note here is with regard to the economy of Roman Britain. Chronologically, the south and east of Britain flourished for much of the early part of the occupation, then suffering as a result of the 'Crisis of the third century' (see Chapter 9) before flourishing again in the fourth century when other parts of north-western Europe were suffering further as the western Empire came under increasing pressure from both without and within.

Trade, both national and international, was driven by a number of factors during the period of existence of the *Classis Britannica* in Britain. The two key factors though were firstly the desire on the part of many elites to attain and display the trappings of *Romanitas*, this being magnified by the proximity of the south and east to the Continent. Secondly, yet again, was the disproportionately large military presence in occupied Britain. James (2011, 155) says that demand for 'Roman' goods would have been particularly strong among the legionaries who saw themselves as Roman and yet lived for the most part distant from Rome, such goods therefore helping them to distinguish themselves from the natives among whom they lived at the periphery of Empire. Similarly auxiliaries, raised elsewhere in the Empire but based in Britain, would have encouraged trade with their own homelands to maintain their own identity.

While this demand for goods from the military clearly benefited the south and east of Britain through which most of the trade would have arrived, the military presence in the north and west where most of the troops were based had a completely different effect. Here, all the data available indicates that the economy was stunted and totally subverted to the needs of the military. It is therefore no surprise that out-side some notable examples such as York (Roman *Eboracum*) and Corbridge (Roman *Coria*, with even these two examples owing their existence to a military presence), the vast majority of the urban and elite settlement in occupied Britain were a feature of the south and the east of the province, not the north and the west.

Sources and Data

As detailed in the introduction, the data from which the detail of this work has been sourced originates from the archaeo-logical record, the historical record, scientific observation and analogy, together with supporting anecdotal evidence where appropriate.

In terms of the archaeological record there are many exam-ples of vessels of all sizes dating to the occupation period being found and examined across north-western Europe, some of which have a commonality of design that a number of com-mentators have interpreted as indicating an association with the regional fleets of the time (including in our case the *Classis Britannica*). These exciting finds are fully detailed in Chapter 2. Additionally, the archaeological record also provides data from the infrastructure that facilitated the operation of the *Classis Britannica*, for example the forts and harbours that supported the British regional fleet. Such evidence is fully detailed in Chapter 4. Finally, with reference to archaeological data, we have the thousands of tiles and bricks dating to the occupation that have been found on both sides of the English Channel bearing the 'CLBR' stamp of the *Classis Britannica*. These are detailed in Chapters 4 and 8.

Data from the historical record comes in the form of pri-mary sources dating to the classical world, and from epigraphy. Among more than 100 ancient works that mention Britain, a number of authors go into great detail with some specifically highlighting the regional navy in action. The most important for this work are Julius Caesar himself with his *Gallic Wars* (first century BC but useful to set the scene for pre-conquest Britain), Strabo with his *Geography* (late first century BC/ early first century AD, useful again for pre-conquest context), Cornelius Tacitus with his *Annals*, *Histories* and *Agricola* (late first century AD to early second century, and hugely important for the conquest period), Suetonius with *The Twelve Caesars* (late first century AD to early second century, and again relevant to the conquest period), Cassius Dio with his *Roman History* (late second to early third centuries AD, his extensive work covering most of the existence of the *Classis Britannica*), Herodian with his *History of the Empire* (late second century AD to mid-third, and particularly important for the campaigns in Britain of Septimius Severus), and Ammianus Marcellinus (fourth century, with his *Roman History* and useful for analogy). To these authors and their titles we can add the now anonymous *Historia Augusta*, a collection of biographies of emperors from AD 117 to AD 284 written in the later Empire.

Next we can examine a number of official itineraries and codices that include occupation-period Britain when giving details of the main travel routes across the Empire, crucially including place names for towns and key sites such as fortresses, and the distances between them. Firstly we have the *Tabula Peutingeriana*, a damaged thirteenth-century AD reproduction of a Roman road map that only includes the south-east corner of Britain (the remainder having been lost). Specifically detailed on the map are the Kentish ports that played a major role in the activities of the *Classis Britannica*, namely Richborough (Roman *Rutupiae*, a multi-purpose site featuring a harbour, the monumental arch and later a key Saxon Shore fort), Dover (Roman *Dubris*) and Lympne (Roman *Lemavio*). Next we have the *Antonine Itinerary*, this surviving as a manuscript that details the 225 most important roads in the Empire and the key sites along them. This provides a huge amount of information about occupied Britain, including details of all of the main civic centres and fortresses. Appearing to date from the reign of Caracalla (sole Emperor from AD 211 to AD 217), it therefore overlaps with the period of activity of the *Classis Britannica*. Next, though not strictly an itinerary, we have the *Ravenna Cosmography*, an early eighth-century AD list of names of places in the Empire based on earlier sources and thus including 300 locations in Britain (three centuries after the latter had ceased to be part of the crumbling western Empire). To this we can add the *Notitia Dignitatum*, a late Roman collection of the key officials and military formations in the Empire and their locations. Though outside the period of chronological interest of this book the *Notitia* is useful by way of analogy. Finally we have the *Codex Theodosianus*, a compilation of all legal rulings since the time of Constantine I dating to the first half of the fifth century. Again outside the time of interest for our period of study, it is useful by way of analogy.

We now move on to the epigraphy that specifically mentions the *Classis Britannica*, a number of references surviving in the context of memorials detailing the careers or activities of *praefectus classis* (fleet admirals), *trierarchi* (captains) and crew members of the fleet. In the case of the former a good example is provided by an inscription from Ostia naming Q. Baienus Blassianus as the *praefectus* of the *Classis Britannica* during the reign of Trajan. Another, closer to home, comes in the form of an altar dedicated to Neptune that was found reused in the walls of the later third century Saxon Shore at Lympne (almost certainly originating from the original *Classis Britannica* fort on the site). The epigraphy on the altar says it was set up by Admiral of the British fleet Lucius Aufidius Pantera and has been dated to the mid-second century. Further, a Marcus Maenius Agrippa is detailed on an inscription from Camerinum in Umbria that states he commanded the *Classis Britannica*, again in the mid-second century and with him likely being the successor to Pantera commanding the regional fleet. He is also mentioned on an altar inscription to 'Jupiter Best and Greatest' found at Maryport (Roman Alauna) in Cumbria, where he is also listed as being the overall procurator of the whole province, possibly at the same time as being the *praefectus classis*. Next we have Sextus Flavius Quietus on whose tombstone in Rome is detailed the fact he became the commander of the British fleet, again in the mid-second century. Meanwhile, an inscription from Celeia in Noricum details that one Titus Varius Priscus was also the *praefectus* of the *Classis Britannica*, though no date is available here, while finally for admirals we also have an unknown individual who is detailed in a partial inscription from Rome as having commanded four regional fleets – the $\overline{Classis}$ *Britannica*, *Classis Germanica*, *Classis Moesic* and *Classis Pannonica*. This latter is particularly interesting as it is not clear if the reference is to consecutive commands or to an unusual combination of all four. One theory is that it refers to the state of affairs after the defeat of usurping British Governor Decimus Clodius Albinus by Septimius Severus in the late second century. In Chapter 7 I make the case that the *Classis Britannica* would have supported Albinus, and was then 'reformed' by the new governor and military commissioners sent to the province after Albinus' death. It may well be that while the 'reforms' were taking place a single commander could have controlled the British, Rhine and Danube fleets.

In terms of references to *trierarchus* of the *Classis Britannica*, we have five, the first four on gravestones at the regional fleet's headquarters in Boulogne. Firstly there is Quintus Arrenius Verecundo, then Tiberius Claudius Seleucus, followed by P. Graecius Tertinus (in the context of his son's memorial) and B. Domitianus (again in the context of a memorial to his son). Finally we have the North African Saturninus, known to have been a *trierarchus* of the *Classis Britannica* from an inscription

found at Arles in southern France. This is a particularly important piece of epigraphy as it is dated to between AD 244 and
AD 249 and is the last reference known to the *Classis Britannica*.
To conclude the personalised epigraphic evidence we have
one Didio, marine of the *Classis Britannica*, who is known from
his gravestone at Boulogne, and finally Demetrius, another
marine of the regional fleet also buried at Boulogne where a
fragment of his gravestone has been found. The former originated in Thrace, while the latter came from Syria.

Epigraphy regarding the *Classis Britannica* not specific
to an individual is also found in Britain. This includes the
well-known inscription on a stone block on Hadrian's Wall
between Birdoswald and Castlesteads referencing a detachment of *Pedites Classicorum Britanniorum* (marines of the
British fleet), and a similar inscription on a stone block in the
portico of the granary of the Roman fort at Benwell, also on
Hadrian's Wall, this referencing a *Vexillatio Classis Britannicae*.
Both of these inscriptions have traditionally being interpreted
as an indication that the detachments actually built the section
of wall or structure rather than them being permanently based
there fulfilling a military mission. Additionally, the regional
fleet is mentioned in the context of a *Cohors 1 Aelia Classica*
(First Cohort of the Hadrianic Fleet, see Chapter 7) dating
to AD 146 on a list of units detailed on a bronze discharge
diploma from Chesters fort on Hadrian's Wall. This appears
to be the same unit mentioned in another diploma dated
to AD 158 found in three pieces outside the Roman Fort at
Ravenglass, and on a lead seal from the same location.

Of the other forms of data, scientific observation is threaded
throughout the whole narrative. Analogy is also used extensively, for example in the comparison of the experiences of
other regional fleets across the Empire with that of the *Classis
Britannica*. Finally here anecdote too is used extensively, for
example when comparing the modern understanding of the
academic application of sea power (see the discussion of the

military roles of the *Classis Britannica* in Chapter 4) with what is known of the campaigns and activities of the regional fleet around the islands of Britain and across the North Sea during the occupation. Additionally, anecdote is used in the context of the numerous examples of occupation-period jewellery and graffiti found in Britain that carry enigmatic and stylised images of galleys. These are included here as anecdote rather than as hard archaeological data given the lack of provenance regarding their origins and also because, though resplendent with their maritime imagery, they lack a specific mention of the *Classis Britannica*. They are particularly important from a phenomenological perspective given they may actually portray such a vessel operating around the islands of Britain during the occupation. Specific examples include an amber intaglio brooch featuring a galley and pharos, and similarly a graffiti on a lead sheet with a galley prominent, both found at Caistor-by-Norwich (Roman *Venta Icenorum*) and the former now in the collection of Norwich Castle Museum and Art Gallery.

Naval Operations Around Britain in the Classical World

In this final section of the background chapter I discuss the tidal regime around the islands of Britain and across the North Sea that would have had an impact on the operations of the *Classis Britannica*, the changes of sea level between then and now that certainly impact our understanding of these operations from a phenomenological perspective, the weather patterns across our area of interest during the Roman period, and examine the models that enable us to interpret the patterns of maritime trade in the region during the period of existence of the regional navy.

It is the gravitational attraction of the moon and to a lesser extent sun (the closeness of the former countering the far great mass of the latter) on the rotating earth that create the tides. Then as now they had a major impact on naval operations, and a regional understanding of them was vital to any form of successful maritime activity. In that regard one only has to look at the damage inflicted on Caesar's invasion fleet in 55 BC by a violent storm associated with a very strong tide off the east Kent coast. Tidal regimes differ around the world, but in Britain today there are usually two high tides (every twelve hours and twenty-five minutes) and two low tides per day, this being called a semi-diurnal regime. In addition to this twice daily rise and fall, the specific positioning of the moon then also provides additional influence such that the highest high tides and lowest low tides are spring tides (with full and new moons), and the lowest high tides and highest low tides are neap tides, this being a fortnightly cycle. Finally, a seasonal cycle also has an impact such that the highest of the spring tides peak during the spring and autumn equinoxes. Thus it is likely that Caesar's experience above was associated with a very high spring tide (he specifically describes a full moon being present), possibly combined with a storm surge travelling south from the North Sea.

Within this tidal regime the difference between high tide and low tide is known as the tidal range, this additionally differing around the coasts of Britain based on regional littoral and riparian topography, and also water depth (bathymetry). In that regard, at one extreme the Bristol Channel has the third highest global tidal range while Lowestoft on the East Anglian coast one of the lowest. Similarly, for all the same reasons above starting with the twelve hours, twenty-five minutes differential between high tides, the tidal times around Britain also differ within the semi-diurnal regime.

To illustrate the impact that knowledge of the tidal flows around Britain has on maritime operations one only has to look at the English Channel. The principal point of connectivity for the Roman province with the Continent, the tidal regime in this vital waterway changes significantly depending on location. In the eastern part of the crossing, the tidal streams change direction alternately east and west every six and a quarter hours. In the Straits of Dover, however, the tidal alternation is between the north-east and south-west, though again every six and a quarter hours. Matters are further complicated by the fact the same factors that influence the tidal range also impact the speed of the stream in either direction. Therefore local knowledge is essential, which perhaps Caesar was lacking in 55 BC.

Differences in tidal range and times during the occupation compared to today would have been caused by one principal key factor, namely the depth of the sea, which differed then when compared to today (see following comments on weather patterns). Sea levels around Britain have been rising since the Last Glacial Maximum (LGM) as part of the Flandrian Marine Transgression, with the chronological differential being exacerbated by isostatic processes that have seen post-glacial land levels fall in the south of Britain at the same time as they have risen in the north and Scotland. Devoy (1990, 17) has argued that relative sea level (RSL) by the beginning of the occupation would have been between 0.5 and 1m below current levels when looking at mean high water spring tides. Hall and Merrifield (1986, 18) go further, saying that the River Thames was 4m below its current level in the first century AD, while at the extreme end of this argument and in a source quoted by a number of more recent scholars, Briquet (1930, 439) argued there had been a rise in RSL of 5m since the occupation period. Some of this rise in sea levels actually occurred during the occupation, with Waddlelove and Waddlelove (1990, 253) arguing there was a marine transgression spike early in the first millennium AD that caused sea levels to rise significantly higher. Cunliffe (1988, 83) agrees, explaining that the change within the occupation period is readily visible on Romney Marsh where a layer of alluvium up to 2m thick, and dating to the later Roman period, covers settlement from earlier in the occupation. Even given this rise during the occupation, however, sea levels still seem to have been lower at the end of the period of Roman presence in Britain than they are today.

These lower sea levels during the occupation would definitely have seen a moderately different coastline around Britain than the one today, with many inlets as of then now being silted up. Good examples include the Wantsum Channel that then separated Thanet at the north-eastern tip of Kent from the rest of the mainland. During the Roman period this provided a ready channel to enable those travelling from the English Channel to the Thames Estuary to bypass the treacherous Goodwin Sands, and is the reason why the Saxon Shore forts at Reculver and Richborough were built at its northern and southern ends. Similarly, Cunliffe's Romney Marsh was then open water, semi-enclosed by a spit of land that provided a safe anchorage and the reason for the Saxon Shore fort built there at Lympne (and almost certainly an earlier *Classis Britannica* fort, see Chapter 4).

One novelty regarding the seas around Britain that emerged following the conquest was for the first time the various *oceanus* were named, with titles that would have become familiar and, indeed, second nature to the crews of the *Classis Britannica* (Mason, 2003, 78). In this regard, the *oceanus Britannica* covered the region off the south coast of Britain heading out into the Atlantic, while the *oceanus Hibernicus* covered the Irish Sea. Meanwhile, the *oceanus Hyperboreus* described the seas off the western highlands and islands of Scotland, the *oceanus Duecaledonius* the seas off eastern Scotland (very important to the northern campaigns of Gnaeus Julius Agricola and Septimius Severus, see Chapters 6 and 8) and the *oceanus*

Germanicus the North Sea. Finally, the English Channel was titled the *fretum Gallicum*.

Moving on to weather conditions and how these may have impacted those carrying out maritime activity around Britain during the occupation, this is clearly a less precise discipline than understanding the tidal regime given the latter's reliance on known astronomical phenomenon. Nevertheless, modern scientific research has provided us with a picture that seems to indicate the weather in the province was not that far removed from that we experience today, except it was perhaps slightly wetter earlier in the occupation (Grainge, 2005, 37). Taking this analogical evidence as a starting point, we can then argue the principal type of system dominating weather patterns over and around Britain during the occupation would have been Atlantic lows, leading to the prevailing winds originating usually from the westerly quadrant. Such winds would be created by North Atlantic depressions moving east or north-easterly across the open ocean and then over the north-western European landmass, often hitting Ireland and Britain first. It is this type of system that Caesar describes as delaying the sailing of his 54 BC expedition to Britain. These lows are often modified as they interact with high-pressure systems when they approach the Continental landmass, leading to the cheerfully unpredictable weather that is so much a part of the modern British cultural experience. For the Romans, yet again the phrase 'then as now' is relevant, noting Britain being famous throughout the Empire for the *birrus* rain-proofed hooded cloak.

Finally in this chapter I briefly touch on the models we can use to understand the maritime transport networks around occupied Britain with which the *Classis Britannica* would have interacted. Maritime transport by sea, canal and river was essential to the smooth running of the Roman economy and had a direct impact on the prosperity of a given region. Carriage by such means was the preferred choice of transporting heavy goods over long distances in the pre-modern world and even today, specifically because of cost given it is significantly cheaper than land transport. The wider importance of transport costs is illustrated by Russell (2013, 95), who cites the example of the Baths of Caracalla in Rome where half the construction costs were taken up by shipping and haulage. Therefore any advantage regarding this cost would be taken, and in this context the below table by Selkirk is particularly instructive:

Vessel/Animal/Vehicle	Fuel Type	Distance able to carry 1 ton on 1 gallon
Roman merchant ship	Food/cooking fuel	1,280 miles
Roman codicaria (towed river barge)	Food/cooking fuel	32 miles
Mule	Fodder	2.4 miles
Roman ox-wagon	Fodder	0.8 miles

(Selkirk, 1995, 144.)

Hard occupation-period data for this transport price differential is embedded in the Edict of Diocletian, which highlighted sea travel as the cheapest means of transporting goods, then inland waterways, and finally (by a distance) roads. With regard to the transport of Egyptian papyrus, the figures in the edict show waterways being 4.9 times more expensive than travel by sea, with roadways being up to 56 times more expensive than by sea (Campbell, 2011, 216). More recent examples of similar economics can be found in the sixteenth-century accounts of Corpus Christi College in Cambridge, which detail that it cost the same amount to move a load of stone 130km by water as it cost to move it 16km by land (Russell, 2013, 96). Emphasising the point, Russell provides one further example, saying:

Sea Eagles of Empire

As recently as 1962, limestone from Portland in Dorset was cheaper to purchase at Dublin (*c*.625km distant), to where it was to be transported by sea, than at inland Birmingham (*c*.210km distant).

Two models are particularly useful in providing context when considering occupation-period sea traffic around the British Isles and across the North Sea. Firstly, Morris (2010, 1) argues that from the LIA through to the end of the occupation period, three specific regional maritime exchange systems existed. These facilitated the transfer of peoples and materials (which he terms 'connectivity'), and their interaction with each other, though at any given time this was dependent on political and economic conditions. The three systems were:

- The Atlantic System, ranging from the Atlantic coasts of Britain and western Europe to the Western Channel
- The southern North Sea and Eastern Channel System, ranging from the Eastern Channel to the east coast of Britain (and centred around the Straits of Dover)
- The eastern North Sea System, linking settlement from the mouth of the Rhine to Scandinavia.

More recently, Evans (2014, 433) has argued in favour of a two-trade-route model around the British Isles, one on the west coast and one the east coast. He argues that both were driven by the need to supply the exponentially large military presence in the north, with the west coast route having as its principal channel-crossing route that between Brittany–Normandy and Poole Harbour. He uses ceramic data to show that it was to the latter that Continental imports of spices, olive oil, fish sauce, dried fruit and Samian ware arrived for trans-shipment along the south coast and then up the west coast.

Meanwhile, he argues that the east coast route featured London as its principal international emporium with strong

Continental links to Gaul and the Rhineland. Archaeological data supporting this interpretation includes evidence for imports of spices, olive oil, fish sauce, Samian ware, other Gallic and Rhenish fine wares, and Noyon and Rhenish mortaria. Once again he says that such imported goods were then trans-shipped north, this time along the east coast. Allen and Fulford (1999, 177) earlier demonstrated through their own analysis of regional ceramic exports that trade along the east coast was two-way in nature, with local black-burnished ware from the Thames Estuary joining the elite goods going north and then appearing along Hadrian's Wall and even on the Antonine Wall. By way of reciprocation, Dales ware and coal of north-eastern origin were then shipped back to the south-east.

Richardson (pers. comm. 21 June 2013) believes vessels plying their trade between the Continent and Britain along the east coast (and indeed the west coast through Dorset Harbour) were following a formalised schedule designed to make the most ergonomical use of their time and carrying capacity. He says:

> Clearly what was happening was that merchant ships were sailing a circuit between a variety of Continental and British ports. Stopping off at Folkestone for example, they would drop off some of their cargo of luxury goods and replace it with locally made Greensand querns. These would then be sold with other goods as the vessel stopped off along the Wantsum Channel, in the Thames Estuary (and onto the London emporium), and then around the East Anglian and North Sea coast.

Allen and Fulford (1999, 178) also argue that while this trade along the east coast into the North Sea and onwards to the Continent was common throughout the occupation, it increased markedly from the Hadrianic period and then declined from the middle of the third century (around the time of the disappearance of the *Classis Britannica*, discussed in depth in Chapter 9). They continue that north Kent and south-east Essex were specifically the origin of much of the material transported to the north (much of which Evans argues would have been trans-shipped through London [2014, 433]), and say that epigraphic evidence for the presence of units of the *Classis Britannica* during the building of Hadrian's Wall is evidence of the important role the regional fleet had in the east coast trade (see Chapters 4 and 5).

Given the prominence of the *Classis Britannica* in maritime activities around Britain until its demise in the middle of the third century (see Chapter 9), it is likely that the frequency of the regional maritime trade in both Morris' and Evans' models would have become more problematic later in the occupation (with Evans' reference to the decline of east coast trade from the middle of the third century noted above).

A final point to note here is the cosmopolitan nature of those engaged in the maritime trade networks around Britain at all stages of the occupation. From a phenomenological perspective it is these merchants and their crews who perhaps best illustrate the multiplicity of identities of many living in Britain at that time, and indeed throughout the Empire (also reflecting the cosmopolitan origins of many in the *Classis Britannica* such as the marines Didio and Demetrius). In that regard de la Bédoyère (2015, 32) provides a first-class example, one Tiberinius Celerianus, a maritime merchant who we know of from a temple dedication to the Spirits of the Emperors in Southwark. In this epigraphy he emphasises at the same time his trade, his loyalty to Rome, his allegiance to his tribe and community, and finally to his home city. Indeed, his is the first reference we have in the historical record of someone calling himself or herself a Londoner.

2

THE ROMAN NAVY: HISTORY, TECHNOLOGY AND CREW

In this chapter I provide military context for all that follows regarding the activities of the *Classis Britannica*. In the first instance Roman naval power through to the advent of the regional navies is discussed, followed by a review of Roman maritime technology, before finally looking at the command and control infrastructure and the crews of the Roman fleets of the time of the *Classis Britannica*.

Roman Naval History

Despite the high profile of maritime power in the Mediterranean in the millennia before the birth of Christ (take the definitive Battle of Salamis in 480 BC in the Greek and Persian Wars, for example), Rome came late to naval warfare. The earliest record we have of a Roman warship dates to 394 BC when such a vessel transported three senators to the Oracle at Delphi to present a votive offering. Sadly the

gods were not listening on this trip as the ship was captured
on its journey! By 349 BC the nascent Roman navy was still
too small to engage a single squadron of Greek pirates cruis-
ing up the Italian peninsula, they being encouraged to depart
by Rome's land troops. A growing capability does emerge by
338 BC when the first Roman naval victory is recorded in the
context of the Latin War (340–338 BC). This event was significant enough to prompt Greek Taranto (*Tarentum*), the major
regional navy at the time, to invite Rome to sign a treaty limit-
ing the latter's naval activity off its coast. The Roman fleet was
still small at this stage, perhaps only twenty vessels by the time
of the Second Samnite War from 328–304 BC. It slowly grew
in size though as the Republic matured, particularly when
Rome expanded its influence south along the Italian peninsula where Greek Italiote colonies were increasingly obligated
to provide additional naval resources for their powerful northern neighbour.

Flexing of naval power continued on a small scale as the
century came to a close, with the Roman navy seizing the
Pontine Islands to protect the coast between the Bay of Naples
and Ostia in 312 BC. The growing importance of this fledgling
part of the Roman military establishment was then recognised
in 311 BC when a 'navy board' comprising two officers called
the *duoviri navales* was established. Their role was to ensure that
the evolving Roman naval military capability was fit for pur-
pose when called on for action. By the end of the century the
Roman fleet seems to have numbered around forty vessels of
various sizes, this being used to varying degrees of success, but
it was the next century that was to see Roman naval power
mature in the context of the epic struggle across the western
Mediterranean known as the Punic Wars.

By 272 BC, with the capture of Taranto and the end of the
Pyrrhic Wars, Rome was the dominant power in the Italian
peninsula south of the River Po. This led to an increase
both in the coastline it controlled and associated maritime

trade, causing an inevitable clash with Carthage, the existing regional superpower. By this time the Carthaginian Empire, heavily based on maritime prowess (reflecting its Phoenician origins), included core territory along the Tunisian North African coast, part of Corsica, most of Sardinia and a large swathe of southern Spain. As such it presented a solid barrier to any Roman expansion westwards into the Mediterranean.

Conflict with a Rome now expecting continued expansion was inevitable and finally broke out in 264 BC in what became known as the First Punic War, with the pretext being control over the key Sicilian city of Messina. Spotting an opportunity when the Carthaginian squadron there left on patrol, the Romans transported a consular army by sea that soon occupied the city and ejected the Carthaginian garrison. Somewhat at odds with the earlier sources that detail the steady if unimpressive growth of Roman naval power, Polybius (1.20.7) says at the time of the crossing to Messina Rome possessed no warships at all, not even light transport craft, and had to source the quinqueremes and triremes used from the unconquered Greek cities of southern Italy. This may be a plot device on the part of Polybius to show the disparity at the time between Roman and Carthaginian naval power, but even in a best-case scenario the latter clearly greatly outnumbered the former in terms of fleet size, even before experience is considered.

Whatever the truth regarding Polybius' comment, the inequality in the number of warships was soon addressed. Responding to Carthaginian raiding up and down the Italian coast, the Senate approved the construction of the first 'official' Roman fleet. This comprised 100 quinqueremes to fight as line-of-battle ships and twenty triremes to act as fast scouts. Roman innovation now came to the fore as, recognising they lacked the nautical skills to tackle the Carthaginians in a full naval battle, they played to their main strength. This was in land warfare where the Romans considered themselves superior to the Carthaginians. To this end they fitted the new ships with the *corvus*, an 11m boarding ramp fitted to the bow of their ships that featured a large iron spike designed to penetrate the deck of the vessel being engaged when the ramp was dropped. Roman soldiers would then board the enemy vessel, engaging opposing marines and crew hand-to-hand. Equipped with *lorica hamata* (chain mail) armour, the *scutum* body shield and a lethal stabbing sword (it was during the First Punic War that the Romans were first introduced to the famous *gladius*), the Roman infantry would usually overwhelm the defending Carthaginians if the engagement got to this stage.

In an early naval engagement the Carthaginian fleet managed to trick a much smaller Roman force into a one-sided engagement where seventeen Roman vessels were captured, though the Carthaginians came off worst in a subsequent minor engagement. The first major naval engagement of the war took place in 260 BC, however, when 143 Roman ships (the fleet having grown) engaged 130 Carthaginian vessels at the Battle of Mylae off the Sicilian coast. The Romans used the *corvus* for the first time *en masse* and secured a huge victory, capturing fifty Carthaginian vessels and at a stroke overturning Punic sea control of the oceanic western Mediterranean. Further engagements over the next few years saw Rome taking Corsica and most of Sardinia, then defeating the Carthaginian fleet twice at Sulci in 258 BC. In 257 BC Malta was captured, with the Roman fleet again defeating the Carthaginians. By 256 BC the respective fleets had reached 300 ships in number and Rome decided to take the war to the Carthaginian homeland in North Africa. The crossing was made carrying a huge force of 50,000 troops, successfully avoiding the Punic fleet sent to intercept it and with the subsequent landing being carried out unopposed on the North African coast. Against expectations though, Roman land forces were beaten by the Carthaginian army and fell back on the town of Nabeul on the Tunisian coast, which they fortified. The following spring a Roman fleet of 200 vessels plus transports set off to carry out an evacuation, heavily defeating a Carthaginian naval force sent to intercept it. In the engagement, which featured an additional forty Roman vessels that had sallied from Nabeul, 114 Carthaginian ships were driven ashore and destroyed or captured. A successful evacuation followed, though this relative success turned into a monumental disaster when the returning fleet of up to 400 vessels (including those captured from the Carthaginians) ran into a great storm that destroyed all but eighty vessels. The loss of life of around 100,000 (including many of the most experienced sailors and veteran soldiers) was the largest in a single seafaring event in history and may be an indication that, while the Romans' military prowess at sea had clearly grown, they still had much to learn about long-range nautical skills.

Despite this catastrophe the Romans managed to bring together a new fleet of 170 warships within a year which, despite having untrained crews, helped capture the major Sicilian city of Palermo before successfully raiding the North African coast. On the return journey fate intervened again, however, with twenty-seven Roman vessels being lost on the rocky coastline off Cape Palinuro.

The war dragged on, a Roman fleet being defeated in 249 BC in their first lost naval engagement. The surviving vessels yet again succumbed to a storm that reduced the overall Roman fleet to only twenty vessels. With typical Roman grit, though, the growing Republic soon replaced the losses, this time with an improved line-of-battle design with better handling characteristics and a new, lighter version of the *corvus*. Major naval success followed in 241 BC when a Roman fleet intercepted a Punic resupply fleet destined for Sicily, where the Carthaginian garrison was in desperate need. When this failed to get through, with the loss of 120 Punic vessels, the Carthaginians sued for peace. The war ended in 240 BC with the withdrawal of Carthaginian troops from Sicily.

The First Punic War was a dramatic coming of age for Roman naval power. From a standing start, with no fleet capable of operating in the oceanic zone, the Romans had established complete blue water sea control in the open ocean around Sicily, as well as control of the littoral zone around the coast of the island and most of the Italian peninsula. In terms of naval losses in the war, the Carthaginians lost more vessels to naval combat, though Rome lost more overall given their losses to storms. Rome finished the conflict, however, with the larger navy, and within a few years had added the remainder of Sardinia to its capture of Sicily (except Syracuse).

Following the conflict Rome continued to expand, with naval power playing a major role. One fleet campaigned in Liguria in the north-west of the Italian peninsula in the 220s BC, while another tackled Illyrian piracy in the Adriatic. The latter saw Rome establish a physical presence in the Balkans in what is now modern Albania, leading the Republic for the first time into the sphere of influence of Macedonia, one of the eastern Mediterranean's superpowers.

With the Roman Republic continuing to flex its power to satisfy growing Imperial ambitions, renewed conflict with Carthage was inevitable. The Second Punic War broke out in 218 BC, with Rome generally able to exercise sea control in the oceanic zone throughout the conflict, and additionally control the littoral zone around the key areas of land activity.

Rome began the war with a fleet of sixty ships ready to support a landing in the Punic-controlled region of Spain (by now greatly expanded), and another of 160 vessels ready to descend on the Carthaginian North African homeland. With the Punic navy strangely reticent to challenge Roman sea control, which effectively cut off Carthage from its Spanish colonies and vital raw materials, the Carthaginian leader Hannibal was forced to take his great gamble by invading Italy across the Alps in 218 BC. Despite tactical victories of huge proportions, over the next two years he failed to bring Rome to heel, the latter again showing immense grit to continually recover from huge defeats by fielding new armies. The Roman fleet also won the first naval engagement of the war, at Lilybaeum off the Sicilian coast where victory thwarted any ambitions Carthage had of re-establishing a presence there. Making best use of its naval prowess, the Republic next took the battle to the Punic colonies, establishing a naval base at Tarragona (Tarraco) in Spain that cut Hannibal off from the launch pad of his invasion. A naval battle followed at the mouth of the River Ebro in 217 BC where Rome broke any naval power Carthage retained in Spain, capturing twenty-five Punic ships.

Naval conflict continued to play a major role as the war progressed, with Hannibal now stranded outside the citadel of Taranto in southern Italy. This held out against him through supply by sea and denied him access to the city's extensive harbouring facilities. Rome captured the key Sicilian city of Syracuse in 212 BC after seeing off a last desperate Carthaginian naval resupply attempt. Naval exchanges continued for the next decade, with the Roman fleet usually dominant as at the Battle of Carteia in 206 BC, before the final defeat of Hannibal at the Battle of Zama in 202 BC. To show that Rome was once and for all the dominant naval power in the western Mediterranean, the remaining Punic vessels in Carthage were towed out to sea and burned. This was very fitting, for in final analysis of this important conflict, while Hannibal was able to achieve the spectacular victories on his march down the Italian peninsula that have resonated throughout history, it was actually Rome's aggressive dominance at sea that meant the Carthaginians never had a chance of ultimate strategic victory.

One additional outcome of the Second Punic War was that Rome became engaged in conflict with Macedonia, whose intentions became clear when the Roman navy intercepted five vessels off the coast of southern Italy carrying envoys and a treaty between Hannibal (then in Italy) and the Macedonian King Philip V. From this point onwards, the next fifty years of Roman expansion eastwards saw the Republic in conflict with the Hellenistic kingdoms of the eastern Mediterranean, with naval campaigning again playing a great role. Over time the various opponents were beaten one by one, such that by 146 BC the Macedonian and Seleucid kingdoms and various combinations of Greek city-states had been vanquished. Last man standing in opposition to the monolithic Roman expansion eastwards was the Pontic King Mithridates, this obstacle finally disappearing with his death in 63 BC.

The Roman fleets of this period in the early to mid-first century BC were considerably smaller than at their height during the Second Punic War, with many ships being decommissioned as Rome's opponents were successively defeated. A by-product of this was an increase in piracy, particularly in the eastern Mediterranean (and especially along the Anatolian coast), exacerbated by the flood of former sailors and marines now without work following the draw-down of naval conflict in the region. They found ready employment manning the pirate vessels that began to plague the regional sea routes, challenging Roman sea control in the oceanic zone (and threatening its grain supply from Egypt) as well as dominating the littoral. Ultimately something had to be done, this coming in the form of Gnaeus Pompeuis Magnus (Pompey the Great), whose cleansing of the eastern Mediterranean from 67 BC added another victory to his growing reputation. To carry out this task the former consul took a very modern approach by dividing the Mediterranean into thirteen zones (seven in the east and six in the west) and assigning a fleet to each, though clearly the critical mass in terms of naval power would have been in the east. This sophisticated approach was highly successful and within a year the pirate scourge had been swept from the Mediterranean. To give an idea of the scale of the problem, Pompey's campaign is credited with killing 10,000 pirates, capturing another 20,000 and taking or destroying 600 vessels, his fame rising to the extent that he was next given command of the campaign that ultimately finished off Mithridates.

The next character to enter the stage of Roman naval history is Julius Caesar in the form of his conquest of Gaul in the 50s BC and two subsequent naval incursions to Britain. In the first instance, as his Gallic campaign progressed into north-western Gaul, Caesar came into contact with the tribes of the Atlantic seaboard who had a totally different maritime technological tradition when compared to those of the Mediterranean with which Rome was familiar. Pre-eminent were the Veneti of southern Brittany (Caesar, 3.8), who seem to have controlled most of the cross-Channel marine traffic to Britain. This trade was thriving well before the Roman conquest in terms of Mediterranean goods (as well as those produced in north-western Europe), this being evidenced by finds at sites such as Hengistbury Head and Poole Harbour in Dorset of large quantities of pre-conquest wine amphora and elite pottery. Chronological insight into this trade is available in the context of LIA jetties and wharfing that have been found at Poole Harbour dating to 250 BC. Mason (2003, 68) adds that the four specific Continental locations where trade originated for onward marine carriage to British coastal emporia were the mouths of the Garonne, Loire, Seine and Rhine, though clearly given their prominent role, traffic from the region controlled by the Veneti would have been the most important.

Although the Veneti originally submitted to Caesar's authority in 57 BC, including yielding hostages and signing treaties, the Gallic coastal tribe captured some Roman hostages of their own to use as bargaining chips a year later in an attempt to regain those held by the Romans (Caesar, 3.9). The result, however, was full-scale war with Caesar, who regarded the move as a breach of trust and realised quickly he would have to engage the Veneti at sea to defeat them. To prosecute the war Caesar raised a fleet in the Mediterranean that travelled in short order to the north-west European coast, comprised largely of triremes though including a few larger quadriremes and quinqueremes. This fleet eventually overcame a Veneti fleet of some 220 ships at the Battle of Morbihan Gulf in the late summer of 56 BC. Caesar had to innovate to defeat his Gallic opponents given the latter, vessels were more suitable for conflict in the regional sea conditions, having a much higher freeboard than the Roman galleys. In this regard the Romans deployed sickle-shaped hooks on the end of long poles to cut the rigging of the Veneti vessels, making them more vulnerable to boarding (once again the Roman marines being far better equipped than their opponents), this leading to the capture of a number of Gallic vessels. The remaining Veneti ships scattered and were picked off one by one in the littoral zone along the coast of Brittany, the Roman galleys being more manoeuvrable in this environment. The destruction of the fleet of the Veneti once again saw the Gallic tribe fall under the control of Rome, and indeed from this point onwards they began to supply much maritime expertise to the late Republic as the expansion across the north-west of Europe continued apace.

As detailed in his Gallic Wars (Caesar, 4.20), Caesar's next focus was clearly linked to his defeat of the Veneti, for with this naval challenge removed he next turned his attention to Britain where the tribes of the south and east had been providing support and succor to their Continental Gallic neighbours (see Chapter 3). The Veneti had been particularly dominant as the regional naval power because, very unusually in the context of British history, in this period of the LIA the island of Britain seems to have featured very little maritime military capability of its own. Caesar would also have been encouraged in his new enterprise by the wealth of intelligence he would have been able to gather from the defeated Veneti concerning the mysterious island and its inhabitants across *oceanus britannicus* (as detailed by Ptolemy, see Chapter 1). He would also for the first time have been able to tap into the naval prowess of the Veneti for such a challenging operation.

We are fortunate that Caesar provides great detail concerning his two incursions to Britain in 55 BC and 54 BC (with the obvious safety warning concerning source material reliability). The make-up of the land forces for these two missions, effectively large-scale armed reconnaissances, are detailed in Chapter 3. However, in terms of the naval component, for the first attempt Caesar marched his army north to the territory of the Morini opposite Kent where the Channel crossing was at its closest. Here he gathered eighty transports and eighteen additional vessels modified to carry horses, together with galleys from the fleet that had defeated the Veneti to provide close-in protection in the littoral zone either side of the Channel for the crossing. Interestingly, in a precursor to the intelligence gathering and patrol functions of the later *Classis Britannica*, Caesar then sent the tribune Gaius Volusenus in a trireme to identify a safe landing area on the coast of Britain (it being noteworthy that the war galley was used rather than the more usual *speculatoria navigia*, these being specialist *myoparo* and *scapha* cutters and skiffs converted for scouting purposes).

Caesar next waited for favourable conditions before crossing the Channel, arriving in late August off the coast of Dover in Kent (though his cavalry transports missed the tide and were never to arrive). Finding native British troops massed on the coast awaiting his arrival (clearly tipped off by their Gallic allies), he headed north, weighing anchor off Walmer. However, the Britons had tracked his fleet as it travelled along the coast and were once again arrayed along the shore. The Romans were therefore forced to carry out an amphibious assault (one of the military roles of the later *Classis Britannica*), with the war galleys of the fleet driving hard ashore to the north of the landing area in order to turn the Britons' right flank (the transport ships having got into difficulty closing with the shore). From this position the quinqueremes, quadriremes and triremes were able to enfilade the landing area using ballista and handheld missile weapons. Though heavily contested the landing was ultimately successful, with the leaders of the Britons eventually suing for peace. However, bad weather (see Chapter 4 for detail) later damaged many of the ships that had facilitated the crossing and, after some regional campaigning (the Britons being emboldened by Caesar's naval difficulties), the Romans returned to the Continent using the remaining serviceable ships. The lessons here were clear. The scale of the operation had been too small, the transports used unsuitable for amphibious operations and intelligence regarding local tides and weather lacking.

Caesar, never one to turn down a challenge, was determined to return to Britain and did so the following year. This operation was on a much bigger scale, however, with the fleet carrying his troops much larger. The Romans had also learned from their experiences the previous year regarding the type of vessel best suited for amphibious operations because Caesar ordered the construction of 600 specially built ships, most probably making use of the ship construction skills of the Veneti. These vessels featured lower freeboards than usual to enable easier disembarkation and wider beams to carry bulkier loads. To these vessels the Romans added 200 locally chartered transports, a further eighty ships that had survived the previous year's incursion and twenty-eight war galleys (again a mix of quinqueremes, quadriremes and triremes, the latter once more being in the majority). Once again the land component of the new invasion is detailed in Chapter 3, but suffice to say the size of Caesar's force clearly intimidated the Britons as the landing on the east coast of Kent was this time unopposed. Just as in 55 BC, however, bad weather intervened. While Caesar was campaigning inland against a large British force that had eventually gathered to confront him, a storm badly damaged many of his transports anchored off the coast of Kent. Realising the vulnerability to his rear he returned quickly to the landing area and initiated an urgent repair operation (with many of the vessels being dragged on to the beach to prevent further damage in bad weather). The Roman land force then renewed its campaign against the Britons, with Caesar forcing a crossing of the Thames (supported by his war galleys) and capturing the main base of the British leader Cassivellaunus, who then sued for peace. Honour satisfied, Caesar then returned to the landing area in Kent and re-embarked his forces for the return journey to north-eastern Gaul, this taking place in two waves given the scale of ship losses in the earlier storm. The first wave travelled to the Continent safely but these vessels were prevented from returning by bad weather, with Caesar then deciding to risk cramming his remaining troops into the few serviceable vessels left in Britain (almost certainly the war galleys). These arrived safely back at the end of September.

Caesar concluded his conquest of Gaul in 51 BC, though his ambition and success inevitably led to conflict with his rivals back in Rome, most notably Pompey. The latter was well respected by the naval forces of the Republic following his leadership role in the campaigns against the Anatolian pirates and he received their support, with Caesar being left without a large fleet of his own in the Adriatic. Pompey's attempt to exercise sea control here ultimately failed, however, when Caesar was able to transport his army across to the Balkans by sea, though Pompey's fleet did break his opponent's attempts to besiege him. This forced Caesar to withdraw eastwards across Greece, where matters were decided at the Battle of Pharsalus with a Caesarian victory. Caesar was able to match this victory in the eastern Mediterranean with similar success in the west, where his fleet prevented two attempts by Pompey's supporters to break out of besieged Marseille (though fire ships destroyed half a Caesarian fleet operating off Sicily). After Pompey's defeat at Pharsalus and subsequent flight to Egypt, his remaining naval forces re-gathered in North Africa, leaving just one admiral at large in the Adriatic.

Caesar used his naval forces in the eastern Mediterranean to chase down Pompey, who was promptly killed on arriving in Alexandria. Caesar's subsequent appearance in the Ptolemaic capital again saw his naval forces in action as part of the civil war between Ptolemy VIII and his sister Cleopatra, and then again in the final defeat of Pompey's remaining naval forces. Caesar, of course, did not have long to enjoy his success, being assassinated in 44 BC. Naval power once again played a major role in the next phase of civil war that followed, first between Mark Anthony and Octavian against the assassins, then after the principal defeat of the latter at Philippi in 42 BC, between the alliance of Mark Anthony and Cleopatra against Octavian. This final conflict in the round of civil wars came to a head with the crucial naval Battle of Actium in 31 BC, when Octavian's military commander, Marcus Agrippa, first achieved sea control around the coast of Greece to choke off his opponent's supply routes and then forced the decisive engagement on his own terms. Victory soon followed.

By the end of this struggle for power in Rome Octavian had amassed more than 700 warships, many of which he laid up or decommissioned as he consolidated power, he taking the title of Augustus in 27 BC. From this point onwards until the onset of the Gothic naval raids of the mid-third century AD Rome exercised complete sea control in the Mediterranean, and for much of the period around the Atlantic coastline, too.

With the beginning of the Principate and Imperial Roman history, Augustus initiated a series of reforms of the Roman navy that were to remain in place throughout this period of undisputed sea control. This reflected the growth of Roman power into regions of the known world previously outside its sphere of influence and involved the creation of specific regional navies tasked with exercising sea control where a coastline was present or the dominance of a river frontier where not. The two principal regional navies were the *Classis*

Ravennate and *Classis Misenensis*, effectively the official state fleets based at Ravenna and Misenum and so controlling access from the Italian peninsula into the Adriatic and Tyrrhenian Seas. Others followed, for example the *Classis Germanica* on the Rhine being incorporated very late in the first century BC. Ultimately there were ten such regional navies (including the two in Italy), and the story of these and what was to follow after the middle of the third century is told in the context of the *Classis Britannica* in Chapter 3. For reference purposes, overleaf I detail the full list of the regional navies, together with the level of stipend paid to its *praefectus* commander to give some idea of its size and importance.

Fleet	Annual Stipend
Classis Ravennate	300,000 sesterces
Classis Misenensis	200,000 sesterces
Classis Britannica	100,000 sesterces
Classis Germanica	100,000 sesterces
Classis Pannonica	60,000 sesterces
Classis Moesica	60,000 sesterces
Classis Pontica	60,000 sesterces
Classis Syriaca	60,000 sesterces
Classis Nova Libica	60,000 sesterces
Classis Alexandrina	60,000 sesterces

(Ellis Jones, 2012, 61.)

Roman Maritime Technology

In north-western Europe at the time of the *Classis Britannica* two distinct shipbuilding traditions are visible in the archaeological and historical record, with vessels built in either the Mediterranean tradition or the Romano-Celtic tradition.

Each will be considered in turn in the context of the British regional fleet.

In the case of the Mediterranean tradition, the key distinction was the use of locked mortise and tenon plank fastenings (originally a Phoenician invention). Many of these ships would have been military in nature, and in the context of the *Classis Britannica*, principally war galleys. Such vessels had their origins at the beginning of the first millennia BC in the form of pentaconters, which featured a single bank of oars either side of the vessel. By the time of the Greek and Persian Wars the principal line of battle ships had grown to include biremes and triremes (the latter invented by the Corinthians around 530 BC), so called because they featured two and three banks of oars either side respectively. As the millennia progressed larger and larger polyremes appeared, including quadriremes (the '4', and so on), quinqueremes (allegedly invented by Syracusian dictator Dionysius I in 399 BC), hexaremes, septiremes, octeres, enneres and deceres. The pattern here was for vessels to get larger and larger, clearly a symptom of an arms race in the fairly symmetrical conflicts between the Hellenistic kingdoms and later during Rome's expansion across the Mediterranean. In the case of the wars of the eastern Mediterranean in the third and second centuries, Demetrius the Besieger, his son Antigonus Gonatas, and Ptolemy IV built even bigger ships, the latter apparently a '40'. The larger vessels would have been much fewer in number, however, serving principally as flagships, with the main line of battle ships at the time of the Punic Wars being the quinquereme and the main scout ship, the trireme.

In terms of the naming of the vessel types based on the oaring system, the larger polyremes derived their names not from the number of banks of oars but from the number of men rowing on a given bank. In this context a quinquereme would feature a trireme arrangement but with two oarsmen rowing the top two tiers of oars. Whatever the size, the vessels would come in aphract (oarsmen unprotected), semi-cataphract (oarsmen partially protected) and cataphract (oarsmen fully protected) versions, though clearly the larger line of battle ships would have been cataphracts.

By the time of the *Classis Britannica*, with the lack of a symmetrical threat to justify the investment in the expensive larger polyremes, the standard vessel for the regional fleets was the *liburna* bireme. The name originates from the Liburni tribe in Dalmatia, whose fast biremes were renowned in the Roman world for their feats of piracy. Such ships are the most common type depicted on the second century Trajan's Column in the context of the conquest of Dacia. We also know that at least one trireme served in the *Classis Britannica* as we have an inscription at Boulogne that mentions such a vessel in the service of the regional fleet, but by and large the vessels carrying out the majority of military activity in the waters around Britain would have been *liburnae*.

From an early stage war galleys carried the same suit of weaponry, principally the bronze or iron ram designed to impact an opposing vessel below the waterline at speed and thus sink it, or alternatively to run down the length of a target vessel with the aim of immobilising the opposing vessel by destroying the oars (and oarsmen) on that side. Marines would also have been carried from an early stage, in the form of troops equipped with missile weapons (mainly bows, slings and javelins), with artillery appearing later in the form of bolt or stone-throwing ballista and stone-throwing onagers. These weapons could be used in direct ship-to-ship engagements with standard ammunition, or more problematically with lit ammunition designed to set their opponents afire. Additionally, we know from Caesar's accounts of his war with the Veneti that sickle-shaped hooks on the end of long poles were deployed to cut the rigging of enemy vessels (making them easier to board), while later Agrippa also introduced the *harpax* (harpoon), a simple grapnel attached to a 2.3m shaft

trailing a line and designed to be fired from the larger ballista. Metal strips were often attached to the line to prevent
it being cut, and once ensnared the opposing vessel was then
reeled in and once again engaged hand-to-hand through
boarding. Of course, the artillery aboard ship also allowed land
targets to be engaged effectively when carrying out military
operations in the littoral, for example by Caesar during his
incursion into Britain in 55 BC. The Roman, Carthaginian and
Hellenistic polyremes of the wars of the western and eastern
Mediterranean would also have featured towers of increasing size to provide fighting platforms for the missile-armed
marines, while finally the Roman line-of-battle ships would
also have featured the *corvus*.

The commonality of *liburnae* in northern waters during
the occupation is testified by an analysis of Roman ship fittings found at Richborough using data from the 1922–38
excavations that shows such vessels were the most common
type present. The best-known example of a Mediterranean-
style vessel from occupied Britain in the archaeological record,
however, is the County Hall ship discovered in London in
1910. Built using locally sourced oak from the south-east of
England, this ship has been dated to the late third or early
fourth century. The vessel is not actually thought to have
been military in nature and seems to have been used as a ferry
between the capital and the Continent. Other vessels built
in the Mediterranean style known from across north-west
Europe from this period include a galley found at the Roman
fort at Laurum in the Netherlands (Lendering, 2012, 1), a
first- or second-century boat excavated at the Roman fort at
Vechten in the Netherlands in 1893, two first- or second-century boats excavated at the Roman fort at Zwammerdam in
the Netherlands in 1968–71, and finally two riverboats found
at Oberstimm in central Germany.

A final point of interest here regarding the *liburnae* of the
regional fleets is that they seem to have been individually

named. An example is provided by the grave stele of a junior officer of the *Classis Ravennate* that describes him as the captain of the *liburna Aurata* (Golden).

More common in north-west Europe, however, and of equal relevance to this study of the *Classis Britannica*, are vessels of Romano-Celtic design. They are so called because of their similarity to the ships of the Veneti mentioned by Caesar, who describes them thus (3:1):

> The Gaul's own ships were built and rigged in a different manner from ours. They were made with much flatter bottom, to help them ride shallow water caused by shoals or ebb tides. Exceptionally high bows and sterns fitted them for use in heavy seas and violent gales, and the hulls were made entirely of oak, to enable them to stand any amount of shocks and rough usage. The cross-timbers, which consisted of beams a foot wide, were fastened with iron bolts as thick as a man's thumb. The anchors were secured with iron chains instead of ropes. They used sails made of raw hides or thin leather, either because they had no flax and were ignorant of its use, or more probably because they thought ordinary sails would not stand the violent storms and squalls of the Atlantic and were not suitable for such heavy vessels.

While this is a generalisation based on one type of vessel, what is clear is that this is a very different maritime technology to that originating in the Mediterranean, and one which Caesar interestingly says was superior (certainly in the context of the northern waters where they operated) to his own vessels in everything save speed and the ability to use oars. The Romano-Celtic tradition has been identified through some thirty wrecks found in the Severn Estuary, the Thames, the Channel Islands, the Scheldt–Meuse–Rhine Delta, the Rhine at Zanten and at Mainz (Roman *Mogontiacum*). Ships of this tradition broadly have the following features:

- A framing of closely spaced, large timbers with half-frames spanning the sides and bottom, and with a floor covering the bilges and bottom (the individual timbers often not being fastened together)
- Planking that is flush laid and fastened to the frame with large iron nails
- Caulking within the plank seam using macerated twigs, moss or twisted fibre
- Where a mast is used, the mast step being well forward

Leading naval historian Sean McGrail (2015, 125) believes that within the Romano–Celtic ship tradition there are two distinct groupings, styling them Type A and Type B. The former are keel-less and flat-bottomed, designed for use in the littoral and on canals, lakes and rivers. Though some types had sails and oars, many examples used a towing post set forward, the latter being best illustrated by the numerous examples of *codicaria* river barges found in the archaeological record and in epigraphy across the region. Such vessels are heavily referenced by the fourth-century Roman poet Ausonius (Mosella, 5), who speaks of the use of hawsers by the men towing them from the riverbanks. Analogously we can get phenomenological insight into such riverine barge operations during the occupation by examining the experiences of those commercially using rivers such as the Medway in Kent in the eighteenth and nineteenth centuries after the Medway Navigation Company had opened up this river to navigation. These barges were pulled by gangs of men, called 'halers' or 'hufflers', as opposed to barge horses. Generally, once a vessel was underway and there was little or no current, a single person could reasonably be able to pull a 50-tonne barge load, though it was normal practice at that time for a number of men to be employed in this regard. For context, in this period it took a barge being pulled in this way twelve hours to get to Maidstone from Tonbridge. Maintenance of the bank was essential here to ensure the commercial success of the barging operations, this being carried out at the same time as riverbed maintenance to ensure the river remained fully navigable. The experiences of those operating the barges during the eighteenth and nineteenth centuries seems to have been broadly similar to that of their Roman forebears taking barges from Ostia to Rome, when we know the barge teams operating on the River Tiber comprised a helmsman aboard the barge and four *codicarii infra pontem sub(licium)* (Roman 'hufflers') on the towpath.

Other common examples of Type A vessels would have been flat-bottomed varieties of the ubiquitous smaller monoreme *myoparo* and *scapha* (specialist military scout versions of such vessels were called *speculatoria navigia* and often featured azure or sea grey camouflaged sails and hulls). Civilian *myoparo* and *scapha* are memorably described by Ausonius (Mosella, 19), who said:

> What bright regattas charm us when, mid-stream, oar-driven skiffs engage in mimic war … the exultant captains move lightly on stern or prow, the youthful crew racing across the water … the picture of these painted prows, and crews of laughing lads, reflected in the river.

Type A vessels found in the archaeological record include further examples at Laurum to join the galleys (Lendering, 2012, 1), a range of flat-bottomed river barges found during excavations of the harbour at Cologne (Colonia Claudia Ara Agrippinensium, Schäfer and Trier, 2013, 36), the Bevaix Boat from Lake Neuchatel in Switzerland, and flat-bottomed barges found at Pommeroeul in Belgium (Campbell, 2011, 146) on a tributary of the River Haine. The largest of these vessels had a central gangplank and is similar in size to a *codicaria*, while the smallest was skiff-sized, oar-propelled and likely a *scapha*. One of these vessels is now on display at the Gallo-Roman Museum in Ath.

Type B Romano-Celtic vessels are seagoing, though often capable of riverine use, and have a full-bodied hull form with firm bilge, posts and a plank keel. They were propelled by a sail in estuaries and when at sea, and a number of examples have been found in Britain dating to the occupation. London provides two excellent candidates in the New Guy's House boat found in 1958 and the larger Blackfriars 1 vessel excavated by Peter Marsden in 1962. The Blackfriars 1 ship is of particular importance given it was found to be carrying 26 tonnes of Kentish ragstone, this being petrologically identified as originating in the Medway Valley and thus being a direct illustration of Roman trade and industry in action in Britain during the occupation. This ship was 14m in length and 6.5m wide, with a shallow draught of 1.5m and a maximum speed of around 7 knots in favourable conditions. The maximum load capacity would have been up to 50 tonnes. Built of oak, it had no keel but featured two broad keel-planks, a stempost with corresponding sternpost and hazel twig caulking for the carvel planking. The mast was supported by a rectangular socket mast-step, in the base of which a bronze coin of Domitian was found. Based on dendro-analysis, the vessel was built in the south-east of Britain around AD 140.

Roman naval expert Gustav Milne (2000, 131) has argued that the close similarity in design of the New Guy's House boat, the Blackfriars 1 vessel and others found at Bruges in Belgium, St Peter Port in Guernsey (estimated to have had a crew of three, Rule and Monaghan, 1993) and Barland's Farm in Gwent (this boat was half the size of the Blackfriars boat, though again the same design) indicates a close association with the *Classis Britannica* given the regional footprint of the finds. However, many other Type B-style vessels of differing types to these ships have also been found across Europe, for example once again at Laurum, Cologne and Pommeroeul. What is not in doubt though is the commonality of these vessel types across north-west Europe, this ubiquity again being shown by analysis of Richborough ship fittings that show them to be the second most common types after the Mediterranean-style *liburnae* (the latter's dominance not surprising given the military nature of this site).

The above analysis of the vessels used by the *Classis Britannica* should, of course, be understood in the context that then, as now, there was a tremendous amount of variation regionally in the types of maritime technology used by communities across the entire Empire. A good example, completely outside of the discussion regarding Mediterranean and Romano-Celtic designs, is again provided by the ship fittings analysis at Richborough. Here, the third most common type of vessel found is a Germani-style clinker-built (overlapping-plank) fast-rowing design. These ships were of a late occupation date and appear to have been the vessels of north German foederates, raiders or settlers, and while limited in number they are nevertheless a direct example of a completely different shipbuilding tradition in action during the (late) occupation. However, where the state was involved in maritime activity, through the regional fleets or otherwise, there is no doubt in my mind that there was an enormous amount of commonality in the technology used, whether in the Mediterranean or Romano-Celtic traditions. Hence the similarity of many of the vessels described by Milne or found at Laurum, Cologne and Pommeroeul, many of which were built to a set pattern. A direct analogy here would be the *fabricae* state-owned manufactories large and small across the Empire making standardised equipment for the Roman military and state.

Therefore, while acknowledging what is clearly a generalisation, one can therefore make a strong case that during its period of operations the *Classis Britannica* would have operated a mixed fleet of locally built, Mediterranean-tradition *liburnae* and Romano-Celtic-tradition Type A-style *myoparo* and *scapha* for military operations – the latter together with various types of Type A *codicarii* and Type B Blackfriars 1-style vessels also being used for transport purposes (both in a military and civilian context). This fleet of vessels, built to a set standard per type, would have found itself intermingling with a wide variety of vessel types as it carried out its duties on behalf of the Emperor.

Command, Control and Crews

Next we can consider perhaps the most important component of Roman naval capability during the period of activity of the *Classis Britannica*, namely the men who facilitated its operation from top to bottom. In that context I start here with a brief overview of provincial governance in the Principate to give insight into how the control of the regional fleets fitted into this structure (and to emphasise the importance of the naval component of a given province's military capability). I then move down the entire command chain to consider all ranks and their experiences of life in a Roman regional navy.

In terms of governance, a major Imperial Roman province until the Diocletian reformation had two different chains of command to ensure its smooth running. The first was the staff of the Imperial governor, and the second that of the procurator. The former was tasked with ruling the province, was the chief administrator of Roman law and sat at the top of the military command chain. A consular status Imperial legate, he would be supported by an *iuridicus* (legal expert), three senatorial rank legionary legates and three senior senatorial rank military tribunes. Equestrian-rank officers would make up the remaining military hierarchy, with fifteen legionary tribunes and up to sixty auxiliary commanders (Mattingly, 2011, 219).

The second chain of command was that of the procurator, who was tasked with making the province pay, reporting directly to the Emperor's *fiscus* (exchequer). The term procurator derives from the Latin verb *procurare* ('to take care') and referred to the individuals, usually freedmen, hired by the wealthy to manage agricultural or financial estates (Furhman, 2012, 195). The use in an Imperial context originated in the reforms of Augustus (Birley, 2005, 298) as he began to establish the apparatus of Empire, with the name being applied at this senior level to those managing the Imperial private and public estates.

The individuals so employed proved particularly useful in a provincial role given the lack of senatorial interest in this regard. By the beginning of the reign of Claudius the first full provincial procurators had appeared, for example in Judea in AD 41, they being independent of the governor and thus acting as a useful political counterweight. Very shortly thereafter they also began to be recruited from equestrian ranks. The procurators of Britain were equestrian rank from the beginning (Birley, 2005, 298), with the lesser *procuratores* employed below them including other equestrians and also freedmen, some of the latter from the *familia caesaris* (the Emperor's own freedmen and slaves). Though there might appear to be parallels with a modern civil service here, note should be taken that we are talking about a strictly limited number of individuals, so the analogy is not as useful as it might appear. The *procuratores* would have been registrars, finance officers and the superintendents and specialists tasked with running major state-sponsored industrial activity (for example the *procurator metallorum* tasked with running the *metalla* state mines and quarries, see Chapter 5).

In Britain the procurator was styled the *procurator Augusti* (reflecting the provincial pecking order, regarding similar titles for *praefectus classis*), with the first holder of the post being Publius Graecinius from AD 43 to AD 60 (he, at least initially, also being the procurator in Gaul). A key point here is that the procurator in *Britannia* was appointed immediately after the Claudian invasion – the Emperor intended to make the new province pay from the word go. After all, it had to be shown that the new province was *pretium victoria* – worth the conquest. The procurator had specific responsibility for collecting taxes which, as Pearson (2006, 39) explains, would have included responsibility for mines, quarries, Imperial estates and other state monopolies where the superintendents and specialists would have been stationed.

In terms of total numbers, taking both the governor and procurator's staffs together, this would give a combined number of fewer than eighty senior officials to run the province legally and financially. As Mattingly (2011, 219) says:

> Even if we include legionary centurions and unknown numbers of Imperial freedmen and Imperial slaves, the core bureaucratic team in the province was very small.

Later, following the Diocletian reformation, the procurator's role was replaced by a *vicarius* who had responsibility for the wider *diocese* (the original province having been broken up), with each of the new smaller provinces in Britain being governed by a *praeses*-rank governor (who combined the role of the original governor and procurator). With this reformation the constellation of civil servants supporting state activity would have been greatly expanded, given the additional tiers of governance.

Returning to the period of activity of the *Classis Britannica*, and to the discussion on military naval capability, from the Augustan period a new command structure was put in place reflecting the emergence of the regional fleets. No longer would there be a single command structure as in the late Republic led by a consular-level individual (with perhaps a *praetor* army commander beneath him), this arrangement instead being replaced by a devolved structure with a *praefectus classis* being appointed for each fleet who was answerable only to the Emperor, the latter making each appointment personally. This was initially an unusual post given the fact that it was clearly a military position, but followed the procuratorial reporting line direct to the Emperor (with Birley, for example, saying that the *praefectus classis Britannicae* was second only to the procurator in terms of importance in the civilian chain of command in Britain, 2005, 298). The solution to this bipolar position was an elegant one, with the *praefectus classis* coming under the local military control of the governor when in theatre (and sitting with the legates and tribunes of the governor's military headquarters), while at the same time being equally comfortable engaging with the parallel procuratorial chain of command (given the official reporting line direct to the Emperor, Pittasi, 2012, 54). Hence we are able to consider the *Classis Britannica* in this book not just in the context of its fighting capability, but also its service to the province in a civilian capacity (see Chapter 5). In this regard, clearly the navy was not required for conflict at all times and was therefore a sizeable resource that the governor, procurator and indeed Emperor would not have wanted to see idle. The procurator would have used whatever resource was to hand to make the province pay, and it is in this context that we should therefore not simply think of the fleet in a military context, but also as a tool to perform other functions. Parfitt (2013, 45) is explicit about this, saying:

> The Classis Britannica seems to have [often] functioned ... as some kind of army service corps, supporting the Government and provincial army, rather than [just] as a Navy in the modern sense.

This use of the military, whether it be land forces or naval, in a civilian context would have been entirely normal in the Roman world (see Chapter 5). Even after the Diocletianic reformation of the late third and early fourth centuries AD, when a new level of bureaucracy was installed to help manage the creaking Empire, these new officials were classified as being part of the army and styled *militia officialis*. Wearing military uniforms, these bureaucrats were even attached to defunct and largely fictitious military units with, for example, the former *legio* I *Adiutrix* providing an administrative home for the clerks of the Praetorian Prefect in Rome. We have a spectacular example of this crossover role from our period of interest earlier in the Empire in the form of the Marcus Maenius Agrippa detailed in Chapter 1 who, when one cross references the two epigraphic mentions of his career from Umbria and Maryport, seems to have held the posts of procurator and *praefectus classis Britannicae* in the mid-second century at the same time. This dual role for the regional fleet and its commander was sometimes assisted by the governor's appointment of a *beneficiarii procuratoris* from his own staff to serve on the procurator's staff, acting as a go between.

Over time the position of *praefectus classis* grew into a very senior position on the equestrian career path, with the commanders of the *Classis Ravennate* and *Classis Misenensis* having the same status as the head of the Praetorian Guard in Rome. Initially former legionary tribunes and later legates, it is clear from the epigraphic data detailed in Chapter 1 that it was common for the *praefectus classis* to switch between legionary and *classis* command, and indeed between both and senior civilian positions. Later, after Claudius' integration of the civil and military branches of the Imperial administration, the post *praefectus classis* was opened up to freedmen of the Imperial household. This changed back after the Year of the Four Emperors in AD 69 when sea power was one of the keys to the eventual victory of Vespasian, and after this time the post reverted back to being an equestrian-only position again. One can judge from the table on page 46 listing the pay of the *praefectus classis* of each of the regional fleets their order of seniority, but from this point new titles also began to be added to those of the fleet commander, further indicating levels of importance. Thus the commanders of the two senior fleets received the added title of *praetoria* to the *praefectus*, leading to the titles *praefectus classis praetorii Ravennate* and *praefectus classis praetorii Misenensis*. Similarly, the commanders of the Pannonian and Moesian regional navies gained the title of *flavia*, in terms of importance below *praetoria*, to add to the title of the commanders of these two fleets. Similarly, the commanders of the German and Egyptian regional fleets also gained an additional title, this time *augusta*. We do not know of any added title for the commander of the *Classis Britannica* but analogy may shed some light here given that the procurator in Britain also carried the title *augusta*.

As an aside here, and relevant given it overlaps with the final years of the *Classis Britannica*, the division of command of the Roman military in Britain is unclear following Septimius Severus' creation of the two provinces in the islands of Britain in the early third century. Common sense dictates, however, that the troops on the northern and western frontiers would have reported to the governor in York while those having a wider regional responsibility (for example the *Classis Britannica*) would have reported to the governor in London (Roman *Londinium*).

Meanwhile, in the same way that the procurator had a specialist staff working beneath him, so did the *praefectus classis* of the regional fleets. These would have included his second-in-command, the *subpraefectus* (who would have fulfilled the modern roles of executive officer and aide-de-camp), and a *cornicularius* as a third-in-command and acting as chief of staff. Other functionaries of the staff of the *praefectus classis* would have included *beneficiarii* (headquarters staff), *actuarii* (clerks), *scribae* (writers) and *dupliarii* (leading ratings).

Below the level of the headquarters staff the structural hierarchy of the Roman regional navy relied heavily on Hellenistic nomenclature adopted from the initial Roman contact with Greek culture in the eastern Mediterranean. In this context, the commander of a squadron of ships was called a *navarchus* (with the most senior being styled *navarchus princepes*), while the captain of an individual ship was called a *trierarchus* (referencing the title's origins with the captain of a trireme). Below this level, land-based Roman military nomenclature was added to the mix, reflecting the experiences of the Roman navies in the Punic Wars when they would prefer to close with an enemy and use the *corvus* rather than fighting from afar. Therefore the *trierarchus'* executive team, which sat outside the military component of the wider ship's company, included the ship's *gubernator* (senior officer and responsible for supervising the steering oars), a *proretus* (acting as a second lieutenant) and a *pausarius* (rowing master). More junior officers on the *trierarchus'* staff included the *secutor* (master at arms), *nauphylax* (officers of the watch) and specialists such as a *velarii* (in charge of the sails) and a *fabri* (the ship's carpenter). This gathering was completed by a number of *scribae*. The *navarchus*, *trierarchus* and their executive team exercised command and control when at sea through the use of either signal flags or the use of highly polished metal discs in the form of heliographs.

As for the ship's company itself, this was called a century whether it corresponded to a legionary century or not in terms of size, and included everybody else aboard outside the *trierarchus'* own executive team. As with its land counterpart, the century was commanded by a centurion who was assisted by his own team comprising an *optio* (second-in-command), *suboptio* (a more junior assistant), *bucinator* (bugler) or *cornice* (horn player), and an *armorum custus* (armourer). Below the level of these specialists the rest of the complement comprised marines (whether *sagitarri* archers, *ballistarii* artillery crew or *propugnatores* deck soldiers), some *valarius* (sailors) and, of course, plenty of oarsmen (*remiges*, who were professionals, never slaves as depicted by Hollywood), this whole ship's company being generically known as *milites* (soldiers, the singular being *miles*) rather than *nautae* (sailors), reflecting once again the original preference of the Roman navy for close action.

At the beginning of the Principate, service as a *milites* aboard ship was less well regarded than service on land in the legions or auxilia, though this did change over the period of existence of the *Classis Britannica*. Initially, as detailed in Chapter 3 with regard to the British regional navy once it was established, recruits came from local communities with maritime experience. This was a tradition that dated back to the late Republic when allied nations were frequently encouraged to supply experienced sailors for the Roman fleets, Cicero (XI.5), for example, highlighting Proconsul C. Cassius being urged by the Senate to use Asian sailors for the fleet in the eastern Mediterranean. This recruiting base widened as the Empire matured, and into the second and third centuries recruits were also sourced from inland communities (sometimes from far afield), the new *milites* then simply being trained on the job once they had joined a ship's crew. Such crews were extremely skilled, with Mason (2009, 31) explaining:

> The crews were highly trained, professional soldiers proud of their abilities and with a strong espirit de corps.

Only in extremis were criminals or slaves drafted into service, and then (as indicated by historical precedent) only after being made freedmen (Appian, V.1). Once in the service of the Emperor the *milites* (whether from a nautical background or not) went through an extensive training regime, particularly the *remiges* who manned the oars of the galleys. Their training began ashore in specially set up *icria*, mock-ups of the oaring systems. Meanwhile, marines seem to have been recruited from even farther afield than the other *milites*, for example the two detailed in Chapter 1 with regard to their gravestones found in Boulogne originating from Thrace and Syria.

Terms of service for all ranks of the regional navy, up to and including the *trierarch*, were similar to though slightly longer than those of the auxilia of the Principate, with a normal length of service of twenty-six years being ultimately rewarded with Roman citizenship. Only a *navarchus* could gain citizenship within the twenty-six years. This pattern seems to have been set up by Augustus at the same time as he set the length of service for legionaries at twenty years and auxilia at twenty-five. The difference of the year between the auxilia and *milites* may reflect the lesser status for the latter at the beginning of Augustus reign, though after AD 160 (and at a time when the status of the *milites* had improved) the term of service was increased to twenty-eight years, so the original difference may be for a reason unclear to us today.

The *milites* all received three gold pieces or 75 *denarii* as a one-off upfront payment when they enlisted, interestingly the same amount as both legionaries and auxilia. Basic annual pay at the beginning of the Principate for the lowest ranked *milites* was around 100 denarii, the same as for an auxilia. Those given greater responsibilities were paid an additional bonus on top, with those paid one and a half times the basic salary being called *sesquiplicarii* and those paid double being called *duplicarii*. From this annual salary, just like his land-based equivalents, the *milites* would have had deducted a certain amount to cover the cost of arms, equipment and food, and an additional amount that would be paid into the squadron's savings bank for his retirement fund.

Clothing aboard ship would have differed between the regional fleets given the differing weather conditions, except perhaps the marines, but even here there would have been regional variations in the choice of helmet and armour. One can be sure that for the *Classis Britannica* an essential item of clothing would have been the *birrus*. Staple clothing for the *milites* in northern waters would also have included a *pilos* conical felt hat, a belted tunic and trousers, and either *caligae* (sandals) or felt stockings and low-cut leather boots as footwear. When on official duty the *sagum* military cloak would also have been added. A final point to note here is that the *milites* serving aboard the *speculatoria navigia* scouting *myoparo* and *scapha* would have had their clothing camouflaged an azure blue or sea grey to match the similarly coloured sails and hulls.

For weaponry the *milites* of the *Classis Britannica* would have been armed in a similar fashion to their land-based auxiliary counterparts. Aside from artillery the principal missile weapons would have been bows and slings, with javelins and darts also being used at close range. At the point of boarding an enemy vessel, *pilae* armour-penetrating javelins would also have been used, while for close work the *milites* of this period would have been armed with boarding pikes, *hasta navalis* (naval spear), stabbing swords (such as the *gladius* rather than the slashing swords preferred by their regional opponents) and the *dolabra* boarding axe. Armour, while noting the likelihood of regional variations, would usually again have mirrored the land-based auxilia, with the *navarchus* and *trierarchus* wearing an iron-muscled cuirass (this based on the numerous grave stele of senior naval officers) while the marines in the ranks would have worn a hip-length shirt of iron chain mail (*lorica hamata*) or iron scales (*lorica squamata*). Helmets would have ranged from those of a standard military pattern made at a state-run *fabricae* workshop (for example the Gallic type, offering protection not only to the head but also the cheeks and back of the neck) to the simple *pilos* conical type. For a shield the auxiliary wood and leather oval design would have been used rather than the larger and heavier *scutum* of the legionaries, it being much more flexible in the close confines of hand-to-hand fighting at sea. Such shields would have been stowed along the sides of the *liburnae* above the oar ports when not in use, in much the same way those aboard Viking longboats are often depicted.

Given the overall crew size of up to 200 men in a vessel at best 30m in length (and with a narrow beam to boot), life aboard the *liburnae* of the *Classis Britannica* would have been cramped with little privacy (with even less on the *myoparo*, *scapha* and *codicarii* though more so on the larger merchant vessels). To that end it is likely the officers and *milites* would have shared their food and drink while on service, given the likely friction in such a confined space if the officers were treated significantly better. Examples abound of problems aboard ship with the morale of the crew if their superiors were treated too ostentatiously, a good example perhaps being the Imperial German Navy in the later stages of the First World War. If possible, even when on patrol and on long-range journeys, meals would have been taken ashore. The food and drink was stored wherever possible, the latter in animal skins or large terracotta containers called *dolia* or *pithoi*. Water was, of course, vital, and the first provision catered for after the ship's gear, sails, cordage and spare oars had been loaded aboard. To get an idea of the amount needed, a quinquereme '5' of the Punic Wars with some 250 *remiges* needed half a ton of water a day. Wine would also have been carried, but the clear priority was water. In terms of food, ships seem to have carried around ten days' worth, together with the means of processing it (*mortaria*, basins, hand mills and similar). Staple foods for the officers and *milites* of the *Classis Britannica* would have included bread, various *pulmentum* porridge recipes and the ubiquitous ship's biscuit (which derives its name from the latin *bis coctus*, literally twice cooked). One reference to the diet of Greek galley crews also references the oarsmen eating a mix of barley meal with wine and oil while rowing. Fresh and dried fruit and vegetables would have been added to the diet when available, as well as meat and fish. In the case of the latter two, cattle, sheep and pigs were the most common farm animals across Roman-occupied Britain, while eel, herring, plaice/flounder, cyprinids (such as carp) and salmonids were the most common fish. All would have been liberally doused in the ubiquitous *garum* fish sauce when available!

Finally, here we can again get phenomenological insight into the lives of those manning the *Classis Britannica* and the regional fleets through an appreciation of the role religion played in their daily lives. Even in the age in which we live, with its astonishing levels of science and technology, those regularly sailing on the open ocean are notably superstitious. This was writ large in the classical world given the lack of such modern technology to predict weather and sea conditions accurately. Of course, those living in the past would have had their own ways of compensating to an extent in this regard, with their own detailed understandings of the environments in which they lived and worked. However, one should equally note, as an example of the inherent dangers, the huge losses of ships and men suffered by Republican Rome during the Punic Wars to storms, a poignant reminder of the risks taken by those travelling at sea in the ancient world. It is no surprise that Caligula singularly failed to convince his troops to invade Britain from northern France in AD 40, and that Claudius similarly had to overcome superstitious fears on the part of the troops used to invade across the English Channel in AD 43 (see discussion of both in Chapters 4 and 6). Even riverine travel was viewed as problematic, noting here the number of Romano-Celtic temples found in north-western Europe in association with a riparian setting. Examples of the latter include East Farleigh on the River Medway, and Domburg and Colijnsplaat at the mouth of the River Scheldt (Cunliffe, 2013, 383). Such temples are described as providing a religious 'hello-goodbye' function for those using the rivers in their daily lives.

This superstition with regard to naval travel had many manifestations in the ancient world, over and above the temples mentioned above. For example, one of the earliest known designs used to decorate a seagoing ship was the *oculus* 'all-seeing eye' painted on to the bow of a vessel to 'see the way forward'. Similarly, it was common practice for a statuette or

shrine of the patron deity of a given ship to be placed in its
stern (though the Hollywood example of Hera as seen in the
film *Jason and the Argonauts* may be stretching things a little!).
Indeed, it was equally common for the ship's name to be associated with the deity concerned, while as another example of
superstition at sea, sailing on a Friday was also considered bad
luck in the Roman world.

Deities associated with sea travel in the classical world
included god of the sea Neptune (the Greek Poseidon,
although in the Roman world he was also associated with
unpredictability), Oceanus (the divine manifestation of the sea
in the form of a river encircling the known world) and Castor
and Pollux, the *dioscuri*. The latter, sons of Zeus and Leda (wife
of Tyndareus) in Greek mythology, were said to have been
sent as two balls of flame to help Jason's *Argo* when the ship
was caught in a storm. Thereafter they were often linked with
sea travel, this continuing into the Roman world where they
were depicted as silver-clad armoured horsemen. Even today
they are associated with St Elmo's Fire, the weather phenomenon whereby luminous plasma dances on the rigging of ships
during electrical storms, almost certainly the source of the
original *dioscuri* association with sea travel. Given the procliv-
ity in the Roman world for the integration of local deities
into the wider system of worship (a good example being Sulis
Minerva in Bath), it is no surprise that the provincial fleets also
had associations with their regional pantheons.

A good example would be the *Classis Alexandrina* in Egypt
where Isis was the local goddess linked to sea travel, while
the *Classis Syriaca* had links to the eastern cult of Mithras (a
deity heavily associated with the Roman military from the
first century AD). The Roman Empire being what it was, however, it comes as no surprise that these local deities were also
found being worshipped at the opposite ends of the Empire
in a marine context, for example Isis along the Rhine frontier and Mithras at a temple at Burham on the banks of the

River Medway in Kent. This spread of ideas is indicative of the distance through which the *milites* of the regional fleets were recruited as the regional fleets matured (note above the marines from Thrace and Syria whose tombstones were found in Boulogne). Links of Mithras with the regional fleets continued until their ultimate demise with, for example, a *praefectus* of the *Classis Misenensis* on the eastern coast of Italy dedicating an altar to the deity in the mid-third century AD. A last consideration here is with regard to Christianity, whose rise to dominance among the religions of the Roman Empire sits outside the chronological span of this book. Nevertheless, the arrival of this eastern cult in Britain would have just overlapped the period of activity of the *Classis Britannica* given what we think St Alban was martyred in the middle of the third century (Lambert, 2010, 6).

Now, having set out the detailed background regarding Roman naval power above, it is time to review the Roman military presence in the province (and later provinces) of Britain within which the *Classis Britannica* sat.

3

THE ROMAN MILITARY
IN BRITAIN AND THE
CLASSIS BRITANNICA

This chapter provides in-depth analysis of the composition of the Roman military presence in Britain during the occupation, paying particular attention to the *Classis Britannica*. In particular I set out here the full chronological history of the *Classis Britannica*, allowing the later detail regarding the campaigns of the regional fleet to be better understood.

The Size of the Roman Military in Britain

To start with the land forces, the initial invasion force under Aulus Plautius totalled up to 40,000 men (Grainge, 2005, 111) comprising four legions (*legio* II *Augusta*, *legio* IX *Hispana*, *legio* XIV *Gemina* and *legio* XX *Valeria Victrix*) and 20,000 auxiliaries carried by 900 ships (Grainge, 2005, 129). It is worth noting the huge size of this force (which does not count the thousands of servants and slaves who would have accompanied it), reflecting Caesar's experiences in his ultimately abortive landings in 55 BC and 54 BC. With regard to the first of these, Caesar arrived with just two legions (*legio* VII *Claudia Pia Fidelis* and *legio* X *Fretensis*) totalling some 10,000 men, while the latter featured five legions (*legio* VII and four others) totalling 25,000 men plus 2,000 auxiliary cavalry. As detailed in Chapter 1, the Roman poet Horace certainly indicates that the failure of these two operations definitely had a big impact on the psyche of a Roman military, and indeed wider society, by this time well used to victory. The fact that Horace references the 'fierce Britons' alongside the Parthians is a key indicator here, the latter famously having withstood repeated Roman attempts at military engagement and conquest.'

In the case of both of Caesar's incursions his force was clearly insufficient, a matter definitively addressed for the AD 43 invasion (which itself can be argued nearly failed during the Boudican revolt of AD 60/61).

With regard to the size of the military presence in Britain in the post-conquest period, Martin Millett (1990, 181) has calculated that the army totalled up to 20,000 troops in normal circumstances. David Mattingly (2006, 131) goes further, saying that it numbered up to 55,000 in the second century (this before Severus' northern campaigns in Scotland in the early third century when his invasion force totalled 50,000 alone), and between 20,000 and 25,000 in the fourth century. A useful statistic to consider here is that the British Army in early 2014 numbered just under 100,000 regular and reserve-trained personnel. Therefore Mattingly's figure of up to 55,000 troops in the second century is clearly a huge number for this north-western archipelago of Empire, especially given a likely maximum population at the time of just over 3.5 million (see Chapter 1) compared to the 64 million today. To provide even more context, Mattingly's military figure of 55,000 represented up to 12 per cent of the entire Roman army at that time, in just 4 per cent of the overall Imperial territory. It is

also worth noting here that both Millett and Mattingly, in the
same calculations that determined the size of the military in
Britain, also look at the size of the associated garrison settlements, with the former estimating a figure of between 50,000
and 200,000 and the latter 100,000 in the second century and
50,000 in the fourth century.

Turning to the maritime component of the military presence in Britain, the *Classis Britannica* had its origins in the
Claudian invasion of AD 43 when the naval force of 900 ships
was created to facilitate the incursion. Initially formed around
a core of experienced men from the *Classis Misenensis*, it
was not actually called the *Classis Britannica* until the Flavian
period, when regional stability gave the province the opportunity to formalise its activities. By that time Cunliffe (2013,
386) speculates that the majority of its sailors and shipbuilders
would have originated from the Morini and Menapii coastal
tribes of Belgic Gaul and from the Batavi in the Rhine Delta,
on the basis that these were the tribes in the region with
the most experience in shipbuilding and maritime activity.
Mason (2003, 31) adds that other regional communities who
may have provided ship's crew included the Chauci, Frisi and
Veneti, all well known for their nautical skills.

The manpower complement of the *Classis Britannica* can
be inferred from the size of the wider Roman fleet, and its
regional components, over time. The original Roman war
fleets created to fight the First and Second Punic Wars (see
Chapter 2) were extensive, given the nature of the conflict
across the western Mediterranean, numbering up to 60,000
men in terms of crew for the second iteration. Most of these
would have been *remiges*, for example 30,000 such oarsmen
being needed for the 203 BC invasion of Africa to man the 160
warships that landed the troops who would ultimately win
the war at the Battle of Zama. This overall figure of 60,000
fell to around 30,000 by the reign of Augustus at the turn
of the first century BC, before rising back to around 50,000

again by the reign of Hadrian in the second century AD as the regional fleets reached maturity. Key factors in this increase over 140 or so years would have been the growth of the *Classis Germanica* and creation of the *Classis Britannica*. As can be seen in Chapter 2, based on the stipend paid to their commanders, these two were jointly the third most important fleets in the Empire after the Italy-based *Classis Misenensis* and *Classis Ravennate*. It is from the complements of these two latter fleets that we can start to infer the size of the *Classis Britannica*, with Mason (2003, 31) arguing that during the reigns of Otho and Vitellius in AD 69 the former had a complement of 6,000 and the latter 10,000 (using a calculation based on the number of *milites* converted for legionary land-based warfare during the Year of the Four Emperors). He then looks at the military mission of the *Classis Britannica*, arguing it would need three squadrons to maintain sea control in the oceanic zone and to control the littoral in its areas of activity, these squadrons operating on the east and west coasts of Britain and in the Bristol Channel. Finally, he looks at the known fleet bases at Boulogne (the headquarters, detailed in Chapter 4, where he says the fort would have accommodated 3,500), Dover (640 men) and other bases such as Richborough, Lympne and Pevensey (all detailed in Chapter 4). Based on all these factors he calculates the complement of the *Classis Britannica* would have been around 7,000 men.

As detailed in Chapter 1, the last epigraphic testament to the existence of the *Classis Britannica* is that of Saturninus, ex-*trierarchus* in the British Fleet, dated to AD 244–249 (Russel, 2002). Ingleton (2012, 10) and Cleere (1977, 19) add that around this time the *Classis Britannica* fort at Dover also fell out of use, the latter saying it was slighted deliberately and comprehensively. Meanwhile, Morris (2010, 147) also argues that around this time there is a marked decline in North Sea trade. Such data and anecdote has traditionally been used to argue the case that the *Classis Britannica* ceased to exist in the mid-third century, for example by Cunliffe (2013, 389). There is no clear data to indicate why the regional navy disappears at this time, this being discussed in detail in Chapter 9. For our purposes regarding the size of the Roman military presence in Britain, however, we can return to the second century when the *Classis Britannica* was at its height, taking Mattingly's 55,000 figure for the army and adding to it the 7,000 personnel of the regional fleet, giving a huge total of 62,000 military personnel operating in and around the islands of Britain. This would represent an eighth of the entire Imperial military complement at the time, a figure large enough to prompt Herodian (2.15) to comment on its size and power. No wonder Britain was regarded as the wild west of the Empire!

Military Infrastructure

This huge Roman military presence in Britain during the occupation required a serious support infrastructure to enable it to be used effectively without weighing too heavily on the regional economy. In the first instance the most telling manifestation of this was the new network of major roadways built in Britain both during the conquest period, this tracking the legions as they advanced across the country, and afterwards as the economy of the new province grew. The major roads included Watling Street from Richborough through London to Wroexter (Roman *Viroconium*), Ermine Street from London through Lincoln (Roman *Lindum*) to York, Dere Street from York to the northern frontier, and the Fosse Way from Lincoln to Exeter (Roman *Isca Dumnoniorum*). These principal roadways provided the Roman military in the province with the ability to move rapidly from one end of the country to another, with additional routes such as Akeman Street from London to Gloucester and Stane Street from London to Chichester (Roman *Noviomagus Reginorum*) providing short cuts as required. To these roads we can add a plethora of similarly well-built minor roads such that Britain was threaded for the first time with a circulatory system fit to support one of the fastest growing economies of the Empire, and one that as can be seen in Chapters 6, 7 and 8 was in an almost constant state of military engagement, particularly to the north and west. This network linked up directly with the similar road network across the English Channel through Boulogne and the other ports along the North Sea and Atlantic coasts of north-western Europe (see discussion in Chapter 4 regarding the Roman perception of water barriers, whether sea or river based, that differed to ours today), fully integrating the new province with the heart of the Roman Empire. The Antonine Itinerary is of particular interest here as it clearly shows three of the key roadways in the south-east of Britain start or finish at the Channel ports.

Finally on roads, when considering this network across occupied Britain, we can reflect on how the Romans themselves would have viewed this new transport network. Such infrastructure to modern eyes is exactly as it appears, a means of facilitating economic activity. To the Romans though it was an expression of power and the might of Rome. In this regard, the laying down of this organised, versatile and long-lasting means of connectivity was a means of putting the stamp of Roman authority on the local landscape and peoples newly integrated into the Empire. Thus, wherever there was a road, there was Roman power and authority.

These roads then linked together another new manifestation of Rome that appeared in Britain for the first time, namely stone-built urban centres. These came in three forms, in the first instance *coloniae*, which were chartered towns for Roman citizens, often established to settle discharged veterans. A good example in occupied Britain would be Colchester (Roman *Camulodunum*). Next we can consider the *municipia*, these again being chartered towns but with more of a mercantile focus, a

good example being St Albans (Roman *Verulamium*). Finally
we have the *civitas capitals*, which functioned very much as
modern county towns do, being the principal cities of a given
tribe or people. Good examples include Caerwent (Roman
Venta Silurum, the tribal centre of the Silures) and Canterbury
(Roman *Durovurnum Catiacorum*, the tribal centre of the
Cantiaci). To these we can add what archaeologists today call
small towns, they being quite literally that and usually having
an association with either industry (for example salt production or iron manufacturing), religion or being located on a key
transport node. A good example of a small town in the latter
context is Rochester (Roman *Durobrivae*), sitting as it does on
the junction of Watling Street with the River Medway. The
importance of towns of all sizes with regard to providing the
infrastructure to facilitate military activity is writ large when
you consider how many of the roads detailed above transit
through them. For example, the Antonine Itinerary shows that
eight out of the fifteen most important routes in occupied
Britain start, finish or pass through London, while similarly
four are linked with York.

Back to our Roman focus on military infrastructure, the
next major manifestation of the Roman presence in Britain
would have come in the form of the legionary and *vexillation*-
size fortresses (respectively 20ha and 8–12ha in size) that
dotted the landscape, tracking the initial conquest period
(and subsequent campaigns) and later the incorporation of
the new province into the Empire. Noting that the individual
sites waxed and waned in importance and use throughout the
occupation, key examples of the former included Colchester,
Exeter, Caerleon (Roman *Isca Silurum*), Gloucester (Roman
Glevum), Wroxeter (Roman *Veroconium Cornoviorum*), Chester
(Roman *Castra Deva*), Lincoln, York and Inchtuthil (Roman
Pinnata Castra and, the most northerly of all legionary
fortresses, abandoned early following the Agricolan offensive
discussed in Chapter 6). Legionary fortresses were huge

investments in capital and man-hours and were designed to house an entire legion, more than 5,000 men.

Meanwhile, the British landscape also featured lesser *vexillation* fortresses designed to accommodate smaller bodies of men. Many have an early date (being associated with the conquest period) and were designed to accommodate not just legionaries but also auxilia in mixed battle groups. Good examples of such forts include Corbridge and Mancetter (Roman *Manduessedum*). To these we can add the multitude of smaller auxiliary forts across the entire province, for example those such as Vindolanda on the Stanegate roadway marking the pre-Hadrian's Wall northern frontier and others at the heads of the valleys in the conquered north and west where they were designed to provide security in the less stable border regions.

The location of these forts of all sizes is one of the best indicators we have of the geographical deployment of military force in occupied Britain, showing clearly this was not spread evenly across the province but was largely a feature of the border regions of the north and west (though note the comments in Chapter 4 regarding Kent and the Imperial gateway). We are fortunate in this regard in that we can track, through epigraphy and other aspects of the historical record, the presence of the key military formations in Britain over time. To that end we know that at various times the *legio* II *Augustus* was based at Caerleon (see Chapter 6), Corbridge and Carpow (a fort on the confluence of the rivers Tay and Earn in Perth and Kinross). Similarly, the *legio* VI *Victrix* that came to Britain with the Emperor Hadrian can be found at various times at York, Corbridge and Carpow. Such movement of the legions between various locations was common, even when not on campaign. Thus, movements of entire legions around, or in and out of, Britain saw successive legions occupying the key legionary fortresses at Chester, Lincoln, Wroxeter and York. Early in the occupation there were usually four legions in

Britain, one for each of these forts, but by the early second century there were only three, with the legionary fortresses at Caerleon, Chester and York becoming the fixed centres of the defence of the northern and western borders (Wroxeter had by this time become the *civitas capital* of the Cornovii).

Later in the occupation, but outside the context of this book on the period of activity of the *Classis Britannica*, a new set of coastal fortresses were built around Britain, notably those of the Saxon Shore from the early second century (though most were later) and at other key locations such as Cardiff (possibly Roman *Tamium*). Meanwhile, the final set of bases to consider in this appreciation of the infrastructure required to support the military presence in occupied Britain are those used specifically by the *Classis Britannica*. This analysis is actually carried out in Chapter 4 in the context of the military roles of the *Classis Britannica*.

Having considered the roads, towns and fortresses of Britain and how they supported the military presence in occupied Britain, I finally detail here the means by which the legionaries and *milites* were equipped. Much military equipment in the Empire was manufactured in *fabricae* of various sizes, and there is indeed evidence of these in Britain. Such workshops, large and small, were vital to ensure the readiness for action of the military in all of its roles, and are thus an indication of an extensive military presence in a given region.

In the first instance there is a strong and recognised association for smaller *fabricae* to be located within legionary fortresses. Examples include Caerleon, Inchtuthil and Exeter, with geophysical data at the former highlighting a courtyard building featuring extensive burnt deposits, which has been interpreted as the legionary metalworking workshop. This stone-built structure, to the immediate west of the *principia*, featured the central courtyard square with an ambulatory and four surrounding ranges in which sat the workshops. At Inchtuthil a similar structure, this time built from timber, has been identified as a small *fabricae* by data, including a smithing hearth and a slag pit. Another similar structure within the walls of the legionary fortress at Exeter has also been interpreted as a fabricate. Such workshops have also been found at smaller fortress locations, for example at Corbridge. Here, archaeological data including arrowheads, iron scales and iron slag found alongside hearths and tempering tanks has resulted in one of the buildings within the site of the Agricolan-period *vexillation* fort being interpreted as a small military manufactory.

On a larger scale, however, a similar dataset has been found in a non-fortress context at the Ickham Water Mills site on the Little Stour River to the east of Canterbury. Well known as the location of an extensive occupation-period water-milling facility, it was one of only five major water-milling sites known from the occupation in Britain. With four mills known to have operated from the second through to the fourth century, other evidence now suggests it also had other functions. Excavated in the 1970s, material culture finds included five official lead seals, four stamped with the heads of late Roman Emperors (one of Constantine II, AD 337–340, and three of Julian, AD 360–363) while the fifth has a stamp indicating it originated from Smyrna in Anatolia. The excavators themselves additionally detailed the finding of spearheads, ballista bolt heads, lorica hamata chain mail and late period helmet components, while Young (1984, 35) also highlights the finding of late Roman fittings for *cingulum* military belts. Most enigmatic though is a large iron hammerhead found at the site featuring mechanical deformation on one side. The presence of this find, together with the military equipment and large quantities of iron, bronze and pewter waste, has led to speculation that the water courses were also being used to power water hammers to produce or maintain military equipment in support of the nearby military presence in Canterbury and the regional Saxon Shore forts.

R.J. Spain (1981, 32), in his detailed study of Roman water-mills in Britain, argues that the site was indeed being used by the Roman state to support the military, while Young (1981, 36) also gives some idea of scale, saying:

> Ickham … was most probably in the 4th century an official works depot for local units of the Saxon shore, supplying them with flour and metal work. The presence of lead seals may suggest also that it was used for storage. It should not be regarded as a full-scale fabricae, the Imperial arms factories recorded [on the Continent] in the Notitia Dignitatum. There were few of them and, according to the Notitia, none were located in Britain apart from a clothing factory. A much better parallel would be the legionary works compound [detailed above] at Corbridge.

This seems a reasonable interpretation to me based on the available data, though more work is clearly required to definitively identify the site as a state-controlled military enterprise.

Military Identity

Finally in this section we can consider the current debate about the nature of the Roman military's sense of its own identity and how this impacted the legionaries, auxilia and *milites* in occupied Britain. Gardner (2013, 11) argues that current historical and archaeological thinking actually fails to consider how to make sense of large political units (such as the military) in favour of a focus on the experiences of the smaller units and lower levels of society. He says, however, that new theoretical approaches such as post-colonialism (which acknowledges the inherent power inequalities of Imperialism and colonialism) and globalisation (for example looking at the connections between different social scales in a given society) are now providing a platform to begin a re-evaluation of the nature of the Roman military. Fundamental to this is a debate about whether the Roman military was actually a homogenous whole (as it is often portrayed) or whether it had a multitude of identities, and in this regard the *Classis Britannica* can provide some serious insight.

The Roman military was clearly separate in its own right from the rest of society, and indeed possessed its own manifestations of Roman material culture that are known readily to the specialist archaeologist, for example Germanic belt buckles in the later period. However, the question about whether it was comprised of multiple identities within its own community of soldiery is clearly important, as the answer has a huge impact on how we might expect the military to be experienced both internally (within the armed forces) and externally (by the rest of society). The question has prompted a lively debate in Roman archaeology, with Gardner (2013, 10) explaining that:

> … some Roman archaeologists … [are] significantly re-conceptualising the Roman military, and focusing upon the understanding of multiple military communities and identities, rather than a monolithic 'Roman Army'.

To this point, James (1999, 16) also argues in favour of a significant degree of regional variation in Roman military identity, saying that military identity was far from static and was refashioned regularly. In that regard, paradigms that can serve as templates to allow concepts of such multiple identities for the Roman military to be studied include:

Capability and specialisation, for example at a very basic level the land-based legionaries and auxilia and the naval *milites*, but also noting the prevalence in the Roman military for building complex armies with specialist units (Whitby, 2002, 23).

Chronology. At a basic level, in the case of land forces one can look at the differences between the composition of armies in the early Empire (with their legionaries and auxiliaries) and the *comitatenses, limitanei* and *foederates* of the later Empire (Goldsworthy, 2003, 200). In the case of maritime forces, a prime example would be the British regional fleet, with the formal *Classis Britannica* in the earlier Empire and more localised naval capability later (see Chapter 9).

Geography. This impacts military identity on two levels, firstly with regard to the place of origin of each military unit. Very clearly troops (at least originally) raised in a certain area maintained an association with it. This is visible at a macro level, for example the *legio* III *Cyrenaica*, which may have been founded in Libya (Goldsworthy, 2003, 51), and at a micro level, for example the Batavian auxiliaries who accompanied the Claudian invasion of Britain and fought at the Battle of Mons Graupius in AD 84 (Tacitus, xxxvi.1–2), and the *numerous barcariorum Tigrisiensum Tigris* boatmen operating from South Shields in the fourth century (Hodgson, 23, 2007). Finkle (2014, 138) argues these bargees maintained their identity on arrival to the extent they introduced the classic bitumen-coated Mesopotamian Guffa oracles to the rivers of north-eastern England. In the case of the focus of our study on the *Classis Britannica*, we also have the *milites* detailed in Chapters 1 and 2 whose gravestones have been found in Boulogne, which show they originated from Thrace and Syria.

The second impact of geography on a unit's military identity reflects its base of operations, which will clearly (over time) impact the evolution of its self-appreciation, however firmly this is rooted in its place of origin, and however separate one can argue the military was from the rest of society (Gardner, 2013,10). This process accelerated towards the end of the Empire in the west, Britain being a useful example where Gardner (2007, 255) highlights the gradual changes in the sense of identity over a period of generations for troops/warriors at the former edge of Empire.

Useful ciphers with which to look at such differentiated military identities are the legionary, *vexillation* and smaller fortresses detailed above, given their prominent position in the range of sites benefiting from detailed archaeological examination and historical interpretation. In particular, such sites allow examination both of the interaction actually within the residing military unit, and of the unit with the inhabitants of surrounding local communities.

In the case of the former, Gardner (2013, 11) speaks of the 'dialectic of control' in the military unit whereby power is both exerted over the individual soldier or *milite*, but is also contested by him. It is with such contestation that one might see examples of differing identities emerge. By way of example, Gardner talks of the baths at the major legionary fortress at Caerleon, saying (2013, 12):

> Evidence [here] speaks to both the imposition of discipline and the potential for discord that defined military practice in dynamic ways over time. The baths were a priority in the construction of the fortress … and although later modifications would expand the complex, the importance of bathing as a practice was promoted, both solidarity and bodily transformation [in conjunction with equipment and training] was clearly paramount. Yet the baths were also an area for more unstructured interaction, with the finds providing evidence of gambling, casual food consumption and the potential for socializing with non-soldiers.

This dialectic becomes even more pronounced as the occupation in Britain (and the Roman experience elsewhere) progressed, with on the one hand the extra layers of public administration following the Diocletianic Reformation increasing the coercive experience of being within the Roman military, and on the other very different building styles emerging within military sites and once again showing evidence of individuality. In the latter regard Gardner (2013, 12) references the different ways in which barracks were rebuilt at Caerleon.

Meanwhile, with regard to using a fortress garrison's interaction with the surrounding community as a means of examining differentiated identities within the military, one of the best indicators is that of scale. Both Millett (1990, 185) and Mattingly (2011, 223) argue that the garrison settlements associated with the military had a population at least twice that of the military establishment. The former says that an army presence in the islands of between 10,000 and 20,000 attracted a garrison settlement population of between 50,000 and 200,000 (an enormous figure) while the latter says that when the military presence in Britain peaked in the second century at between 45,000 and 55,000, the associated settlement population was 100,000. While many inhabitants of these settlements would have been members of the military train, many others would be local. Mattingly (2011, 223) describes such communities thus:

> These were the families [official and unofficial] of the soldiery and veterans, the traders, the craftspeople, and servicers of the needs and desires of the army.

Common sense alone dictates that the presence of this community in close proximity to the military unit would have impacted the identity of the latter.

This is an interesting debate and continues to be the subject of much discussion in Roman archaeological circles. However, for the purposes of this work on the *Classis Britannica*, the Roman military is considered as one body, with references to regional variations being made at specific points if relevant and appropriate.

4

THE MILITARY ROLES OF THE
CLASSIS BRITANNICA

Having set out detail concerning Roman naval power, and a narrative about the Roman military presence in Britain during the occupation, here I look in detail at the military roles fulfilled by the *Classis Britannica* and the infrastructure needed to facilitate these multifarious activities.

As a starting point we can reflect on the traditional objectives of warfare at sea, both in the classical world and indeed today. These are sea control, sea denial, the control or denial of choke points, the control or denial of basing and deployment areas, and the preservation of one's own and the denial of the enemy's ability to use the sea for economic activity. In the context of the *Classis Britannica*, these objectives extrapolate into the following roles: blue water military operations in the oceanic zone, coastal military operations in the littoral zone, intelligence gathering and patrol (in both zones, though principally the littoral), transport and amphibious operations, supply, and finally communications. Each is considered in turn, with the experiences of the *Classis Britannica* of each studied therein.

Blue water naval capability is associated with power projection in the oceanic zone, for example in a counter-force role against enemy naval forces and also in the context of intervention against enemy maritime trade links and infrastructure to disrupt economic activity. The ultimate aim is sea control, that is 'command of the sea' as achieved by the Roman Empire through much of its existence and, by way of analogy, by Britain in the nineteenth century (Rubel, 2012, 1). A significant amount of activity in blue water naval operations takes place at the strategic level, with Vego (2014, 30) highlighting that opportunities to carry out major naval operations are much more prevalent in this environment than in littoral operations. Blue water warfare was less common in the classical world than the modern era, with most engagements at that time taking place in the littoral zone. This reflects the level of maritime technology available (see Chapter 2 for detail), with the ensuing preference of any naval commander to keep his fleet in sight of the coast if possible during transit (not precluding travelling out of sight of the coast totally, but mitigating against it where possible). Further, for much of the period of Roman naval military activity, symmetrical threats were few and far between, ruling out the need for a Mahan-esque 'sea power' capability for much of the history of the Empire. Exceptions would have included the Gothic naval raids in the Black Sea and eastern Mediterranean from the third century AD onwards given their scale and frequency, and perhaps during the frequent bouts of civil war that threatened sporadically the stability of the Empire.

Neither of the above examples mention the region of operations of the *Classis Britannica*, namely around the British Isles, the North Sea, the English Channel and the northern Continental coast as far as the Rhine. This is largely due to the lack of a regional symmetrical open ocean threat throughout the period of the *Classis Britannica*'s existence (and indeed throughout the majority of the occupation). By the time the regional fleet came officially into being, any Gallic Atlantic-coast threat was a distant memory given Caesar's conquests a century earlier. In fact, as set out above, many of the experienced sailors of the *Classis Britannica* would have originated from the Atlantic coast tribes given their maritime expertise. We do, of course, know of the maritime threat of northern Germanic raiders from the early third century onwards (see Chapter 8), it being notable that the fortification of key British cities such as London date to this period, together with the likely origins of the Saxon Shore forts in the south and east (their name being a giveaway here). However, the maritime technology of these Germanic raiders appears to have been less than that of their Viking successors later in the millennium, for while the hull forms of their rowing vessels seem similar (if smaller), their vessels lacked sails (McGrail, 2014, 142, again discussed in full in Chapter 8). Therefore the common perception is that instead of challenging a passage boldly straight across the North Sea to raid the superpower salient to their west, they followed a coastal route down the north-western European coast, then crossing to Britain at one of the closest crossing points, for example across the English Channel to Kent. Supporters of this argument say in this regard it is no surprise that the densest cluster of Saxon Shore forts was in Kent (see discussion at the end of this chapter), featuring the chain around the county's north-eastern coast from Reculver, then to Richborough, on to Dover and finally in this section of the chain on to Lympne. This view is discussed in Chapter 8 when I consider whether the Saxons actually challenged the later *Classis Britannica* in the oceanic zone of the North Sea to cross directly, though to be clear this threat was asymmetric and not an attempt to wrest sea control here away from the Empire.

Similarly, endemic raiding is also evident down the north-eastern coast of the later *diocese* by the Picts (the tribal confederation who appear in the historical record in Scotland from the later fourth century), and across the Irish Sea by raiders originating in Ireland (as evidenced by the story of St Patrick). Though famously co-ordinating their attacks on the *diocese* of *Britannia* in AD 367, with north Germans also joining in on this occasion, the level of maritime technology available to the Picts and Irish would have been even less in terms of sophistication than that of the Germans, so the need to keep clear if possible of the oceanic zone would have been much greater for these northern British and Irish raiders (again accepting there are always exceptions to the rule). Therefore, looking across this German, Pictish and Irish threat environment, the requirement for a blue water military capability would have been even less in these northern waters than in the Mediterranean, except the interdiction of any Germanic raiders crossing the North Sea. And, of course, sticking strictly to our terms of reference regarding the *Classis Britannica*, which as we have seen disappeared in the middle of the third century, even these later threats are almost chronologically irrelevant to the study except perhaps as useful analogies (though with a limited amount of Germanic and perhaps Irish raiding from the early third century).

Therefore, in the oceanic zone, for much of the period of its existence the main role of the *Classis Britannica* was not to project 'sea power' but rather to maintain and protect communications across the North Sea and from the south coast down to southern Gaul and northern Spain. This is considered in more detail later on, and is also the reason that this book does not consider macro-level naval tactics given it is highly unlikely the *Classis Britannica* would have engaged in fleet-scale engagements.

Clearly then, it is in the littoral combat area that the *Classis Britannica* played its greatest role in a military context during the occupation, the term referring to the littoral zone between the coast and the open ocean. It is writ large in all the major campaigns in our area of interest when military success was accompanied by close co-operation between the land forces and the regional fleet (see Chapters 6, 7 and 8). Littoral military action differed then, as today, from blue water operations in a number of ways. Vego (2014, 30) emphasises that most military activity in the littoral zone is tactical in nature, with decentralised command and control being the key to success given the rapidity with which the tactical and operational situation can change. We have a classic example of this in the context of Caesar's first incursion into Britain in 55 BC when he reports (4.25) the standard bearer of *legio* X *Fretensis* having to leap ashore to encourage his fellow legionaries to follow his example, they being surprised to find their landing opposed by British chariots and foot soldiers. Naval military operations in the littoral zone also required a different mix of platforms and capabilities than those needed to operate in the oceanic zone. This may explain the dominance in the Roman Empire of agile *liburnae* biremes in the battle-line force-mix (ideal for littoral warfare) compared to the larger cataphract-style quinqueremes and similar of the Punic Wars in the Republican period, the latter more capable as oceanic zone platforms given the greater relevance to the dominance of blue water sea lanes but less manoeuvrable and thus more vulnerable when close ashore.

The importance of a littoral combat capability is self-evident when one considers that today 95 per cent of the world's population is settled within 600 miles of the coast, and 80 per cent of the world's nations border the sea. This would have been no different throughout the existence of the *Classis Britannica* when the regional navies of the Roman Empire would have had to engage in operations along a sovereign coastline longer than any in a European context before or since (and additionally along major Continental river systems). Vega (2014, 31) provides further insight here regarding the economic importance of the littoral zone, highlighting that all seaborne trade, of course, begins and ends there.

The specific characteristics of carrying out military operations in the littoral zone include restricted space for manoeuvring (note how many naval battles in the pre-modern era took place because one side was trapped against the coastline, for example the key naval Battles of Carteia and the Ebro River and in the Second Punic War, Pitassi, 2012, 6, see Chapter 2), the dangerous marine environment for warships along a coastline (when a sudden change in the weather could prove fatal, as evidenced by the loss of twenty-seven Roman warships off Cape Palinuro in south-eastern Italy in AD 254 in the First Punic War, Polybius, I. 39, and see Chapter 2 for context), and the inherent difficulty in staying undetected by the enemy given the proximity of the coast and the associated reduction in warning time to respond to enemy aggression. For two excellent examples of the latter we can look to the Battle of Lilybaeum in 217 BC in the Second Punic War again, when a tip-off from Hiero of Syracuse led to the Roman interception of a Carthaginian naval raiding force and the capture of seven ships and 1,700 prisoners (Briscoe, 1989, 66), and the destruction of Majorian's African invasion fleet in AD 461 in the Bay of Alicante following its disclosure to the African Vandal King Gaiseric, this latter event sealing the fate of Roman North Africa until the Justinian reconquest (Heather, 2005, 399).

In terms of the *Classis Britannica*'s experiences of littoral warfare, this would have featured multiple tactical actions fought in the context of major land-based military campaigns (for example playing a key supporting role in the northern campaigns of Agricola in the late first century and Septimius Severus in the early third, see Chapters 5 and 7), specifically naval operations of significant size (for example counter-piracy operations in the Irish Sea), and smaller actions in isolation of wider military activity (for example protecting the western edge of the Continental *limes Germanicus* as far as the River Rhine, often overlooked in the context of the wider responsibilities of the *Classis Britannica*). As evidenced by the references to the Agricolan and Severan campaigns, the littoral military activities of the regional fleet form a core element of the wider chronological study of the activities of the *Classis Britannica* that follow, and they will be covered in depth there.

Next we can consider the intelligence gathering and patrol function performed by the *Classis Britannica*. Given its mix of vessel types and capabilities, like all of the Roman regional navies, the fleet would have provided the military around Britain, the North Sea and along the north-western European coast with a vital scouting capability. This would have been in the context of the experiences of littoral warfare detailed above, but also more broadly supporting the provincial governor's staff, for example in a policing function to prevent the smuggling of contraband. The value of good quality reconnaissance and intelligence gathering, particularly in the context of littoral activity, is writ large in a negative context in Caesar's (4.21) description of his first incursion into Britain, where not only were the landing troops surprised to find opposing Britons assembled to meet them, but where the legionaries also had to wade ashore through deep water due to the ships not being able to approach the shore closely. Having seen such a situation during a NATO amphibious operation in Norway while working for *Jane's Defence Weekly*, this author can reflect that troops enduring such an experience are not best pleased!

The *Classis Britannica*'s experience of fulfilling an intelligence gathering and patrol requirement would have been the principal daily activity of the regional navy. In such a role, when on a major campaign the fleet would have acted as the eyes and ears on the maritime flanks of the army, whether along the coast or down the major river networks (by way of analogy, in the case of the latter one should note the example of Vikings much later in the millennium making great use of British river systems to penetrate far inland for plunder and settlement). Once again, this campaigning role in the context of the Agricolan and Severan operations in northern Britain is considered in detail in Chapters 5 and 7.

Outside the context of a major campaign, steady patrolling would have been the daily meat and drink for the *Classis Britannica*. Here one can imagine the *liburnae* bireme patrolling every day, resplendent with marine shields balanced in long rows above ore ports and bedecked with *ballistae*, and the *myoparo* and *scapha* cutters and skiffs skidding in and out of coastal inlets ensuring the steady flow of wealth from the province to the Emperor's *fiscus* was not disrupted by smuggling and commercial illegality. Whether keeping an eye on the coastal Germanic tribes north of the *limes Germanicus* or simply keeping the sea lanes clear around the British Isles and across the North Sea, the *Classis Britannica* would have been on patrol in all weathers throughout the year, except in the most hostile climatic conditions.

Progressing in our analysis of the roles of the *Classis Britannica*, we next come to transport and amphibious operations. This was, of course, a key role for the regional fleet, especially given it was actually created in the first place for such a requirement when the 900 ships detailed in Chapter 3 were gathered for the Claudian invasion in AD 43 (taking the name *Classis Britannica* from the Flavian period). The fleet would have used whatever vessel type was necessary when fulfilling this role, whether large merchantmen (either sailing under the fleet's colours, indentured or contracted) for large-scale activity, or *liburnae*, *myoparo* and *scapha* for the swift insertion of troops into hostile territory on raiding missions to disrupt enemy economic activity. In the case of the former, the Agricolan and Severan campaigns again provide the best examples for study (as in Chapters 5 and 7) when the east coast of Britain in particular would have witnessed the transit northwards of the heavy-lifting vessels of the fleet, laden with troops and material for the attempts at northern conquest. For the latter, disruptive raiding would also have been an ongoing activity (and anecdotally would have been the principal one for the predominantly river-based regional fleets such as the *Classis Germanica*).

The *Classis Britannica* would also, of course, have contributed to the maritime supply network around the British Isles and across the Channel and North Sea. In a military capacity this was vital given the need to maintain the very significant presence in the north and west at this outermost extremity of the Empire, with Selkirk (1983, 72) for example arguing the military installed riverine hydraulic infrastructure (locks, weirs and similar) into the Rivers Tyne and Tees to allow goods transported from the south and east of Britain by *Classis Britannica* supply vessel along the coast to then transit directly along the river networks to the border zone. The requirement for this military supply capability would, of course, have been greatly expanded to support campaigns north of the border, particularly that of Septimius Severus given its enormous size.

Supply would also have been facilitated by the regional navy in a civilian capacity. The *Classis Britannica*, and its 7,000 personnel, was a resource that both the governor and procurator would not want to have seen idle and, when not on campaign or engaged in other military activities, would have been used as the administration saw fit to ensure the efficient flow of capital from the province to the Imperial *fiscus*. Some of the civilian roles for which the *Classis Britannica* was deployed are considered in Chapters 3 and 8, but one would clearly have been to help facilitate the supply of goods and materials around and outside the province. In this regard the vessels of the regional fleet fulfilling this supply role would have fitted neatly into Morris' three systems of maritime commerce around the British Isles (namely the Atlantic System, the southern North Sea or Eastern Channel System, and the eastern North Sea System), or indeed into Evans' east coast and west coast trade systems. A useful modern analogy here for the merchantmen of the fleet operating in a civilian capacity would be the private finance initiative arrangements through which the British military obtain certain capabilities today, for example with its air-to-air refuelling tankers can operate as airliners when not topping up interceptors over the North Sea.

To conclude this review of the multiple roles of the *Classis Britannica* we can consider the regional fleet in the context of it performing a communications function. This vital activity would have been carried out both in the oceanic and littoral zones (noting that then as now lines of communication are fewer in number and shorter in narrow seas such as the North Sea and the Irish Sea than on the open ocean). The communications function was particularly important for the *Classis Britannica* given that the province was physically isolated from the Continental Empire, and not by the comparatively benign environment (as the Romans would have viewed it) experienced by mariners in *mare nostrum* but by the much more hostile waters around Britain. Analogously, the crossing of the English Channel to the Romans at this time would have been more akin to space travel today than simply a sea voyage, given the mythology surrounding the various surrounding *oceanus* and these being islands at the extremity of the European landmass (see Chapter 1 for detail). We have specific examples here to illustrate this interpretation, for example Caligula's failed invasion attempt in AD 40 when faced with reluctant troops (he famously ordering them to gather sea shells on the Gallic coast instead, Dio, 59.25), while similarly Claudius' AD 43 invasion also almost failed were it not for the intervention of the Emperor's freedman, Narcissus, in shaming the troops to board the invasion fleet (Dio, 60.19).

Crucial to understanding this is the way the Romans would have considered today's English Channel. To them after getting over their pre-conquest trepidation it was not a barrier, a view that has more in common with recent culture history than it does with the Roman occupation. Instead, at that time it would have been viewed specifically as a crucial means of connectivity without which there would be no province of *Britannia*. This explains the physical monumentalisation of the Imperial gateway at Richborough on the eastern Kentish coast with its huge arch that lasted for the entirety of the *Classis Britannica*'s existence. The arch symbolically marked the landing place of the Claudian invasion in AD 43, and was physically the starting point of Watling Street, the major roadway travelling across northern Kent to London and then on to Wroxeter in the west of the province. It was also the exact place every new governor to the province would have appeared for the first time and walked through wearing his official military uniform and sword, he being forbidden to do so outside his own province where he had no jurisdiction. Given this theatre, it was in every possible way connectivity writ large, a bold statement illustrating the English Channel as a 'bridge' between the Continental and the Britannic provinces of the Empire. In this regard it is no coincidence that, of the two invasion fleets dispatched to defeat the usurper Carausius' successor Allectus in the late third century (see Chapter 10), that directly commanded by Constantius Chlorus landed in Kent with the western *caesares*, then headed directly along Watling Street to London (with the hard fighting being done by troops commanded by his Praetorian Prefect Asclepiodotus who landed near the Isle of Wight, Grainge, 2005, 141). We can similarly view the hazardous winter crossing of the English Channel to Kent in AD 343 by Constans following the defeat of his brother, Constantine II, three years earlier, with the recalcitrant elites of Britain in his sights, and also to briefly campaign in the north (Moorhead & Stuttard, 2012, 200).

If one takes this crucial connectivity context to the next stage, clearly there would have been a desire to protect the ends of this connection – Kent and north-eastern Gaul – over and beyond the initial Claudian invasion bridgeheads. Control over such crossing points was very important to the Empire and there are a number of specific examples that illustrate this, with Carroll (2009, 251), for example, highlighting the bridgehead fortress of *Divitia*, which was built by Constantine on the eastern bank of the Rhine directly across from the city of Cologne (Roman *Colonia Claudia Ara Agrippinensium*) to protect the crossing point. James (2011, 241) says the sophisticated military design and technology used in this fortress rivalled anything in later medieval Europe, emphasising the importance of the bridgehead role. Another example closer to home is provided by the second century bridgehead defence system at Catterick (Wilson, 2002, 127).

Focusing back on our period of study and the experiences of the regional fleet from the first through to the mid-third century, it would have been the *liburnae* of the *Classis Britannica* carrying out their communications role that would have provided the physical means by which these points of connectivity between Britain and the Continent were kept open. It was thus the fleet that provided the link through which the *cursus publicus* and any other manifestations of official *Romanitas* flowed to and from this north-westerly tip of the Roman Empire.

Finally, having considered the *Classis Britannica* in the context of its communications and other roles, I now move on to consider the actual physical infrastructure that enabled the navy to fulfil its various functions, namely the ports and harbours used. Reflecting its communications role bridging the English Channel and keeping Britain connected to the Continental Empire, it is of interest that the headquarters was actually on the Continent at Boulogne, phenomenologically illustrating this contemporary view of the seaway as a point of connectivity and not a barrier. Here a substantial fort functioned as the fleet's control centre, enclosing an area of 12.5ha, just over half the size of a full legionary fortress (Mason, 2003, 30) and therefore a major installation (see Chapter 3 for context).

On the British side of the Channel the principal centres included Richborough (with its monumental arch), Dover and Lympne on the Kentish coast (Philp, 1982, 176), with Mason (2003, 30) adding Pevensey in East Sussex as a candidate. Each would have featured a detachment of troops (the largest at Boulogne) with their associated harbours hosting a mix of *liburnae, myoparo, scapha* and transport ships of all sizes. In addition to the specific *Classis Britannica* facilities, these vessels would have also used the wider maritime infrastructure around Britain (for example the harbours at the legionary fortresses at Caerleon in South Wales and Chester in the north-west), in northern Gaul and along the Continental North Sea coast to fulfil the fleet's multifarious roles. A useful analogy in this regard is provided by the later chain of Saxon Shore forts around the south-eastern coast of Britain from northern East Anglia through to Portchester in Hampshire, many being built atop *Classis Britannica* predecessors (certainly Richborough, Dover and Lympne, and possibly Pevensey, too). This Saxon Shore system was only part of the later coastal defensive network around Britain and along the Continental coast, which would have also featured, for example, the chain of signal towers/watchtowers built down the north-eastern coast of Britain at locations such as Scarborough, the late third century 4ha fort at Cardiff, and fortresses on the Continent from Brest (Roman *Osismis*) on the French Atlantic coast north to Oudenburg on the Belgian Channel coast.

We know of the *Classis Britannica* association with the forts at Boulogne and around the Kentish coast thanks to the archaeological record, for example roof tiles featuring the stamp of the regional navy. At Boulogne more than 100 such tiles have been found, all manufactured locally (being dubbed *Classis Britannica* tile Fabric 1 by Roman pottery expert Professor David Peacock), but it is Dover that provides the best example. Excavating there in the 1970s and 1980s, Dr Brian Philp (1980, 100) found a concentration of more than 1,000 such tiles at the original Roman fort, all dating to before its demolition and replacement with a Saxon Shore fort in the later third century. The *Classis Britannica* tiles found at Dover were made locally in the Weald (being dubbed Fabric 2) where official naval brickworks produced vast quantities of such building material, the fleet also running the major iron-working sites of the eastern/coastal region of the Weald (both until the middle of the third century when the brickworks and the major iron working sites both disappear at the same time as the regional navy, see Chapter 8 for full detail and discussion). The presence of such tiles has also been used to link the major villa at East Cliff atop East Wear Bay in Folkestone with the *Classis Britannica*, either in the context of the structure being the British headquarters of the fleet or it being a signal station in its own right, but both interpretations have yet to be proved and it seems this villa simply made use of a local abundance of official tiles.

Meanwhile, at Richborough the *Classis Britannica* association is derived from analogy and anecdote, given the presence of the later Saxon Shore fort at this key site, which sat at the southern end of the Wantsum Channel during the occupation, this now silted-up waterway then offering safe passage for vessels transiting the English Channel to the Thames Estuary (by avoiding the treacherous Goodwin Sands). Prior to the building of the Saxon Shore structure in the later third century the site featured the monumental arch (which some believe was reused in the later stages of its existence as a watchtower given that a deep triple defensive ditch was dug around it) and an extensive *vicus*. A Fabric 2 *Classis Britannica* stamped tile has also been found here.

At Lympne, sitting on the north-eastern edge of modern Romney march (then open water partly enclosed by an off-shore sandbar), recent research indicates a *Classis Britannica* fort sat beneath or nearby the later Saxon Short successor, given the reuse of much material from the earlier structure in the later fort. Further, ten *Classis Britannica* Fabric 2 tiles have also been found locally.

Finally, the association of Pevensey in East Sussex with the *Classis Britannica* is again through the presence of Fabric 2 tiles (though only three) and the key location, it sitting atop what would during the occupation have been a fine harbour (and the site, of course, being later reused for the fine Saxon Shore fort, the defensive location being so good that it was last modified for action through the installation of pillboxes in the Second World War).

Many other sites have been associated with the *Classis Britannica*, some with a firm provenance such as the major eastern/coastal Weald iron working sites (these being industrial in scale, see Chapter 8), and the ports there that would have served them. Such harbour facilities included a site on the River Brede, an extensive site at Bodiam on the River Rother and a site on the northern edge of Romney Marsh (noting that large amounts of Roman period material culture around Dymchurch).

Similarly the small town of Kitchenham Farm, featuring a harbour on the River Ashbourne and servicing the more localised iron industry in the central Weald (which was smaller in scale than the huge *Classis Britannica* sites in the eastern/coastal Weald), has been linked to the regional fleet through the finding once again of appropriately stamped tiles. Interestingly here, of the thirty-one most recent stamped tiles found, twenty-nine are of Fabric 1 and so originated in Boulogne, illustrating with great clarity the long-distance trading networks in use at the time.

Meanwhile, an official *Classis Britannica* association, though with less supporting detail, has been suggested for other sites, for example at Brough-on-Humber, Portchester (presumably through the siting there of the later Saxon Shore fort), Chichester, at either end of Hadrian's Wall (Bowness, Roman *Maia*, and South Shields, Roman *Arbeia*, the latter certainly important during the campaigns north of the border, see Chapters 6, 7 and 8), Chester (again see Chapters 6, 7 and 8), the small town of Rochester and also at Faversham (both the latter straddling Watling Street in Kent). The jury remains out on all regarding the official status of these harbours, whether military or civilian, given the lack of hard archaeological data regarding their provenance. Finally, the regional fleet would have made extensive use of the military harbours built during specific campaigns such as those of Vespasian in the south-west of Britain in the mid-first century, Quintus Petillius Cerialis, Sextus Julius Frontinus and Agricola in the later first century (in northern Britain, Wales and Scotland) and Septimius Severus in the early third century (in Scotland). These latter military harbours are all detailed in Chapters 6, 7 and 8.

As can be gathered above, the densest concentration of official *Classis Britannica* sites (at least in Britain) was in Kent and the south-east. This is to an extent counter-intuitive given that the south and east of the province (later, provinces and finally *diocese*) was considered to be the most integrated part of Britain within the Empire (making its full contribution to the *fiscus*), with the north and west being a border zone with a regional economy geared to support the military deployed there at the edge of Empire. My research is now beginning to indicate, however, that within the settled and productive south and east, Kent in particular was more militarised and may have had more in common with the north and west. Kent, of course, has always played a special role in both the defence of the islands of Britain against foreign incursion, and also the projection of military power towards the Continent and more broadly. In the case of the former, historical precedents abound, from the dockyards at Chatham fitting out the Royal Navy to fight Napoleon's challenge on the high seas through to airfields such as Manston hosting the fighters of the Royal Air Force during the Battle of Britain. In the case of the latter, we need look no further than the role the region's ports played in deploying British Expeditionary Force to France and the Low Countries at the outset of both the First and Second World Wars.

Things were, of course, no different during the Roman occupation. Points for consideration here include the fact that Kent was the Imperial gateway into *Britannia*, and the point of connection with the wider Imperial network on the Continent. As Millett (2007, 175) argues:

> One of the unusual features of the archaeology of Kent in comparison with other parts of southern Britain is the continued presence of the Roman military after the initial invasion period ... the harbor facilities were important as a bridge to Gaul and for the provision of military supplies [and] it is in this context that we should understand the continued military presence in the area.

Also for consideration is the fact that, until the mid-third century, Kent featured the dense concentration of state-run industrial enterprises outlined previously and detailed in Chapter 8 with, as I argue, the *Classis Britannica* actually managing the operations as an Imperial Estate for the Emperor. This reflected the early identification by the state of the opportunity provided by the proliferation of the locally available raw materials in Kent and the south-east, and the maritime transport opportunities of a region surrounded on three sides by water and incised with navigable rivers (and with the readily available *Classis Britannica* there to help exploit them), these together explaining the willingness of the state to intervene to ensure maximum returns for the Imperial *fiscus*.

Finally, for consideration in this appreciation of the martial nature of occupied Kent, we have the overt military presence in the county in the form of the forts and harbours of the *Classis Britannica* and the later and more extensive Saxon Shore, effectively turning Kent and the south-east into a bastion projecting into the Channel and North Sea. While debate still continues about the specific role the later forts played (the role of those for the earlier regional fleet being fairly clear), and the exact chronology of their construction, what is clear is that these fortifications began to play a crucial role in protecting Britain from the beginning of the third century. Whether we err to the less militarised viewpoint of the forts being built to control trade and store resources (for example as argued by Pryor, 2004, 80), or to the other extreme with them being bases from which military operations were planned and executed against specific and very real threats (de la Bédoyère, 1999, 29, and Fields, 2006, 7), what is clear is their advent marked a specific, very visible manifestation of the state looming large on the Kentish and south-eastern coast (even more so than during the *Classis Britannica* period). All added together, and also noting that regional centres such as Canterbury seem to have had a preponderance of public rather than private buildings, one gets the distinct impression that the Kentish experience of being the official Imperial gateway, with its state-run extractive industries and fortified coastline, would have had a particularly militarised atmosphere throughout the totality of the occupation.

5

THE CIVILIAN ROLES OF THE
CLASSIS BRITANNICA

To be clear to the reader, this book is about the *Classis Britannica* in its military capacity fulfilling the roles mentioned previously. However, as Parfitt says in Chapter 2, it would be a mistake to simply see the regional navy as a direct parallel to the modern Royal Navy or US Navy. He and others believe that in addition to being fighting forces, the regional navies were also a resource used by the procurator of a province for other purposes, in effect being the equivalent of a modern army service corps (this later being institutionalised in the form of the *militia officialis* after the reforms of Diocletian). In this capacity they helped to ensure the prosperity of the province and the steady flow of revenue to the Imperial *fiscus*.

As mentioned in Chapter 1, this was, after all, an era before the advent of a civil service, nationalised industries or a free market capable of being engaged by the state to complete large-scale capital expenditure projects. In this context, understanding the civilian roles of the *Classis Britannica* therefore provides important insight and context when we begin to consider narrative of its military activities in the next chapter. The specific civilian roles considered here for the *Classis Britannica* are in the context of administration, public service (for example fire fighting), engineering, construction, and managing industry.

Before going into specific detail it is useful to reflect on the mechanisms by which the *Classis Britannica* would have actually been used by the state as a civilian asset. In this regard it was helped by the bipolar nature of the reporting structure into which it fitted. As is set out in Chapter 2, the regional navies followed the procuratorial reporting line direct to the Emperor. However, the service was clearly military in nature, and thus when in theatre came under the direct control of the governor. It was the latter who was best placed to assess the military requirements of the province and how to make best use of the resources at his disposal, both land and sea-based. In this regard, outside the great campaigns detailed in Chapters 6, 7 and 8, the nature of military activity during the period of existence of the *Classis Britannica* was one of constant friction along the northern border (often spilling southwards during major incursions), and increasingly along the west coast as Irish raiding gathered apace. It would therefore have been the land-based forces of the province that provided the heavy lifting with regard to the required military capability, with the *Classis Britannica* patrolling the littoral zone in the Irish Sea and around the flanks of the northern border and also maintaining communications with the northwest of the Empire. This would have left a significant portion of the fleet's 7,000 complement looking for a role to fulfil in normal circumstances, and it is here where both the governor but particularly the procurator would have wanted to make best use of this resource to the economic advantage of the province. In short, the governor would have had no men to spare in the legions and auxilia protecting the borders, but in normal circumstances he would have spare capacity within the

Classis Britannica. It was therefore simply a matter of releasing these assets for civilian use under the control of the procurator, a completely normal practice in the Roman Empire.

Looking specifically at the civilian roles, in the first instance clearly the military was more than capable of providing an administration function for a given province, including Britain. To this end, Goldsworthy (2003, 144) explains:

> One of the principal tasks of the officium [Governor's headquarters staff] was overseeing the administration of the army in the province, but it could also be turned to any of the range of tasks likely to be encountered by the Governor.

A useful analogy here for the *Classis Britannica* fulfilling such a role is provided from the other side of the Empire by one Babatha, an early second-century resident of the province of Arabia, whose private papers were found in Israeli caves at Khirbet Qumran. The papers detail her property assets as recorded in an official census in December AD 127, and indicate her declaration was made to a cavalry commander named Priscus who was acting in this administrative role on behalf of the procurator and governor. In Britain the *Classis Britannica* would have been similarly deployed as the procurator saw fit to help administer the province.

Another public function for the military was that of firefighter, with D'Amato (2009, 14) detailing as an example the two cohorts of military personnel stationed permanently at both Ostia and Puteoli (modern Pozzuoli) to guard against the occurrence of fire at the port facilities there. Roman London would have had similar requirements given its size, this being evidenced by the fact the second phase of London's basilica and *forum* (dating to the late first century) was the single largest built structure north of the Alps (Hall and Merrifield, 1986, 10). Once again the *Classis Britannica* would have been the nearest military resource to hand in Britain given the

deployment of the majority of the land-based military presence in the north and west. The success of such a fire-fighting
force is questionable, however, given the occasional fires
that we know destroyed large parts of the provincial capital
during the occupation, for example the well-known one that
occurred during the reign of Hadrian.

Of course, the Roman military were also highly skilled in
engineering. In particular, Goldsworthy (2003, 146) details the
large number of specialist craftsmen and engineers attached to
military units, whether the legionaries and auxilia of the army
or the *milites* of the regional fleets. Blagg (2002, 182) highlights
that such specialists included highly experienced architects,
surveyors and builders. Additionally, the professional soldiers
themselves were skilled engineers in their own right, able to
fully participate in the construction of not only their own fortifications but civilian structures, too. To this end Connolly (1981,
239) explains that each legionary in the Principate legions had
to carry a saw, pickaxe, sickle, basket, chain and leather strap. The
same was true of the sailors and marines of the regional fleets,
with D'Amato (2009, 15) detailing the remains of one such
individual found during the excavations at Herculaneum who
carried not only his military equipment (for example his sword
and dagger on a military belt) but also a bag of carpenter's tools.
He has been identified as originating in the *Classis Misenensis*.

One of the most obvious examples of the engineering
prowess of such troops, both specialists and regulars, are the
roads built throughout the Empire. Designed to put the stamp
on Rome across the Empire as much as to facilitate transport
(as detailed in Chapter 1), the commonality of their structure reflects the use of the military in their construction, even
when not being built for specific military use. As Goldsworthy
(2003, 146) explains:

Road building was … commonly undertaken by the army.
Such projects benefited the civilian community of the

province, whilst providing the military with improved communications for moving men and material as required.

Other specific examples of the military carrying out purely civilian construction and maintenance are also evident across the Empire. One such is the aqueduct outside the colonia of *Caesarea Maritima* on the coast of Judea, where we know from inscriptions that a *vexillation*, the *legio* X *Fretensis*, was used for maintenance work. Topically for this research given its focus on riverine use, another example is the 3-mile-long canal with bridges constructed near Antioch in AD 75 by *vexillations* from four legions together with twenty auxiliary cohorts. Another fluvial example relates to one Nonius Datus, a veteran of *legio* III *Cyrenaica*, who from epigraphic evidence at Lambaesis in North Africa is known to have participated in the civilian project to bore a tunnel through a mountain to provide a reliable flow of water to a neighbouring town in Mauretania. In Britain, of course, we have two excellent military examples of the *Classis Britannica* being engaged in construction, illustrated by the regional navy inscriptions on Hadrian's Wall between Birdoswald and Castlesteads and at the Roman fort at Benwell, which are detailed in Chapter 1.

Next we can turn our attention to industry. While acknowledging the importance of agriculture in the pre-modern economy, industry nevertheless still played an important part in the Roman economy across the Empire, with the Roman military actively participating in many examples large and small. Evidence of the high levels of this industrial activity can be perceived by us today in a variety of ways, for example the widely recognised data showing high levels of pollutants from Roman industrial activity (particularly lead and copper emissions) found in Greenland ice cores. Here, the only other major pre-later eighteenth century peak occurs during the eleventh century and relates to industrial activities by the

Sung Chinese on the other side of the globe (E. Borsos et al., 2003, 5).

In Britain, examples of this intense industrial activity included mining and quarrying (together, the *metalla*), tile and brick production (see discussion regarding a *Classis Britannica* association), pottery manufacturing, glass production (for example on the south side of the *forum* in London and at Caistor-by-Norwich, Jones and Mattingly, 1990, 216), mosaic manufacturing, *garum* fish sauce production (Biddulph, 2013, 20), milling, clothing manufacture (Britain being well known for the *birrus* detailed in Chapter 2 and also for a form of fine quality tapetia woollen rug, Wild, 2002, 1), industrial-scale brewing (for example at Northfleet in Kent), salt production (from both salterns and brine springs) and coin minting (with copies produced earlier in the Empire and, from the time of Carausius, them being manufactured as new). To these examples of Roman industry we can add the arms manufacturing detailed in Chapter 4. Taken together these industries represented a significant component of the economic output of the province, and indeed a strong case can actually be made that the occupation featured the first industrial revolution in these islands, some 1,700 years prior to that of the later eighteenth century.

For specific examples of the military's involvement with industry in Britain during the occupation we can look to the *metalla*. In this regard de la Bédoyère (1992, 100) is unequivocal that the majority of such extractive industries exploiting natural resources were under state control, saying:

> In the Roman world … mines were owned by the Imperial Government and administered on its behalf by [the] Procurator … He controlled all access on the site.

Using data from mining operations across the Empire, Hirst (2010, 106) details that the actual mechanism of such state control would have been public ownership under the authority of the Emperor rather than them being the Emperor's own private imperial estates.

Given the military were readily to hand, it was invariably the troops of the army and *milites* of the regional navy who initially facilitated each major mining operation. This was clearly common (Goldsworthy, 2003, 148), a fine example being the award of triumphal honours by Emperor Claudius to Curtius Rufus, Governor of Upper Germany, for allowing his troops to facilitate silver mining. Mattingly (2006, 507) adds another example of the military being involved in mining, this time for lead. This metal was an important part of the Roman economy, for use in its own right and also as a source of silver for coin production (in this latter case the silver being extracted from argentiferous lead by the process of cupellation, Jones and Mattingly, 1990, 185). The exploitation of lead during the occupation is a useful tool for the archaeologist given that it was produced in ingots or 'pigs' that were usually stamped and dated, giving insight into their origins both geographically and chronologically. We know the legions were producing lead as early as AD 49 in Britain (only six years after the Claudian invasion) because a 'pig' originating in the Mendips has been found at St Valery-sur-Somme in France stamped with the mark of the *legio* II *Augusta* and dated AD 49. This shows that the lead was not just for local use, with three other examples found in Britain of this period indicating that the export route was through Southampton Water (Jones and Mattingly, 1990, 184). Salway (1981, 634) argues the early exploitation of lead in Britain was so important that it was a key factor in the earlier prioritisation of the south-west for conquest in Vespasian's famous campaigns in the mid-late 40s AD when legate of the *legio* II *Augusta*. In this region, at sites such as Charterhouse-on-Mendip, lead production soon reached industrial proportions (the lead here having a particularly high silver content), to be joined quickly by other areas such as Wales and Northumberland. In fact, the industry was so successful that by the AD 70s Britain had surpassed Spain as the leading province supplying the metal, to the extent that the state directly intervened. As Salway (1981, 635) explains:

> By Flavian times the much greater ease with which the surface deposits of Britain could be worked than the mines of Spain … had proved a serious embarrassment to the Imperial Government and production was limited by law, presumably for political reasons such as the protection of interests in other provinces.

Once successfully initiated by the military, the lead mining and manufacturing claims were quickly let to both companies and individuals, thus being completely out of state control, as Salway (1981, 634) details:

> The army may well have continued to provide security and transport. But at an early stage the Government … [handed over] the immediate administration of the workings to concessionaires [conductors].

An example of the latter was freedman entrepreneur C. Nipius Ascanius, the private stamp of whom has been found on a Mendips 'pig' dated AD 59, and who was acquiring lead deposits as early as the AD 60s from the Clwyd region in Wales before this district was actually pacified (Salway, 1981, 634). The limit on lead production seems to have been lifted later in the occupation, possibly during the reign of Hadrian (Salway, 1981, 635) when lead mining in Derbyshire began, the Emperor's name again appearing on 'pigs' from this source. These 'pigs' had no private stamp on them at all, indicating once again that the state was initiating production, though the industry here may not have been as successful as that of the south-west given the comparatively poorer silver content. The same was true of lead-mining operations in Shropshire and Yorkshire. Lead manufacturing did continue into the later period though, to facilitate demand for pewter in addition to its more traditional uses, and once again official stamps on 'pigs' indicate state involvement.

Meanwhile, another strong example of the state being involved in the *metalla* is with regard to iron ore and the associated iron manufacturing industry, one of the best examples in occupied Britain being located in the Weald in Kent, East and West Sussex and Surrey, this flourishing from the first century AD through to the mid-third century AD. Here, in part of the region we have a very strong example of the *Classis Britannica* actually being directly involved in every process of an industry ranging from mining the siderite iron ore, carrying out the iron-manufacturing process and then transporting the resulting products nationally and, indeed, internationally.

The Weald was one of the three principal iron-producing areas in Britain during the occupation, the other two being the Forest of Dean and the East Midlands (both of which superseded the Weald in terms of importance after the middle of the third century AD following the demise of the *Classis Britannica*, Cleere and Crossley, 1995, 72). Iron was also produced on a lesser scale elsewhere in Britain, in areas such as East Yorkshire, Exmoor in the south-west and, later in the occupation, the Thames Valley.

Easily accessible raw materials were at the heart of the location of the Wealden iron industry, for example the region's iron ore which had a healthy average iron ore content of 40 per cent (Jones and Mattingly, 1990, 192). The heavily wooded Weald was also a ready source of the large amounts of timber needed to produce the vast quantities of charcoal needed for the iron-manufacturing process, with oak, beech, hazel and ash all being used in this regard. Hodgkinson (2013) adds that a readily available source of water was also important in the location of individual sites, saying:

A lot of the early iron-working sites are found in stream valleys. This provided water to support all aspects of the operation, with the added bonus that it also facilitated prospecting along the banks of the streams.

Iron production began early in the Weald in the LIA on the northern and southern fringes of the region and it is clear that the arriving Romans had detailed foreknowledge of the industrial potential of the area. This is evident in the Caesarian citation of '*iron in the maritime*' (V.135), which Jones and Mattingly (1990, 192) argue references the Wealden iron industry, believing the same of Greek geographer Strabo's comment about iron being an export from Britain (IV.5). From these LIA beginnings the scale of the iron industry in the Weald then expanded greatly from the beginning of the occupation.

The Roman Wealden iron industry was focused on two specific areas, a central region where most of the sites manufacturing iron were small to medium-sized in nature and which may have been seasonal in their use (catering for regional requirements), and an eastern/coastal region that featured some sites that were so large they would be perceived today as manufactories (and catering for national and international requirements). It was this latter *metalla* in the eastern/coastal Weald that I argue was run by the *Classis Britannica* on behalf of the state.

The siderite iron ore extraction operations would have been in the form of shallow quarries or bowl-shaped opencast pits, with the largest iron ore mining sites being located at Bardown and Beauport Park (both in the eastern/coastal region), though in many cases the siderite would have been mined very close to the iron-working sites themselves. Once extracted the ore was then roasted to create ferrous oxides from the carbonate, this being easier to smelt. Furnaces came in a variety of types and were generally larger than any of their chronological successors until the later Middle Ages at the earliest. The Roman iron workers would have used the 'direct process' when producing their iron, with the iron produced in the furnace being available for forging immediately. The iron was obtained from these furnaces by creating temperatures of around 1,100°C, the slag then being removed and discarded, thus providing the principal evidence today of the occupation-period iron industry (along with other waste products including charcoal refuse, ore refuse and furnace debris). In his most recent calculations, Hodgkinson has used this slag to determine the total amount of iron produced in the Weald during the occupation. Working with Crew's (1998, 51) estimates for the occupation-period iron industry at Laxton in Northamptonshire, where he determined that the total iron produced was equivalent to 15 per cent of the total slag volume, Hodgkinson now believes the estimated 75,000–100,000 tonnes of slag and waste in the Weald indicates a huge total of 10,000–15,000 tonnes of iron being produced. In terms of the output of each site, the exceptionally large 10ha operation at Beauport Park (again, which I argue was run by the *Classis Britannica*, see commentary regarding *Classis Britannica* stamped tile) would have produced 210 tonnes of iron per year, with a huge volume of coppiced woodland needed to support this.

The iron produced by this intensive industry would have been used for four categories of goods, these being:

• Tools and implements
• Weapons
• Construction ironwork (nails and similar)
• Miscellaneous (horseshoes, boat fittings, barrel hoops and similar).

Additionally, the iron slag that was a by-product of the manufacturing process was also used in compacted form as metalling for Roman roadways in the region. As an example, the Roman road running northwards from Lewes to London is surfaced with slag for more than 30km.

As mentioned above, I believe the *Classis Britannica* managed the entire iron-manufacturing operation in the eastern/coastal region of the Weald. Context here is provided by Cleere and Crossley (1995, 66), who say:

> It is generally accepted that the State owned the mineral rights in all of the provinces in the ... Empire: in practice this meant that they were vested in the Imperial patrimonium or private estate and therefore made a contribution to the fiscus or 'Privy Purse'.

A number of leading archaeologists and historians (for example Brodribb, 1979, 141) have long hypothesised that the *Classis Britannica* is a specific example of this practice in the eastern/coastal Weald. Many take this view further, making the case for the region being an official Imperial estate, for example Cleere (1977, 18). There is certainly a large amount of archaeological data to support such a view, together with anecdote, which I set out later on.

The most frequent data referenced by commentators linking the eastern/coastal region of the occupation-period Wealden iron industry to the state are the huge numbers of tiles and bricks stamped with a *Classis Britannica* mark (Brodribb et al., 1988, 275), this proliferating at sites such as Bardown, Beauport Park, Kitchenham Farm and Little Farningham. In a specific example, Brodribb (1979, 141) details that of the forty-one complete *tegula* (flat roof tiles) found in his excavations at Beauport Park in the 1960s and 1970s, all but one featured a *Classis Britannica* stamp. It is worth noting here that of the 3.35 tonnes of tile actually found on the site during these excavations (the vast majority of them only partial survivals), nearly all featured full or partial *Classis Britannica* marks. To further emphasise the scale of this occurrence, Brodribb (1979,

141) says given the fact the overall size of the site was 114 square metres, and the fact that in total 1,320 *Classis Britannica* stamps had been found, this represented eleven such stamps per square metre. Such use of *Classis Britannica*-stamped tile to identify the nature of an occupation-period site has other regional parallels, with Philp (1980, 100) using the very dense concentration of more than 1,000 such tiles at the original pre-Saxon Shore Roman fort at Dover as evidence that it was directly associated with the regional navy (see Chapter 4).

Tile is not the only form of data available either when interpreting the state presence in the Weald, with numismatics also having a role to play. An excellent example is presented by the controversial 2008 East Sussex coin hoard found at an occupation-period satellite iron working site near Bardown in the eastern/coastal region (the exact location being undisclosed). This contained 2,891 radiates dating from AD 215 through to AD 268 (with all Emperors from Caracalla to the Gallic Emperor Postumous being represented apart from Alexander Severus and Maximinus) and is very unusual in that it contains no examples of smaller denomination *denarii*. A mercantile origin for many of the coins can be inferred from this fact and from the wide geographic range of mints from where the coins originated. This includes Rome, Antioch, Milan and Lyons. The hoard also contains a comparatively high number of rare coins, for example a radiate of Gordian III's wife Sabina Tranquillina and coins documenting the Secular Games of Philip I (the last to be held in Roman history). These coins, together with the small number of highly debased radiates and also the evident parallels with well-known and similar coin hoards from Eastbourne and Selsey, indicate the hoard had a high-status origin and therefore a state association. As such it can be viewed as some kind of official Imperial pay cheque that for some reason ended up being hoarded, perhaps at a time when the *Classis Britannica* had either disappeared or was in the process of disappearing, and contemporaneously the Wealden iron industry ending.

The transport infrastructure of the occupation-period Weald, especially in the eastern/coastal region, also provides data to support a state presence, with the north–south alignments of the key regional Roman roads, particularly the vital Rochester through Maidstone to Beauport Park example linking the iron industry north of Hastings with the north Kent coast, speaking to their being built specifically to enable official communications for the *Classis Britannica* with the Medway Valley and the north Kent coast. The location of extensive port facilities at sites such as Bodiam (see Chapter 4) to facilitate the industrial-scale transport of manufactured iron out of the region also indicates the involvement of the *Classis Britannica*. The unusual settlement pattern of the occupied Weald, with little elite settlement in the centre and most of the villas on the periphery or in the Medway Valley, also supports an Imperial estate interpretation.

Beyond the hard archaeological data supporting the regional navy as the agent of the state running the eastern/ coastal Wealden iron industry during the occupation, data from analogy also presents compelling evidence. For example, while outside the stamped *Classis Britannica* tile and brick (significant though it is) there is little other epigraphic evidence in the Weald, other useful epigraphic examples proliferate in other *metalla* across the Empire. Particularly useful are those that define mining activity in a specific territory. Examples include inscriptions on boundary markers, funerary monuments, other types of stamped brick and tile, worked blocks of stone and graffiti. Hirt (2010, 48) says this is particularly valuable with regard to mining enterprises because such activities, at least those on a large scale, took place in strictly defined territorial entities separate from the colonial, municipal and other official territories within a province. The two key words used in the epigraphy to show such official territorial boundaries

are *prata* and *territorium*, both being used in association with
military units or state activity. An example of the former is a
boundary stone separating the *prata* of *legio* IV from the lands
of the town of Segisamo in Spain, while for the latter one
can look to a pronouncement by Alexander Severus (Emperor
from AD 222 to 235) regarding a bath house built on the *territorium* of *legio* II *Augusta*. The most relevant to state-run industry
appears to be *territorium*, another good example being the use
of *territoria metallorum* on the famous bronze tablets found in
the early twentieth century at the Roman copper, gold and
silver mines at Vipasca in Portugal, clearly identifying the area
as an administrative district (Hirt, 2010, 48). The tablets also
identify a *procurator metallorum* as the state official managing
this enterprise (see Chapter 2), definitive evidence that the site
was state run, although it is not clear if the official managed all
the mines and quarries of the province, some of them, or just
this one (and by extrapolation whether *territorium*, or indeed
prata, referred holistically to an Imperial estate, or to part of
one). Whatever the breadth of his responsibilities, he would
have reported directly to the provincial procurator and thence
to the Imperial *fiscus*.

With regard to the Weald, especially the eastern/coastal
area where there appears to be the strong *Classis Britannica*
association, while there is no reference in the stamped tiles
and bricks to *prata* or *territorium*, or to a *procurator metallorum*,
the scale of activities parallels that at Vipasca, hence it being
a useful analogy. Meanwhile, a final additional piece of epigraphic insight comes from an iron die found in London
that features a stamp declaring its provenance as *m(etalla)
p(rovinciae) B(ritanniae)*, referring to its origins in a provincial iron-manufacturing facility (Birley, 2005, 300). Sadly no
direct link can be made with this and the Wealden iron industry, though anecdotally it is the nearest major area of such
activity. Analogous data is also in evidence outside the context
of epigraphy, with, for example, state involvement in other

major industries such as Egyptian agriculture and the Indian silk trade being well known.

Taking into account all the data, I believe one can reasonably conclude my hypothesis regarding the *Classis Britannica* running the major eastern/coastal iron-manufacturing sites in the Weald as an Imperial estate is correct. We can also look to anecdotal evidence here to support such an interpretation, with the sheer scale of the eastern/coastal operations being particularly instructive. In the case of Beauport Park alone with its *Classis Britannica* tile, this site produced some 30,000 tonnes of slag and waste, making it one of the largest such sites across the whole Empire. Additionally, all the major sites in this area of the eastern/coastal region (including the other two very large sites at Footlands and Oaklands Park) had easy access to the port facilities on the Rivers Brede and Rother (see Chapter 4). In this regard Cunliffe (1988, 84) argues the only sensible means of distributing the iron manufactured in this region was from such facilities and hence to the sea. These key sites also all had additional easy access to the key Rochester to Beauport Park Wealden road, again with its *Classis Britannica* association.

The end of the iron industry in the occupation-period Weald in the third century is well recorded in the archaeological record, but as a final reflection in this section it is noteworthy that this decline is particularly evident in the eastern/coastal region where the state presence is strongest. Here, Hodgkinson (2008, 34) says all data (stamped tile and brick, numanistic and other) indicates the *Classis Britannica* presence disappears completely by the mid-third century, coinciding with the general decline of the region.

As an aside here, before moving on to another example of the *Classis Britannica* managing the *metalla* in occupied Britain, many archaeologists and historians also believe that in an eastern/coastal Wealden context the regional navy also managed the tile and brick industry that produced the huge numbers of tiles stamped with the mark of the *Classis Britannica* that is detailed previously at sites such as Beauport Park.

There is no evidence of tile manufacture in quantity in Britain before the occupation, this industry in locations such as the Weald beginning in the mid–late first century AD (in this latter case in parallel to the growth of the iron industry there). The military and settling veterans were the principal vector for the introduction of tile use in Britain, with the soldiers (or in the case of the Weald, *milites*) physically participating in the manufacture of tiles in the same way they would have carried out stone quarrying and wood cutting.

The first municipal or official stamps in Britain appear in AD 90 (in a legionary context), with the tile industry in the eastern/coastal Weald maturing somewhat later in the form of huge state-run brick and tile manufactories. This industry peaked in the mid-second century, by which time its *Classis Britannica* stamped tiles were ubiquitous across the eastern/coastal region, around the eastern Kentish coast and, indeed, further afield. As to why such stamps were used, regional iron-manufacturing and tile industry expert Gerald Brodribb (1979, 141) says such official branding was used for prestige reasons and to ensure their quality.

As detailed in Chapter 4, there are two distinct tile types featuring a *Classis Britannica* stamp, those from the Weald (Fabric 2) and those manufactured near the *Classis Britannica* headquarters in Boulogne (Fabric 1). Fortunately for our purposes, those originating in the eastern/coastal Weald make up the vast majority and are almost ubiquitous in Britain (except one from Dover and those found recently at the central Wealden occupation port site at Kitchenham Farm). Roman pottery and ceramics expert David Peacock says (1977, 237) the Wealden tiles, with their distinctive reddish-pink colour threaded with streaks and lenses of creamy white clay, were manufactured from Fairlight Clay, which sits within the Ashdown Formation in the Hasting Beds rock formation.

He specifically believes the principal *Classis Britannica* naval brickyards used were located near where this clay actually out-crops at Fairlight Head, or from deposits beneath the alluvium of Romney Marsh between Rye and Dungeness. In the first case he argues there is a good chance the principal brickworks have been lost through coastal erosion, while in the case of the second the evidence would have been covered over by recent alluvium deposition in Romney Marsh. While predominantly found in the eastern/coastal region of the Weald (for exam-ple at Little Farningham near Cranbrook, Bardown, Bodiam, Beauport Park, Lympne and Pevensey), the use of the Wealden *Classis Britannica* tiles was widespread, with Pearson (2002, 81) detailing that such tiles can still be seen in the east gate of the Saxon Shore fort at Reculver and reused in the walls of nearby St Mary's church. Cleere (1977, 17) adds that such tiles can also be found at Richborough, Dover, Folkestone, London and Boulogne (a unique example of ceramic building mate-rial being exported to the Continent from occupation-period Britain, Mills, 2013, 461).

In terms of the longevity of the industry, one can reasonably speculate that the tile industry would have continued to thrive while the *Classis Britannica*-run iron industry in the region was still running at full capacity (this seemingly generating most of the demand, despite the widespread export of the tiles), similarly declining after the mid-third century. It was certainly still in operation at the beginning of the third century when newly manufactured Wealden *Classis Britannica*-stamped box-flue tiles were being used to build the Painted House mansion in Dover (Philp, 1989, 101).

Meanwhile, focusing back on examples of the *Classis Britannica* specifically running the *metalla* in Britain, from iron manufacturing we can move on to another example of state involvement in industry, namely quarrying. There are a number of British examples of occupation-period military-run stone cutting and extraction, including the various types of freestone used for pre-Flavian memorials around fortresses such as Colchester, Gloucester, Lincoln and Alchester. The manifestation of the state in this case were the legions themselves, with Hayward (2009, 112) in this context saying:

> The army [legions] would have had the necessary specialists, manpower, equipment and organization at this time to survey, quarry and supply two-metre long blocks [of freestone for monuments].

These localised examples were dwarfed, however, by the enormous ragstone quarrying industry of the upper Medway Valley that from the mid-first century AD through to the middle of the third century AD provided much of the building material to urbanise and later fortify the south and east of the province. This quarrying enterprise was run by the *Classis Britannica* on behalf of the state, and almost certainly in a combined Imperial Estate *metalla* alongside the iron industry in the Weald and under the same *procurator metallorum*. These quarries were located at Allington on the tidal reach of the Medway, and then at Boughton Monchelsea, Dean Street, Quarry Wood in West Farleigh and finally at Teston, all above the tidal reach. While all these quarries are impressive in size, the one at Dean Street to the south-west of Maidstone is especially deserving of attention. At 2.5km in length, it has been compared to the similarly sized main opencast gold mine at the Las Medulas complex in north-western Spain, which is recognised as the biggest pre-industrial man-made hole on the planet. In terms of human endeavour the Dean Street quarry can perhaps be spoken of in the same terms as Hadrian's Wall, the Antonine Wall, the Foss Dyke and Car Dyke as a monumental example of Roman engineering and industrial expertise and enterprise (Pearson, 2006, 98).

All the quarries in the Medway Valley are associated with fine villas along the upper Medway Valley where the elites who

managed them on behalf of the state lived, with the industry lasting such a lengthy period of time because of the good
quality of the extracted stone (ragstone being a fine limestone
that is both durable and yet comparatively easy to work).
Examples of the worked stone dating to the occupation have
been found throughout the region. In London alone we know
it was used to construct the basilica, *forum*, at least three public
baths (located at Huggin Hill, another near today's Upper
Thames Street and another on Cheapside), the building suggested to be the governor's palatial residence, the second phase
of the amphitheatre in the north-west corner of the city, in a
pre-Boudican revolt temple built for Emperor worship and
in the construction of numerous private dwellings. Examples
of the latter include the second-century town house located
at Billingsgate in the south-eastern corner of the city where
ragstone was used as the principal foundation and building
material, and also for the foundations of the slightly later associated bath house there (Rowesome, 1996, 421). Meanwhile,
ragstone cobbles were also used as the foundation of the
walled mausoleum associated with the discovery of a large
oolitic limestone-carved eagle found in 2013 in the Minories
outside the Roman Wall to the east, and most recently has
been found used in two post-Hadrianic fire, ragstone-built
fine town houses that have been found on the eastern banks of
the Wallbrook by Museum of London Archaeology as part of
the Bloomberg excavation.

Some of this stone is still visible today *in situ* at sites such
as the section of the land wall of Roman London still visible next to Tower Hill underground station, and it is in fact
the walls of Roman London that provide the best example
of the immense output of the Medway Valley ragstone quarrying industry. Roman London expert Merrifield (1965, 48)
estimates the ragstone volume for the original 3.2km land-
wall circuit was an impressive 35,000 cubic metres, while Hall
and Merrifield (1986, 28) say this wall would have comprised

more than 1 million squared and dressed ragstone blocks with an inner and an outer facing, together with a rubble ragstone core that was then set with mortar. While a calculation has yet to be agreed on the number of man days needed to build the landward walls of London, insight into this immense undertaking can be taken from the 250,000 man days estimated to have been needed to construct the much smaller walls of Roman Canterbury (partially constructed of ragstone), with Pearson (1999, 102) equally reflecting on the 100,000 man days estimated to have been needed for the walls of the later Saxon Shore fort at Pevensey.

The walls of Roman London also provide compelling chronological insight into the period of activity of the Medway Valley ragstone quarrying industry. This is because the land wall was built in the late second/early third centuries AD, while the riverside wall (together with the bastions that were added on to the entire circuit at the same time as the river wall was constructed) were built later, at the end of the third century. This riverside wall and the bastions were not built with the same well dressed and uniform ragstone blocks as with the land circuit, however, but were constructed in a hurry from reused material recycled from demolished mausolea and public buildings. Many have interpreted this as indicating that in some way, between the two construction periods, the industrial-scale ragstone quarrying in the Medway Valley had ceased to function.

Having established the scale of this enormous quarrying industry, next I consider who actually ran and managed it. As with the iron manufacturing industry in the Weald, within the community of Romano-British archaeologists and historians there is a strong body of opinion this function was actually carried out by the state. For example, Pearson (2002, 44) argues the ragstone quarries were state run and may have been Imperial property and part of an Imperial estate (as I argue above for the Weald). Marsden (1994, 83) agrees, saying the link between the huge quantities of ragstone being quarried around Maidstone and its use in public buildings across the south and east of Britain was a direct indicator of the involvement of the state, adding:

> … it seems likely the area was part of an 'Imperial estate' owned by the Emperor, for this would guarantee the output of the quarries over a long period on this scale.

I have set out in Chapter 3 the means by which the Roman military operated in a civilian context, including the management of state-run industry, and previously I have shown this to be the case in the form of the *Classis Britannica* with regard to the Wealden iron industry until the middle of the third century. As mentioned already, I believe that a strong case can similarly be made here that the ragstone quarrying industry of the upper Medway Valley was governed in the same way, with the regional navy again being the representative of the state and potentially having the same *procurator metallorum* as the Wealden iron industry who controlled the *metalla* in both locations.

Evidence to support the hypothesis that the *Classis Britannica* managed the Medway Valley ragstone industry comes in a variety of forms. In the first instance there is the sheer scale involved. This industry was enormous in size and would stand comfortably side by side with today's industrial-scale quarrying enterprises around the world.

Next we can look to the importance of maritime transport to the success of the Medway Valley ragstone quarrying industry, this bringing the *Classis Britannica* into view as the state representative. Merrifield (1965, 49) is blunt on the subject of the importance of maritime transport in this specific context, saying that:

> The best means of transport for bulk of this kind was by boat, and the Medway and the Thames provided a waterway from quarry to City.

The route taken would have been from harbour facilities on the Medway adjacent to the ragstone quarries using vessels such as the Blackfriars 1 ship described in Chapter 2. Once fully laden with part-finished quarried stone (this being cut and part-worked to order for finishing at the final place of use, a common Roman practice), the vessels would have used riverine hydraulic infrastructure in the form of locks and weirs to navigate the non-tidal part of their journey up to the tidal reach (today at Allington above Maidstone, but in the Roman period further downriver at Snodland given the sea level was lower, see Chapter 1). From there they would have sailed up the Medway, past Rochester and into the Thames Estuary before heading west to London or east around the south-east coastline for destinations elsewhere in the wider region. We, of course, have hard data here in the form of the enigmatic Blackfriars 1 vessel, with Milne (2000, 131) arguing as detailed in Chapter 2 that this and others of similar design were specific to the area of operations of the regional fleet and therefore indicators of the *Classis Britannica*'s involvement in the upper Medway Valley ragstone quarrying industry. In this regard, and specifically using the Blackfriars 1 vessel as his standard vessel type, Marsden (1994, 83) has calculated that to construct the land walls of Roman London, 1,750 voyages by such a ship would have been needed to carry the required 45,000 tonnes of ragstone for the facing alone. From the Maidstone quarries this would have been a journey of some 127km each way. Pearson (2002, 82) provides context here, detailing that 870 boatloads of the material had to be transported from Medway quarries to the Saxon Shore fort of Bradwell to facilitate its construction, with 960 being needed for Richborough and 530 for Reculver. The latter (one of the earlier Saxon Shore forts) is particularly instructive logistically as it shows how in demand the ragstone was as a fine quality building material, it being transported 50km further than any other material used, some 70km from its Medway origins for use as a facing material. Similarly, the same Medway ragstone was being transported to Colchester via the Medway, Thames Estuary, North Sea and River Colne for use in the starting gates of the second-century circus built there.

While considering the archaeological data to support the hypothesis that the *Classis Britannica* managed the occupation-period ragstone quarrying industry in the upper Medway Valley, one question now needs to be addressed directly. This relates to the lack of *Classis Britannica*-stamped tile in the region, or indeed any kind of procuratorial tiles for that matter (the furthest found to the north comes from Cranbrook in mid-Kent, Brodribb, 1970, 1). As is detailed above, a thriving tile-and-brick industry existed alongside the iron industry in the Weald, especially in the eastern and coastal region. This is associated directly with the *Classis Britannica* given the huge quantities of tiles featuring the regional navy's stamp from the major sites in the eastern/coastal region and is particularly important given their use there to help identify the regional fleet's presence. The lack of such tile in the Medway Valley is thus troubling, though I believe the answer is a simple one – there was no need. The lower Medway Valley had its own early occupation period prolific tile industry well before the *Classis Britannica* had officially come into being (the tiles therefore not being stamped, either with the regional navy's or indeed any other procuratorial mark) which pre-dated that of the Weald, potentially by a number of decades. Thus, by the time the *Classis Britannica* had come into being and the Wealden tileries had initiated large-scale production in the early second century, local sourcing of tiles in the Medway Valley was already mature and had been happily catering for regional needs since the beginning of the occupation, so there was no need for the *Classis Britannica* to step in.

We can now move on to analogy to look elsewhere in the Empire where the regional fleets were being used to facili-tate quarrying. As a starting point a good example is the Mons

Claudianus granodiorite mine in the eastern Egyptian desert, where epigraphic evidence provided by letters, passes and receipts shows at least twenty Centurions seconded there from the local legions and, topically for this research, the *Classis Alexandrina* (Russell, 2013, 41). Hirt (2010, 106) also points to the large-scale quarries at sites such as Mons Porphyrites, Tibarian and Mons Ophiates in Egypt, Dokimeoin in Asia Minor, Simitthus in North Africa and Karystos on Euboea as other key examples where epigraphy provides evidence of direct state involvement. Another analogy closer to home would be the *Classis Germanica* and its quarrying activities along the Rhine and its tributaries. Epigraphic evidence of this comes from numerous naval inscriptions in the Trass quarries on the left bank of the Brohol Valley, and from similar evidence that *vexillations* of this fleet quarried Tufa for the Trajanic *colonia Ulpia* at Vetara. Meanwhile, more evidence of provincial fleet quarrying activities comes from even closer to hand, with Russel (2002) saying:

> The fleet also contained specialists in engineering and construction. Inscriptions at [sites such as] Benwell show the fleet not only brought the grain, but constructed the granaries that held it, and contingents of the Classis Britannica were responsible for stretches of Hadrian's Wall.

Such responsibility for building sections of the wall and its associated infrastructure would have included quarrying the necessary stone as well as construction.

Meanwhile, on the doorstep of the upper Medway Valley ragstone industry is, of course, the Wealden iron industry, which is a direct analogy given I have concluded the *Classis Britannica* managed the iron manufacturing *metalla* in the eastern/coastal region there. It is particularly noteworthy that large-scale industry disappeared at the same time in both regions, and at the same time as the regional navy disappears

from the historical record (see Chapter 9). Further, it is notable that both this eastern/coastal region of the Weald and the
upper Medway Valley relied heavily upon maritime transport, whereas the non-*Classis Britannica* central region in the
occupation-period Wealden iron industry relied upon the
north–south Roman road network, aligned as it was with
Southwark (the centre of much metal working during the
occupation) and London.

Anecdote also supports the hypothesis that the *Classis
Britannica* managed the Medway Valley ragstone quarries. In
particular, chronology is important here given the two distinct
periods appear evident in the Medway quarrying industry, an
intense one from around AD 50 (given Kentish ragstone is used
in the original *forum* in London, which dates to this period)
until the middle of the third century, which I argue was
under the aegis of the *Classis Britannica*, and then much more
localised activity following the demise of the industrial-scale
operations in the mid-third century. As mentioned before, this
tracks closely the experience of iron industry in the eastern/
coastal region of the Weald.

A final piece of anecdotal evidence comes in the form of
the Rochester–Wealden Roman road linking the north Kent
coast to the major eastern/coastal iron-working sites to the
north of Hastings. This road actually bisects the Boughton
Monchelsea Roman ragstone quarry, with the author cur-
rently exploring the possibility that a spur from this point
actually travelled direct to the Roman villas on the Medway,
such as that at East Farleigh, and also on to the nearby Roman
ford at Barming. Part of this road has already been found by
the author, linking the Dean Street quarry to the river, with
the focus of the current research now aiming to find the section that links this to the Wealden road. This spur, if found,
would significantly add to proving the hypothesis that the
metalla in both regions was one operation under the control
of the same *procurator metallorum*, and that the elites who ran

the industry (officials from the *Classis Britannica*) lived in the Medway Valley villas.

In the above discussion I have considered the data, together with anecdote, to determine whether a case can be made that the state through the *Classis Britannica* controlled the ragstone quarrying industry in the upper Medway Valley until its demise in the mid-third century. When one considers the sheer scale of the ragstone quarrying industry in the region, the crucial maritime component, the facilitating land links to the eastern/coastal Weald and the wealth of supporting analogy (not least the proximity to the *Classis Britannica*-controlled *metalla* in the Weald as mentioned) and also anecdote, then I do believe the case begins to look compelling.

To address one final issue as I conclude this chapter, I have noted the very early start of the ragstone quarrying industry in the upper Medway Valley, shortly after the Claudian invasion. Of course, as detailed in Chapter 2, the regional fleet was not called the *Classis Britannica* until the Flavian period. However, the entity from which it would be created still existed from the very beginning of the occupation, and would of course have been a resource that the procurator would not have wanted to see idle. Thus, for *Classis Britannica*, one can read its pre-Flavian identity also, acting once again as the agent of the state.

6

THE EARLY CAMPAIGNS OF THE *CLASSIS BRITANNICA* (AD 43–AD 100)

This chapter will examine the role played by the fleet that became the *Classis Britannica* in three distinct periods of campaigning in the first century AD. These are the Claudian invasion of AD 43, the conquest of the new province of Britain through to the mid-50s AD and finally the subsequent campaigns to conquer the whole of the islands up to and including the campaigns of Cerialis, Frontinus and Agricola (by which time the regional fleet had been awarded its official name).

The Claudian Invasion

As detailed in Chapter 2, the naval force that became the *Classis Britannica* was formed to facilitate the Claudian invasion of Britain in AD 43. It had its origins, however, in the earlier and farcical attempt by Caligula to mount such an expedition in AD 40. For this operation, which ultimately resulted as we know in the elite troops of Rome collecting

The Claudian Conquest, AD 43

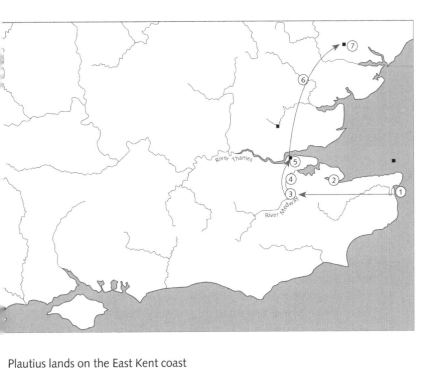

Plautius lands on the East Kent coast

March West along southern slope of North Downs

Medway Crossing Battle

The pursuit to the Thames

Thames Crossing Battle

Claudius and Plautius advance on Camulodunon

Claudius takes British surrender, Province declared

shells on the seashore (see Chapter 4), detailed planning had taken place. This had resulted in the building of a lighthouse at Boulogne, where extensive harbour works and wharfing were also constructed, all still being in place by AD 43 when Claudius turned his attention to the unfinished Julio-Claudian business across the English Channel. It seems certain that, given Caligula's troops were in place for an invasion in AD 40, all the necessary vessels would also have been constructed and in place (note it took less than a year for Caesar to have 600 specially built craft constructed for his 54 BC incursion, see Chapter 2). In addition, the warehouses would have been well stocked with provisions to support the planned campaign, those non-perishable in nature again being available for Claudius three years later.

With all the preparation planning already in place, Claudius was able to act swiftly when the opportunity arose to intervene in Britain. The trigger was provided by the death of Cunobelinus, King of the Catuvellauni, whose territory covered much of the south-east above what is today London. He was succeeded by his two sons, Caratacus and Togodumnus. In order to prove their worthiness they began campaigning against their neighbours, including the Atrebates in the Thames Valley who were Roman allies. The Catuvellauni were evidently successful as Verica, King of the Atrebates, fled to Rome where he sought an audience with Claudius. Instead of consolidating their success, however, Caratacus and Togodumnus overplayed their hand by demanding the extradition of Verica from the Romans. When this was rebuffed by Claudius, disturbances broke out in Britain against the Roman merchants already embedded in the future province, with naval raiding of Continental Roman territory along the Gallic coast also seeming to have occurred (this indicating that British naval prowess had returned to some degree following Caesar's defeat of the Veneti). It was against this backdrop that the physically awkward Claudius was presented with his opportunity to make his name within the dynasty. He now had the means, with much of the organisation in place, and cause in the form of the belligerence of Caratacus and Togodumnus. Thus the scene was set for one of the greatest amphibious operations in the pre-modern world.

Having committed to the invasion, Claudius gathered his army of conquest under the Pannonian Governor Senator Aulus Plautius (whose family were long-term allies of the Julio-Claudians), with the future Emperor Vespasian appointed as one of the legionary legates. It comprised four legions together with auxiliaries, totalling 40,000 men. Noteworthy here in the context of naval operations is the fact that the *Classis Germanica*, the by now maturing Rhine regional fleet, would have played a major role in the movement of these land forces from their original places of deployment to the invasion holding area around the places of embarkation in north-eastern Gaul. In this regard the *legio* II *Augusta*, *legio* XIV *Gemina* and *legio* XX *Valeria Victrix* travelled from their bases on the Rhine frontier itself while Plautius' own *legio* IX *Hispana* travelled with him from Pannonia.

Additionally the fleet would have carried more than 3,000 tonnes of grain to feed the invasion force for at least three months after its arrival. The whole was carried by 900 ships (Grainge, 2005, 129), many of them already having been constructed for the cancelled Caligulan invasion. In terms of design, these vessels would have made much use of the regional Romano-Celtic shipbuilding tradition outlined in Chapter 2 given that the coastal tribes of Gaul such as the Veneti, Morini and Menapii had long been incorporated into the Empire. No need this time for a fleet of Mediterranean-style war galleys to be sailed north from *mare nostrum* as with Caesar's first 55 BC incursion, with many of the new invasion vessels almost certainly featuring the same low freeboards and wide beams as those used by Caesar for his second incursion ninety-one years earlier. Note should be taken, however, that while the ships were produced locally, many of the *milites* for the new fleet originated from the *Classis Misenensis* back in Italy given the need for maritime expertise on a scale never previously seen.

Controversially, our primary sources here do not say either where the invasion force left from, or where it landed. In the case of the former, however, the fact the logistics were already in place at Boulogne following the abandonment of the AD 40 invasion clearly indicates the future location of the headquarters of the *Classis Britannica* was the principal embarkation point (though given the size of the fleet other nearby ports would also have been used). Anecdotally, Boulogne was also the place of embarkation for the Emperor Claudius when he later sailed to Britain to celebrate the ultimate success of the operation (Suetonius, Claudius,17), indicating its provenance as a key crossing point to Britain from the Continent.

Once persuaded to board the invasion fleet (see Chapter 4 for the full details) the huge force set sail in three divisions (Dio, 60,19), arriving in Britain uneventfully and unopposed in mid- to late summer. In this regard the delayed departure of the fleet actually helped the Roman amphibious operation because the British force deployed in eastern Kent to oppose the arriving Plautius had dispersed after concluding the invasion had been cancelled once again. It is also clear there was no attempt to intercept the Roman fleet at sea, despite any resurgence of British naval power following Caesar's defeat of the Veneti, probably reflecting the complete control that the massive fleet had in the littoral zone around both points of the crossing.

Controversy has long surrounded the exact point where Plautius' force disembarked. Given its proximity to the Continent, however, and noting arguments in favour of other potential landing places such as Chichester by Manley (2002, 131) and others, Kent is still widely argued to have been the landing place for this crucial event (Grainge, 117). That being the case, the most likely landing areas would have been on the eastern coast of the county. One candidate would obviously be the beaches between Sandwich and Deal as used by Caesar in 55 BC and 54 BC, though given the huge size of the AD 43 fleet (even accepting it arrived in three waves), a much larger area would have been needed. In that regard it seems likely that the shelter of the then navigable Wantsum Channel to the north of Sandwich, together with the safe harbourage of Pegwell Bay with its broad expanses of beach, would also have been used. As Moody (2008, 141) says:

> Given the size of the operation, it is unlikely that a single location can be identified for the Roman landings. More probably, the ships landed where they could, in the network of harbours, beaches and trading ports on the east and western sides of the Wantsum and troops secured themselves, by units, over a wide area.

Wherever the specific landing places were in north-eastern Kent for this invasion, the locale for the event was later commemorated by the building in the reign of Domitian of the monumental arch at Richborough detailed in Chapter 1 that stood from the late first century through to the late third century, latterly being used as a signal station (Strong, 1968, 72).

It is useful at this point to reflect on the military roles that were fulfilled by the new fleet during the initial phases of the Claudian invasion. In the first instance, control of the blue water environment in the oceanic zone of the North Sea and off the southern coast of Britain into the Atlantic is a given. Without this control, any sea crossing on this scale would have been unthinkable (a recurring theme throughout British history of course). As none of our primary sources speak of any native British naval presence of any size it seems reasonable to make the assumption this was lacking, and it is therefore also clear the Roman naval forces had complete control of the coastal littoral zone on both sides of the English Channel between which the three invasion waves travelled. Throughout the entire crossing one can also be sure that the war galleys (many by this time bireme *liburnae* with a few older models of bireme and trireme rather than the larger polyremes of Caesar's incursions), *myoparo* and *scapha* of the fleet fulfilled an intelligence gathering and patrol function while protecting the flanks of the transport waves.

Clearly, however, the principal military role of the fleet would have been that of transporting this huge army and its stores safely across the English Channel and placing it ashore in Kent. From that point, given the invasion would have taken place in the mid–late summer months, the ships would then have carried out a supply function, transiting to and fro between the east Kent coast and the region around Boulogne (a maritime route that would become one of the busiest in the entire Empire once Britain officially became a province). Finally, the new fleet would have provided a vital communications function to keep the Imperial leadership, military and Roman populace informed as the conquest progressed.

With his forces and provisions building up ashore, but no enemy as yet to engage, Plautius next built an extensive ditch and bank fortification to protect his principal beachhead in Kent at Richborough, this clearly identifying the location as the hub of the various regional invasion sites. Still visible in places today, more than 640m of the defences have been excavated, with the overall site likely to have been rectangular in outline and enclosing a massive 57ha. From this location it would have sealed off the neck of the then promontory on which the arch and later Saxon Shore fort were built. The sophistication of the fortification is indicated by the presence of a gate tower on the western side, this being quickly superseded by a large stores depot built on the same location. This change is indicative of the success of Plautius' breakout from the east Kentish coast, with him clearly making use not only of the experiences of Caesar (and presumably the pre-planning for Augustus' three abortive proposed invasions and similarly that of Caligula) but also of knowledge supplied locally by the inhabitants. His route appears to have headed directly west along the southern foothills of the North Downs, this region of Kent now called the Holmesdale and featuring the most fertile land in Kent. Certainly in AD 43 it would have been heavily settled, and would also have also provided the most sunlight for marches starting in the early morning.

Finally tracking down his elusive foe, Plautius defeated Caratacus and Togodumnus of the Catuvellauni separately in what appear to have been two small engagements, after which the Dobunni (a tribe based in the Welsh Marches who supplied troops to support the Catuvellauni) became the first of the British kingdoms to sue for peace. Advancing rapidly along the Holmesdale, the next engagement is the famous river-crossing battle described by Dio (60.19–60.23) whereby the British forces massed as a great host camped on the western bank of a north–south-running river. The candidates for this river are the Stour in eastern Kent, the Medway – which bisects the centre of the county – and the Darent to the west. The Medway is the most likely location, to the extent that local historians have erected a monument to the battle at the site they argue was the exact location. This is just downriver of Maidstone, with modern Snodland now resident on the western bank and Burham the eastern. The provenance of the site gains credibility when one considers that a mithraeum was located very close by on the eastern bank in the 1890s, this eastern religion having a strong association with the Roman military and thus perhaps marking the site of a major battle.

Assuming the battle did take place here, Plautius used a clever stratagem to turn the flank of the Britons. He ordered some of his native auxiliaries to swim the river in full armour to the north of the confrontation, and from there to attack the British chariot and cavalry horses with bows and slings. These troops were allegedly Batavians, they apparently being specialists in such a manoeuvre. At this point, with panic spreading through the British ranks, Plautius began a forced river crossing. This would have been at one of the fording places on the Medway, with both Lower Halling downriver of Snodland and Aylesford upriver having fords detailed in the historical record. Things did not go according to plan, however, as the Britons gave as good as they got in the close-quarter fighting, the engagement petering out just before nightfall. Battle was renewed at first light the following day and this time the Romans were triumphant, with the defeated British host withdrawing northwards. They crossed the Thames quickly and again prepared to fight a battle defending a major river crossing.

Before moving on we can reflect here on whether a role was played by the fleet in this crucial battle, with the answer appearing to be a resounding no. Knowing the Medway as I do, a smaller war galley such as a *liburnian* bireme or even a trireme would today have no difficulty in navigating upriver to the Snodland/Burham crossing point given that the tidal reach is at Allington. However, as I speculate in Chapter 1, during the occupation the tidal reach would have been further downriver given the lower sea level and indeed may actually have been at Snodland. This would have made navigating to the battle site problematic for a war galley. Nevertheless, enfilading fire could still have been provided by artillery and the *milites* aboard the smaller and more river-appropriate *myoparo* and *scapha* (the former could certainly have carried a small ballista). Further, any of these vessels if present would certainly have been used to transport the auxiliary natives across the Medway to turn the British flank. To my mind the fact that no mention of any such naval activity appears in any of our primary sources is clear evidence that the fleet was not present, with the native auxiliaries therefore having to swim the river (broad at this point) in full armour, probably using inflated animal skins as floats.

The fleet would have been in full view, however, during the next stage of the conquest. After ultimate success in the river-crossing battle on the Medway the Romans stayed hard on the heels of the retreating Britons, arriving on the south bank of the Thames to face off once again against another native army deployed on the north bank (presumably comprising those who survived the Medway battle and reinforcements from across East Anglia). The location of the ensuing engagement is again a matter of discussion, although a healthy antiquarian debate was carried out as to whether it was at the point of the medieval Higham–Tilbury ferry, this being the lowest fordable point on the Thames during the Roman period. If this was indeed the location of the next battle then Plautious would have headed directly north along the western bank of the Medway after the first engagement, then continuing through modern Cuxton, Higham and Church Street before hitting the line of the Thames (this also being the line of a possible later Roman spur road from Watling Street).

Plautius once more decided to force the crossing, again employing the same stratagem as previously though this time on both flanks. In this regard he first sent the auxilia to flank the British defences downriver by crossing the waterway as he had on the Medway, while secondly making use of a 'bridge' to facilitate other troops crossing further upriver. This latter must have been a Roman bridge of boats given it is highly unlikely the Britons would have had the technological capability to build a substantial bridge capable of carrying a large body of heavily armed men over such a major river, even taking into account the numerous islands and marshes in the pre-modern Thames. Further, given their entire strategy to engage the advancing Romans seems to have been to defend river lines, it is improbable that the Britons would have left the only means of crossing the Thames intact.

While I accept none of the primary sources make a specific comment on the use of the fleet in the context of any of the actions I describe, I think we have enough information to glimpse its presence through analogy and anecdote. First up, we can actually picture what such a bridge of boats would have looked like through the excellent analogous example of Trajan's Column. This monument, erected in Rome in AD 113 to celebrate the Emperor Trajan's conquest of Dacia, features numerous scenes of naval craft being used as integral parts of that major campaign, including the building of bridges of boats across the Danube and other rivers. The clue regarding the presence of the fleet in this regard in the Thames to facilitate the crossing is actually in the name, boats. Such vessels could only have been the property of the fleet, which would therefore have had to have been there to provide them, and indeed the expertise to build the bridge. Further, the Thames is a far bigger river than the Medway and it seems unlikely to me that the native auxilia who crossed to flank the Britons downriver would have done so by swimming as on the Medway, even with inflated animal skins. If the fleet was present, which I argue in favour of, then the troops would obviously have been ferried across. In both cases, with the ferried river crossing downriver and the bridge of boats upriver, the fleet would also have provided littoral combat support through the use of missile weapons to keep the opposite banks clear while the ferrying operation was under way and construction of the bridge approached the hostile shore.

Once the engagement began, with the main Roman force fording the river once its flanks were protected downriver and upriver by the above troop deployments, the Britons were this time defeated quickly. A likely scenario would see them being engaged on each flank by the troops who had crossed both downriver and upriver, while their serried ranks were enfiladed by ballista and missile weapons from the fleet in the Thames before their centre was hit by the Roman main troop concentration forcing the crossing. Dio (60.21) says, however, that the fleeing Britons used their knowledge of the local marshy terrain (very evident even today around Tilbury if this was indeed the crossing point) to make good their escape, with many of the pursuing Romans getting into difficulty and some being killed. To all intents and purposes this phase of the campaign was complete, however, with Togodumnus some-how dead and Caratacus fleeing to the west to find sanctuary with the Silures and Ordovices in Wales.

Having successfully crossed the Thames, and about to enter the home territory of the leaderless Catuvellauni, Plautius now paused and consolidated his position. He may have been taking account of Caesar's difficulties during his two incur-sions and was wary of overextending his supply lines. Clearly, however, his fleet was in attendance and in position to sup-port his advance from the line of the Thames Estuary and up the coast of modern Essex and Suffolk. His next action gives much greater clarity to the pause as he now called for the presence of the Emperor Claudius, with Dio (60, 22) saying this was a move that had been pre-planned if Plautius ran into any difficulty. To my mind he had not, however, so a different interpretation is needed here. I think the reason behind his actions actually lies with the close connections between the Emperor's family and that of Plautius. In that regard it seems to me that reaching out to the Emperor now allowed Claudius to elegantly arrive and 'save the day', thus getting the ultimate plaudits for the conquest of Britain. The Emperor arrived in Britain in short order, hot-footing it from Rome with rein-forcements for Plautius, famously including war elephants in an effort to shock and awe the Britons. The Romans then lost no time in driving home their advantage to bring the campaign to a swift conclusion, targeting the Catuvellaunian capital of Camulodunum in a lightning strike that was a resounding success (this again supporting the argument for the Higham–Tilbury crossing point rather than further upriver on the Thames). The Catuvellauni finally defeated, eleven British tribes now submitted voluntarily to Roman rule and it is at this point that Tacitus (Agricola, 14, 11) says the initial province of Britain was founded with Plautius becoming its first governor.

Before moving on to the wider conquest of Britain one can reflect here on the military roles of the fleet during the Claudian invasion. As is set out previously, all the key roles of the later *Classis Britannica* were evident in the actual invasion itself – control of the oceanic and littoral zones, intelligence gathering and patrol, transport and amphibious operations, supply and communications. These would have continued in terms of securing the beachhead on the eastern Kentish coast as Plautius began his westward march to confront Togodumnus and Caratacus, though it is clear the fleet was absent at the river-crossing battle. It was again in evidence, however, and indeed played a major role in terms of littoral control and transport for the successful contested crossing of the Thames, and continued in these roles until Claudius' final victory.

Conquest of the New Province

One could be forgiven for thinking based on the primary sources at this point that, with Claudius' success in defeating the Catuvellaunians, Britain had become a fully fledged part of the Roman Empire. Certainly the Senate back in Rome behaved as though this was the case, voting him a triumph, the title *Britannicus* and a commemorative arch. This was far from the case, however, and from this point onwards a gruelling campaign began over decades to conquer the west (with its lucrative reserves of tin and other metals, noting Rome's desire to make each new province pay as soon as possible) and troublesome north of the main island of Britain. In these campaigns, which of course as we know in the case of Scotland ultimately failed, the Roman fleet played a major role.

As a starting point, after Claudius had headed back to Rome (he actually stayed in Britain only sixteen days), the *legio* XX *Valeria Victrix* began the construction of a fortress at Camulodunum (the town, modern Colchester, being renamed *Colonia Claudia* in AD 49 and re-established as a *colonia* for retiring veterans when the legion left for the south-west that year), firmly implanting the stamp of Rome on the regional natives.

Next the three remaining legions each headed in a different direction with a view to taking as much of the island as possible under Roman control in the shortest time, thus securing the future security and prosperity of the new province. Plautius' own *legio* IX *Hispana* headed north, skirting around the territory of the Iceni tribe in modern Norfolk (this in itself highlighting that while the province had been established a number of client kingdoms still existed to sit alongside Roman territory) and reaching the River Nene, where it established a fortress at Longthorpe. Part of the legion then settled here to consolidate the surrounding territory while the remaining legionaries and their auxiliaries established *vexillation* fortresses (see Chapter 3) in what are now Leicester and Lincoln. We have no evidence of the use of the fleet in support of this campaign, other than the river locations (the River Soar in the case of the former and the River Witham the latter in addition to the Nene). Meanwhile, the *legio* XIV *Gemina* headed north-westwards deep into the Midlands, establishing bases at Manceter, Alchester and Great Chesterford. Once again the fleet is absent in the archaeological record and among the primary sources here.

However, it is with the famous campaigns of the *legio* II *Augusta* under Vespasian, striking out towards the south-west where the tribes were still notably hostile, that we see the fleet once again in action in its military roles fully supporting the land campaign. Suetonius (Vespasian 4) goes into great detail here, saying that the future Emperor:

> … fought 30 battles, subjugated two warlike tribes [the
> Durotriges and Dumnonii], captured more than 20 oppida
> [fortified native urban centres], and took the Isle of White.

Vespasian's westward route was just inland from the coast,
specifically to allow the fleet to provide close support. In
this regard it would have secured his left flank in the littoral
coastal zone to prevent the native Britons outflanking him
by sea and would, of course, have fulfilled the transport role
for the campaign, carrying out all the logistical heavy lifting
to enable him to jump from objective to objective with ease.
The fleet would also have provided intelligence gathering, its
patrols giving advance notice of any British resistance well
ahead of it being encountered.

As each natural harbour was approached by the landward
forces in this pre-modern blitzkrieg the fleet would have
carried out an amphibious operation to secure the anchorage, with analogy from elsewhere in the Empire showing that
legionaries, auxiliaries or even the fleet's own *milites* would
have been used to carry out the task. These front-line harbours
would then have been used as store bases to facilitate the quick
supply of Vespasian's legionary spearheads, not only enabling
rapid progress but building a strong supporting logistics chain
behind the advance to maintain momentum. An extreme
example of this, and also of the flank securing function of the
fleet, would have been the capture of the Isle of Wight early in
Vespasian's campaign. Analogously, this would have featured an
AD 43 Claudian invasion in microcosm, with the fleet display-
ing all its military roles to facilitate the swift conquest of this
significant landmass opposite the vital Solent waterway.

Evidence for the establishment of these regional 'assault'
anchorages along the south coast has been found at a number
of sites, for example at Bitterne at the head of Southampton
Water. Supporting archaeological data comes in the form
of Claudian pottery, and more recently with the finding of

large-scale Claudian period storage buildings on the site of
the later Roman settlement of *Clausentum* (today a suburb of
Southampton), which sits at the tip of the Bitterne Peninsula.
From this location the goods arriving via the regional fleet in
its transport role would have been ideally placed for forward
deployment up the River Itchen to the advancing army.

Vespasian's progress through to his return to Rome in AD 47
can today be tracked by these coastal sites that he established
during his westward progression. For example, a next step
from Bitterne can be found at Wimbourne in Dorset where
he built an early *vexillation* fortress with an associated port
and storage facility (this time on Poole Harbour). Weymouth
Bay would then have been the location of the next fleet base
given its proximity to the major military engagement site at
Maiden Castle (where Vespasian famously stormed the extensive hill fort defended by the Durotriges). Then heading deep
into Dumnonian territory, a key fleet base was established at
Topsham, immediately to the south of the later legionary fortress and *civitas capital* of Exeter (Roman *Isca Dumnoniorum*, of
which it became the port).

After four seasons of campaigning, using this combination
of land-based shock formations supplied and maintained by a
series of new harbours built to keep pace with their advance,
the south-west was subdued. The British fleet, largely deployed
to support Vespasian's campaigning in the region, would by this
point have been strung out along the south coast to maintain
the new anchorages with their extensive wharfs and storage
facilities. The military vessels would also by now have been
forging up into the Bristol Channel and Irish Sea, a brand new
environment where they began scouting the coasts of Wales
and Ireland to take control of the littoral zone. A maritime
threat from those directions was clearly evident, with the early
fort built at Kingsholm, military harbours at Bridgewater, Sea
Mills (Roman *Portus Abonae*) and Barnstable, and signal sta-
tions at Old Burrow, Martinhoe, Morwenstow and St Gennys

evidence of this. Meanwhile, back at Richborough, the site's future role as the Imperial gateway was already being cemented with the beachhead fortifications being demolished and replaced by 62ha worth of massive storage compounds. Already the maritime conveyer of merchant vessels between the east Kent coast and Boulogne was in full swing as the new province began to pay its way.

In AD 47, his work establishing and consolidating the new province done, Plautius returned to Rome along with his most successful legate, Vespasian, being replaced by Publius Ostorius Scapula. At this point the province comprised the entire area below a line from the Wash to the Severn, saving the clients tribes of the Atrebates in East and West Sussex and the Iceni in East Anglia.

We have little visibility in the activities of the fleet in the next phase of the conquest of Britain, this taking in Scapula's campaigns against Welsh raiders led by Caratacus, the early rebellion of the Iceni, his campaign against the Deceangli in northern Wales and a rising of the Brigantes in the north-west against the new province. Mason (2003, 89) argues that as the latter petered out with the deaths of most of the Brigantian ringleaders, Scapula rendezvoused with the fleet in the Dee Estuary, it having travelled north to protect his flank in the littoral zone and to once again provide a supply function.

Naval activity is more evident in the archaeological record as Scapula began to concentrate his resources for a serious assault on firstly southern and then central Wales (targeting in turn the Silures and Ordovices, between them harbouring the fugitive Caratacus), with the *legio* XX *Valeria Victrix* relocating from Colchester to Kingsholm near modern Gloucester. This location was a key site for the conquest of Wales as it was the lowest easily bridgeable point on the River Severn while also being navigable to seagoing transport vessels, this showing maritime supply growing in importance here as Scapula began to build up his forces for the campaign across the Severn. The armed military vessels (smaller war galleys, *myoparo* and *scapha*) of the fleet would also by this time have provided a policing control function in the riparian littoral of the river.

Once the campaign was under way, with the *legio* XX *Valeria Victrix* driving into south Wales to target the Silures (again with the fleet locked on to its southern flank to provide littoral protection, intelligence gathering and supply), Scapula deployed the *legio* XIV *Gemina* to the Welsh Marches to open a new front targeting the Ordovices of central Wales. While progress was slow Caratacus was captured in AD 51 and the following year Scapula returned to Rome, being replaced by Didius Gallus as governor, who relocated the *legio* XX *Valeria Victrix* to a new *vexillation* fortress at Usk (Roman *Burrium*) in south-eastern Wales and the *legio* XIV *Gemina* to a similar fortress at Wroxeter. Both sites were specifically chosen for the access provided to the Bristol Channel by the Rivers Usk and Severn respectively, with maritime supply remaining vital to Rome's continued military success in its Welsh campaigning. This observation is reinforced by the next two fortresses built as the campaign continued, at Chepstow on the mouth of the River Wye and Cardiff on the River Taff (while similarly and around the same time, on the other side of the island of Britain, the *legio* IX *Hispana* built a legionary fortress at Lincoln on the River Witham, which was much broader then than now).

The Welsh campaign continued throughout the AD 50s, with Gallus departing for Rome in AD 57, being replaced by Quintus Veranius Nepos. The latter died within a year of taking office, however, and it is the next governor who gives us our next insight into the activities of the British fleet, Gaius Suetonius Paulinus. By this time, late in the decade, the steady though gruelling campaign had progressed to the north-western tip of Wales (with the construction of many forts to secure each piece of newly conquered territory, Tacitus, *Agricola*, 14, 11) and specifically to the Island of Anglesey deep in the heart of Deceangli territory. This mysterious island was home

to the druids, leaders of LIA religion in pre-Roman Britain
and the emotive centre of resistance against the arrival of the
power of Rome. Just as with the Isle of Wight a decade earlier,
a Claudian invasion in miniature was staged here in AD 60
(with the fleet constructing flat-bottomed transport boats to
cope with the treacherous coastal currents and shallows, possibly building them at a site on the River Dee near the later
legionary fortress of Chester, Roman *Castra Deva*), though this
time the landing was heavily opposed by the Britons deployed
on the shore in a dense mass and driven to a religious fervour.
Control of the littoral zone would have been vital here to iso-
late the native troops from the mainland, as would fire support
from the ballista and missile weapons of the war galleys, *myoparo* and *scapha* (standing well off shore given the issues with
the currents and shallows), which would have provided covering fire for the legionaries, auxilia and *milites* fighting their
way ashore. Though Tacitus (Annals, 14, 29–30) clearly indicates that the fighting was desperate, Paulinus was ultimately
successful and the island captured.

The governor's attempts to consolidate, however, were cut
short by one of the best-known episodes in British history,
namely the revolt of the Iceni under Boudica in AD 60–61
that gathered momentum quickly with other tribes joining a
briefly intense conflagration that saw Colchester, St Albans and
ultimately London put to the torch and 80,000 Romans and
Romano-British massacred (Dio, 62.1). Paulinus eventually
defeated Boudica in a crucial battle at an unnamed site along
Watling Street and restored order to the province, though at
a cost (especially to the *legio* IX *Hispana*) given that his next
move was to draft in 2,000 more legionaries from Germany
together with 1,000 auxiliary cavalry and eight units of auxiliary foot to the province. Our sources make no mention of a
role for the British fleet during the revolt and given its inland
nature in the south and east it is unlikely to have been needed,
especially as most of the vessels of all types would have been

in the north-west supporting the campaigns in Wales, though perhaps some *milites* would have been deployed to bulk up the numbers of the legionaries and auxilia given the desperate nature of events. The final act in Paulinus' governorship in Britain did involve the fleet, however. Clearly skating on thin ice after surviving the Roman equivalent of a military board of inquiry concerning the Boudican revolt, late in AD 61 he took the blame when some ships of the fleet were wrecked and their crews lost (we have no detail of how many and where, though it must have been significant), being ordered back to Rome promptly as a result (Tacitus, Annals, 14.39).

Around this time the conquered areas of Wales began to prove its worth with raw materials such as lead, long a profitable export from Britain, now being slotted firmly into the procurator's economic model for the province as wealth began to flow into the Imperial *fiscus*. We have firm evidence of this in the example of C. Nipius Ascanius detailed in Chapter 5 acquiring lead deposits at this time in north-eastern Wales. With gold, silver and tin also being mined, this would have led to an exponential growth in maritime trade from both Wales and the south-west, with the fleet providing the only immediate means of facilitating transport for the extracted materials in its transport role.

With calm restored to Britain, rebuilding and repair began, once again consolidating the evolving province. Things had settled to such an extent by the mid-AD 60s that the infamous Emperor Nero pulled the *legio* XIV *Gemina* out of the line in Britain, they being redeployed to the eastern frontier for service against Parthia (note Horace's reflection in Chapter 3 regarding the fierce Britons and Parthians, this legion clearly thought an elite fighting formation given it was deployed from one hot spot to another). The legion actually plays a crucial role in our knowledge of the *Classis Britannica* as it is in the context of its next two deployments that the fleet is officially named for the first time, by Tacitus in the context of the

Batavian uprising in Germania Inferior in AD 70 (*Histories*, 4, 79, 3). Thus, having spent three years in Syria, the *legio* XIV *Gemina* is next mentioned being returned to Britain in AD 69 during the Year of the Four Emperors following the fall of Nero. It would have been the fleet that transported the legion once more across the Channel, and then back again later in AD 70 when it was reverse deployed back to the Continent, this time to bolster the Imperial forces along the Rhine frontier where Gaius Julius Civilis had launched his revolt of Batavian auxiliaries. It is here we first see the name of the *Classis Britannica*, though in a rather negative and ignominious light. This is because, having arrived in the Rhineland, the commander of the *legio* XIV *Gemina* (one Fabius Priscus) marched his legionaries and loyal *auxilia* inland to attack the neighbouring Tungri and Nervii tribes who were supporting Civilis rather than mounting a full amphibious assault on the Batavi as it appears he was ordered to do. In so doing he left the fleet at anchor and unguarded, except its own *milites*, where it became an easy target for the Canninefates, another regional tribe supporting Civilis. Tacitus says nearly all the *Classis Britannica*'s vessels were captured or destroyed during a sustained attack on the anchorage. However, Rome being Rome, once Civilis' revolt had been successfully dealt with all the losses for the fleet were made good and it may be at this point that we see the full transition to the bireme *liburnian* as the principal war galley for the *Classis Britannica* and designs such as the Blackfriars 1 type taking on transport responsibilities. Both were ideally suited for their type to operate in northern waters and may reflect the experiences of the fleet from the Claudian invasion in AD 43 through to this stage in the conquest. In AD 71 the freshly rebuilt *Classis Britannica* was in the news again, this time returning to Britain with its new governor, Cerialis (the conqueror of Civilis), and a new legion, the *legio* II *Adiutrix*. The size of the military force in Britain was on the increase again, and plans were afoot for renewed campaigning in the west and the north of the island that would see the *Classis Britannica* playing its greatest role yet in the story of the growing province.

The Campaigns of Cerialis, Frontinus and Agricola

The story of the renewed conquest of Britain now focuses on three great soldier governors sent to Britain under the Flavians, starting with Cerialis, who lost no time in driving forward the frontiers of the province. His target was the Brigantes ('High Ones' or 'Hill Dwellers'), the confederacy of tribes resident in what is now Yorkshire (except part of the east coast, which was the territory of the Parisi), Lancashire, Cumbria, Northumberland and south-western Scotland. The power of this confederation is evident in the size of its pre-Roman tribal capital located at Stanwick in North Yorkshire, an enormous hill fort enclosing almost 300ha surrounded by 9km of ditches and ramparts (Moorhead and Stuttard, 2012, 93). In the post-Claudian invasion period the Brigantes had been allies of Rome under their long-reigning Queen Cartimandua (she is first mentioned by Tacitus in AD 51, *Histories*, 3.45), though whether as a full client state as with the pre-Boudican revolt Iceni is unclear. Her loyalty had been proven in AD 51, the reason for Tacitus introducing her, when she handed over the fugitive Caratacus to the Romans after he had fled to the Brigantes following his defeat in Wales. This event had caused a breach with her husband, Venutius, who she divorced, leading to a conflict that was to see Rome intervening to save her in AD 57. Matters with the Brigantes were then stabilised until the Year of the Four Emperors in AD 69 when Venutius revolted again, taking advantage of the chaos back in Rome. This time he was successful and deposed Cartimandua, she once again asking Rome for assistance (Tacitus, *Histories*, 3.45). This was provided by the then Governor Marcus Vettius Bolanus, who headed north, he being initially successful according to the poet Statius (Silvae, 53–6) who details him campaigning in the 'Caledonian Plains', indicating Bolanus had penetrated to the lowlands of Scotland. Despite this success, however, matters were not resolved satisfactorily in Rome's favour as the new Emperor Vespasian, the ultimate winner in the Year of the Four Emperors, recalled the incumbent governor to Rome in AD 71, hence the arrival of Cerialis.

While the legate of the *legio* IX *Hispana* he had tried to save Colchester from the Boudican revolt but his small army had arrived too late and was decisively defeated by the main British force with him fleeing for his life with his cavalry. They then remained holed up incongruously in a nearby fort until after Paulinus had defeated the insurrection. Cerialis rebuilt his reputation in the Year of the Four Emperors by fighting alongside his kinsman, Vespasian, being rewarded with command of the *legio* XIV *Gemina* on the *limes Germanicus* and leading the campaign to defeat Civilis. He was rewarded yet again, this time with the governorship of the troublesome though now profitable province of Britannia.

As detailed previously, along with Cerialis the *Classis Britannica* also carried the *legio* II *Adiutrix* to the province. This was an interesting choice in the context of the regional fleet given the new legion had been created in AD 70 by Vespasian from the *milites* of the *Classis Ravennate* in Ravenna, whom he had recruited to fight on his side in the Year of the Four Emperors. These troops, as with Cerialis, were totally faithful to the Flavians and their deployment to Britain illustrates the importance to Vespasian of the province where the Emperor had made his name.

Tacitus (Agricola, 17) says that immediately upon arrival Cerialis headed north and set about the Brigantes, indicating that while the campaigns of his predecessor had seen some success, matters were far from concluded. In the first instance he ordered the *legio* IX *Hispana* out from its legionary fortress at Lincoln into Yorkshire where the troops constructed a new fortress at York, deep in Brigantian territory on the River Ouse (again for ease of supply). The *legio* II *Adiutrix* then moved into the vacated fortress at Lincoln to act as a strategic reserve. Next Cerialis split the *Classis Britannica* into two divisions, one on the west coast that gathered in its old hunting ground off the north Welsh coast, and another on the east coast off the Humber Estuary. The former was to support a drive north along the west coast by the *legio* XX *Valeria Victrix*, whose loyalty the Flavians suspected following the Year of the Four Emperors. In that regard the Emperor had already replaced their commander with the Agricola of whom we will hear much more later. Meanwhile, the latter division of the fleet was to support a similar drive up the east coast by the units of the *legio* IX *Hispana* led by the governor himself. Finally, before the campaign began, Cerialis redeployed part of the *legio* II *Adiutrix* from Lincoln to the River Dee, where a new naval facility and fort was constructed at Chester with the double aim of providing a base for the west coast division of the *Classis Britannica* and to secure Agricola's left flank from any insurgency originating in northern Wales.

What is absolutely clear here is the vital importance of the *Classis Britannica* to the success or otherwise of Cerialis' campaign, for example in controlling the littoral zone to secure the exposed maritime flanks of the legionary spearheads, providing the transport and supply function to keep the land forces moving, and scouting out ahead to provide timely intelligence of any gathering opposition. In the latter regard one can imagine the sleek and camouflaged *myoparo* and *scapha* darting in and out of every estuary, creek, river and stream accessible along the coast (their equally camouflaged marines descending on any communities found there in lightning small-scale amphibious operations), with the bireme *liburnae* sitting off the coast to provide fire support and to intercept any local native coastal traffic. One should not lose sight here, of course, of what an undertaking this was for the military, forging ahead into what they would have considered to be the darkest corners of *barbaricum* where very few from their own 'civilised' world had travelled before. They were surely entering the first century AD's equivalent of a Conradian heart of darkness, and the presence of the fleet off the coast and within sight was vital for the morale of the troops.

The parallels of this campaign with that of Vespasian along the south coast in the AD 40s are remarkable, not least with the combination of the land forces following routes along the coast supported by a strong naval presence, with once again military harbours being created along the route as the advance continued. We have strong archaeological data to support this that shows such harbours being built at Wilderspool, Kirkham, Lancaster, Ravenglass and Kirkbride on the west coast (in addition to Chester) and Brough-on-Humber and South Shields (Roman *Arbeia*) on the east coast.

Cerialis' campaign followed a familiar pattern, with each of the two legionary spearheads heading inland to subdue the native tribes from the Brigantian confederation as they reached each estuary and river. Thus, as has happened so many times in British history, rivers such as the Dee, Esk, Ellen and Wampool on the west coast and Humber, Tees and Tyne on the east provided highways along which an invader could take the fight to the enemy. In this instance it was Cerialis and Agricola, they between them wrestling regional control from the Brigantes piece by piece. The progression of this campaign is well evidenced by the multitude of fortresses built as the operation unfolded, with the end never in doubt. The final stand was at the Brigantian capital of Stanwick, with the Romans being totally victorious and Venutius killed. Our sources are silent at this point regarding Cartimandua so it is unclear whether she regained her crown or not, but we do know that by the time Cerialis returned to Rome in AD 74 the whole of the north of

England (and potentially southern Scotland) was occupied by Rome, with the province extending its frontiers (and indeed that of the Empire overall) further north than ever before.

Our next soldier governor is Frontinus, another Flavian favourite who had fought for Vespasian in the Year of the Four Emperors. Famed in his lifetime as a military man of letters, he composed a book on strategy called *Stratagems*, this being heavily used as source material for the later and more famous *Tactics of Aelian*. Arriving in Britain with the north pacified for now, Frontinus turned his attention to the unfinished business in the west, and specifically to Wales. Here, despite the campaigns of Gallus, Nepos and Paulinus, the native tribes were still proving troublesome, especially the Silures in the south. Using the *legio* II *Augusta* from its base in Gloucester (it had been deployed there in the mid-AD 60s), Frontinus mounted yet another lightning campaign, using the River Severn and Bristol Channel to protect his left flank where once again the regional fleet would have played a major role in the now very familiar roles of littoral control, transport and scouting. Within three years all opposition in the south of Wales had been crushed, with a string of forts built across the peninsula to help enforce the rule of Rome. A number of these were on riverine estuaries, again showing the importance of the *Classis Britannica*, they including locations such as Caerhun, Carmarthen, Caernarfon, Lougher, Conwy, Pennal and Neath. Finally, to secure the region even more firmly he redeployed the *legio* II *Augusta* permanently from Gloucester to Caerleon on the River Usk, where they proceeded to build the famous legionary fortress and harbour to oversee southern Wales and the Bristol Channel, and similarly had the *legio* II *Adiutrix* develop the *vexillation* fort and harbour at Chester into a full legionary fortress to keep an eye on northern Wales and the Irish Sea. It is likely that from this point units of the *Classis Britannica* were based permanently at these two sites in southern and northern Wales.

It seems, however, that north Wales continued to be troublesome as it was the initial target of our next and greatest soldier governor, Agricola. His fame, and our knowledge of his campaigns today, owe much to the public relations exercise carried out on his behalf by his son-in-law, Tacitus. One of the finest Roman historians, he details a number of aspects of the history and nature of early occupied Britain in his *Annals* and *Histories*. However, it is his narrative regarding the campaigning of his father-in-law over seven seasons in the *Agricola* that is of most relevance to our review of the *Classis Britannica* given the key role it once again played in the next stage of our story.

Arriving in the late summer of AD 77, Agricola immediately launched a savage offensive against the Ordovices in response to their near annihilation of a detachment of Roman cavalry. Within a month he had hacked his way through to the Isle of Anglesey, surprising the natives with a lightning assault and defeating them completely. Consolidating his position, he had completed what Paulinus had started seventeen years earlier. Wales was now finally pacified and fully incorporated into the Empire.

The new governor now turned his attention to the north of the island, casting the gaze of Rome back once again to the heart of darkness. We have little detail as to why, given the success of Cerealis in defeating the Brigantes, other than the Romans clearly thought the far north of the island still provided the opportunity for Imperial fame and fortune. It may also have been the case that fugitives from the defeated Brigantes had headed north to join their regional cousins, thus presenting the risk of a perpetual threat north of the border, which by this time had been set broadly along the Solway Firth Tyne–Firth Tyne line later made famous by the construction of Hadrian's Wall.

While some tribes engaged throughout Agricola's numerous campaigns in Scotland are named, they are broadly referred to as Caledonians and I stick to that convention here except in specific cases. The use of Caledonian at this time seems to have been a generalisation rather than a reference to an official confederation as with the Brigantes and it is not until much later (see Chapters 7 and 8) that the term is used in the context of a formal political entity.

Whatever the reason for Agricola's northern attention, in AD 78 he redeployed his forces north and spent the year pacifying the local Brigantes to ensure his rear would be secure when he headed further north. This included building a ring of *vexillation* forts around the newly incorporated north of the province (Tacitus, Agricola, 20). He finally launched his assault across the border in the spring of AD 79, following the same pattern as Cerialis in his Brigantian campaign with two spearheads forging northwards, one on the west coast and one (led by *legio* IX *Hispana*) on the east. As always the *Classis Britannica* was on hand just off the coast of each thrust to fulfil the littoral control, transport and scouting roles, with Moorhead and Stuttard (2012, 103) saying that:

> In fact, the fleet was to play a vital role throughout the course of the campaign, sailing ahead to reconnoiter harbours, shadowing the troops as they pressed forward on land, shipping supplies up from the south. Just as importantly, it was a useful tool in Agricola's arsenal for psychological warfare, as the sight of Roman galleys plying up and down the … coast of Scotland, using its sea lanes and its anchorages and beaches as if they were their own, struck fear into the Caledonians' hearts.

This first season north of the border in AD 79 seems to have been relatively problem free, with the remains of a number of fortified marching camps well illustrating the progress of the legions. At Newstead (Roman *Trimontium*) on the River Tweed near modern Melrose in the Scottish Borders a much more substantial fort was also built on the site of the capital of the Selgovae, indicating that any resistance had been short-lived. Tacitus indicates that by the time the campaigning season had ended the east coast spearhead had actually reached as far north as the River Tay (Agricola 22), with Mason (2003, 98) arguing this is an excellent example of the combined land-sea forces strategy being used to such great effect by the Romans. The governor's accomplishments were clearly well regarded back in Rome, with Dio (66, 20) saying the events in the province were so well received that the Emperor Titus (who had succeeded his father Vespasian in AD 79) was given his fifteenth salutation by way of celebration.

The next campaigning year, AD 80, Agricola spent consolidating his position, the south of Scotland up to at least the Clyde and Forth line now effectively under Roman control except the extreme south-west away from the coast where the indigenous Novantae had been bypassed. It was in this year that many of the marching camps were permanently fortified and a road system with supply bases along the way built. Military harbours were also constructed to facilitate the effective use of the *Classis Britannica*, these being located at Kirkbride, Newton Stewart, Glenluce, Stranraer, Gurvan, Ayr and Dumbarton on the west coast, and Camelon on the east. Further north along the east coast a naval base may also have been established at Carpow on the Tay, site of the later fort, given this was the northern extremity of the Roman advance in the first campaigning season. Certainly a harbour was established there by the overall end of Agricola's campaigning in Scotland.

In his third year of campaigning north of the border, AD 81, Agricola turned his attention to the south-west and the unfinished business with the Novantae. In this regard he gathered the west coast units of the *Classis Britannica* in force and launched an amphibious assault (himself in the lead ship, Tacitus, Agricola, 24), either northwards across the Solway

Firth from the occupied south coast or westwards across the River Annan in Dumfries and Galloway, our sources being unclear except their naming the target of Agricola's aggression and the nature of the assault. The determinant here about the geographic origin of the attack would be the extent to which the coast of south-west of Scotland was fully under Roman control, except the military harbours already built. Whatever the exact details, once again this combination of land and naval forces was highly successful, concluding matters rapidly with the total defeat of the Novantae. At this point Tacitus (Agricola, 24) has his protagonist discuss the prospects for a campaign against Ireland with the much quoted suggestion that only one legion would have been needed to complete its conquest. Mason (2003, 100) makes the point that for Agricola to have been even remotely considering such an undertaking, even if only in the context of a Caesarian reconnaissance-in-force, there must have been a very considerable concentration of vessels of the *Classis Britannica* of all types on hand locally (perhaps indicating that the amphibious assault on the Novantae really had been across the wider expanse of the Solway Firth). Gathering in Loch Ryan or Luce Bay in Galloway, this fleet would then only have had to travel 32km to reach Belfast Lough in today's Northern Ireland. However, such a dramatic intervention would certainly have required Imperial approval and Mason (2003, 100) believes the new Emperor Domitian refused Agricola permission, directing him towards the north again now that all of southern Scotland had been subjugated (the *Classis Britannica* clearly playing a major part in facilitating this dialogue in its communications role). Moorhead and Stuttard (2012, 103) believe this decision not to invade Ireland was Agricola's biggest regret of his governorship.

Thus, following Imperial orders, in his next and fourth campaigning season in AD 82 Agricola turned away from this tempting goal across the Irish Sea and headed further into the darkness of the north once more. This time, as the legionary spearheads advanced above the Clyde and Forth line, they focused on the east coast given the inhospitable terrain of the Highlands and islands to the west. Tacitus (Agricola, 25) is clearer here than at any other time about the vital role played by the *Classis Britannica*, detailing it being used to transport troops from the south to replace casualties, harassing the enemy-occupied coast to disrupt economic activity (then as now, for example, fishing would have been a key local industry to support indigenous communities) and maintaining a tight control of the entire littoral zone. He also reflects on the risks of operating in the treacherous littoral and oceanic waters of the far north, highlighting hazards such as the frequent storms and unforgiving tides (Agricola, 25). We have evidence of such dangers back in occupied Britain in the form of the tombstone of an *optio* of the regional fleet at the legionary fortress and harbour at Chester (which at this point would have been the home base for the western squadrons of the *Classis Britannica*), who according to the epigraphy on his memorial died in a storm off the coast of Scotland.

Meanwhile, Tacitus (Agricola, 26) specifically says that at this time, as the campaign progressed inexorably northwards, the two distinct arms of the Roman military began to share the same fortified camps. This is perhaps the best example in our primary sources we have showing the army and fleet working so closely together, whether legionaries, auxilia or *milites*. The *Classis Britannica* was certainly having an impact on the natives of the far north because, with their economic systems so badly disrupted, they began to coalesce for seemingly the first time. Having previously conducted a largely guerrilla campaign while withdrawing glen by glen and loch by loch, they now began to fight for their very survival. Tacitus (Agricola, 27) has them starting out by attacking military installations, though it is unclear which ones. Certainly by this time the most northerly of the legionary fortresses had begun construction at Inchtuthil on the north bank of the River Tay in Perth and Kinross by the *legio* XX *Valeria Victrix*, though this would indeed have been an ambitious objective for the two regional tribes who Ptolemy (*Geography*, Book 2, 150) calls the Venicones and Vacomagi. More likely targets, if not the string of marching camps and forts built to maintain the logistics chain northwards towards the Moray Firth, would have been the military harbours built to preserve the link between the legions and *Classis Britannica*. South to north above the River Tay these have been located at Monifieth (arguably the *horea Classis* granaries of the fleet detailed by Ptolemy, Geographia, 2.3.14), Dun, Aberdeen and Bellie in Moray itself. Given the impact the regional fleet was having on the local tribes, with Tacitus (Agricola, 25) emphasising the psychological factors these harbours would have been prime targets. The Britons were clearly unsuccessful in disrupting such logistical infrastructure, however, as they next decided to advance in columns to meet the Roman forces head on. Agricola responded by dividing his own troops into three columns of his own to avoid encirclement, with the native forces then specifically targeting the *legio* IX *Hispana* (apparently the weakest in terms of numbers of legionaries and supporting auxiliaries). Agricola now marched his other two columns to the rescue and routed the Britons who, backs against the wall, began to move their women, children and elderly to places of safety. Thus concluded the fourth northern campaigning season, although one more piece of information about the year's events gives real-time insight into the naval technology of the *Classis Britannica* at this time. Tacitus (Agricola, 28) says a cohort of Usipi auxiliaries from Germany mutinied for reasons unknown and, murdering their centurion, stole three *liburnian* biremes. Enigmatically described as 'a ghostly apparition as they sailed along the coast' (Tacitus, Agricola, 28) while making their getaway, they eventually crossed the North Sea (showing the seaworthiness of the vessels) before coming to various kinds of grief on the north German coast due to the ineptitude of the crews. This reference to the type of war galley being used by the *Classis Britannica* is clearly indicative that the transformation from the earlier polyremes to the more nimble *liburnae* in northern waters was probably by now complete.

Agricola's fifth and final campaign in the by now very far north took place in AD 83. It marked the culmination of his ambitions to subdue the entire main island of Britain and, given the resistance he had encountered the previous year, he took no chances and fielded the largest force available. This numbered up to 30,000 men, including legionaries, auxiliaries and the *milites* of the *Classis Britannica*, and once again saw the winning combination of land forces and fleet working in close co-operation.

In the first instance Agricola deployed the *liburnae, myoparo* and *scapha* of the fleet forward once again ahead of the legionary spearheads to raid up and the down the coast as far north as the Moray Firth. His aim was once more to prompt the Caledonians to gather en masse with a view to forcing a decisive engagement. This indeed took place, with the famous Battle of Mons Graupius in the Grampians below the Moray Firth. While the exact location of this engagement is not known, a series of large contemporary marching camps heading north from the Tay along the eastern edge of the Highlands seems to indicate its general location. Wherever the battle specifically occurred it was decisive, with the total defeat of the Caledonians, Agricola next leading his troops on a punitive expedition along the Great Glen. Further, he sent specially tasked squadrons of the *Classis Britannica* even further north to complete a circumnavigation of Britain, with Tacitus (Agricola, 10) saying:

The Roman fleet now sailed round the furthest shores for the first time, and so established that Britain is an island.

> At the same time it discovered and overthrew some islands, called the Orkneys, which until then had been unknown. Thule [possibly Iceland, see Chapter 1 regarding Pytheas] too, was sighted.

Total defeat of the natives was now complete, with the Empire believing the entire main island of Britain had been conquered. To further cement control of the north a series of forts and fortlets were built to seal off the various glens in the highlands, in much the same way that trouble had been contained in the conquest of Wales. It was also at this time that the triumphal arch at the Imperial gateway of Richborough was built.

Agricola's campaigns of AD 83 were one of the two high-points in terms of the geographical conquest of Roman Britain (the second came during the campaigns of Septimius Severus, see Chapter 8), but as we know this was not to last. Agricola was recalled by Domitian sometime between AD 83 and AD 85, somewhat ignominiously given his great success. While he was awarded a statue in Rome and triumphal decorations, he never again held high military or civil office, dying in AD 93.

By this time his great achievements had begun to unravel as Rome began to lose interest in northern Scotland, perhaps because of the lack of economic opportunities (remembering the importance to the Imperial *fiscus* of making each province pay, see discussion on the 'open hand alongside sword' strategy in Chapter 1), lack of political interest in Rome or crises elsewhere in the Empire. Within four years of Agricola's departure the forts cutting off the Highland line along the Great Glen had been evacuated and the devastated local populations began to trickle back south. Next the legionary fortress at Inchtuthil was abandoned, even before it was fully completed, with Domitian redeploying the *legio* II *Adiutrix* to the Balkans. The *legio* XX *Valeria Victrix* also deployed south, making its home at the harbour and legionary fortress of Chester. Similarly, while patrolling in the waters of the far north no doubt continued to maintain control of the littoral zone there, the *Classis Britannica* headed south. Thus, as the end of the first century AD approached, the fleet found itself principally operating out of the harbours at Chester and South Shields.

A final point to make in this chapter covering the extensive operations of the *Classis Britannica* during the Claudian invasion, conquest and northern campaigns is that throughout this entire period detachments would have also been operating across the North Sea, where the regional fleet had responsibility for controlling the littoral zone on the Continental coast up to the estuary of the River Rhine (and perhaps as far as the River Elbe). We have little detail here from our primary sources except Tacitus' commentary regarding the fleet and Civilis Revolt in AD 70 (*Histories*, 4, 79, 3). We can be sure, however, that as construction of the *limes Germanicus* began to cement the Continental northern borders of the Empire the British regional fleet would have been busy and active securing its western flank, working in conjunction with its sister fleet the *Classis Germanica*.

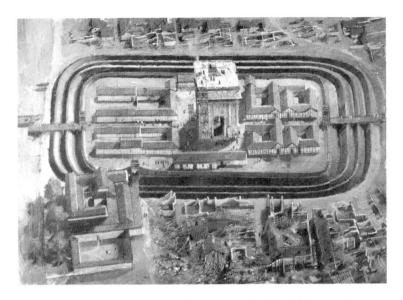

The Imperial Gateway into Britain: the monumental arch at Richborough, reused as a watch tower with surrounding defensive ditches in the third century. (© Historic England)

Wallsend Fort and fortified harbour, the extreme eastern end of Hadrian's Wall with its military port. (© Historic England)

Intaglio showing Roman merchant ship underway with main and bow sails set, with pharos at right (possibly representing one of those at Dover or that at the *Classis Britannica* headquarters in Boulogne). (From Caistor-by-Norwich © Norwich Castle Museum and Art Gallery)

Reconstructed Roman riverine galley. (Römisch-Germanisches Zentralmuseum, Mainz/V. Iserhardt, R. Müller)

Clay oil lamp featuring image of galley with main sail set and oars deployed. (© Museum of London)

Model of Roman merchant ship of Blackfriars 1 vessel size unloading in the Roman port of London. (© Museum of London)

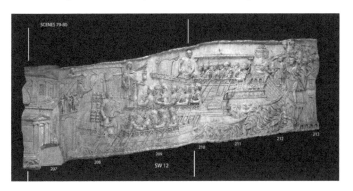

Roman war galleys deploy as Emperor Trajan sets out for the 2nd Dacian War as depicted on Trajan's Column. (Roger B. Ulrich)

Roman biremes from Trajan's column. Note the stern shelter. (Roger B. Ulrich)

The Russian doll effect! Image of Roman war galley as detailed on image of bireme on Trajan's Column. (Roger B. Ulrich)

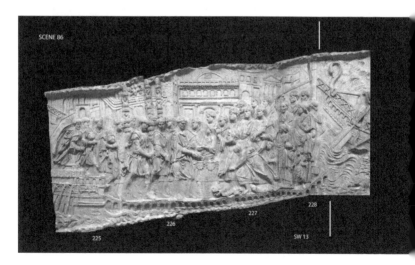

Trajan disembarking from a bireme onto a harbour front, merchant ship at right, from Trajan's Column. (Roger B. Ulrich)

Roman biremes detailed on Trajan's Column with rams prominent. (Roger B. Ulrich)

Artist's reconstruction of Romano-British bloomery furnaces in Little Furnace Wood, Mayfield, the Weald. The *Classis Britannica* played a major role in iron manufacturing in this region of Kent, East and West Sussex, and Surrey. (From *The Wealden Iron Industry* by Jeremy Hodgkinson, courtesy of the estate of the late R. Houghton)

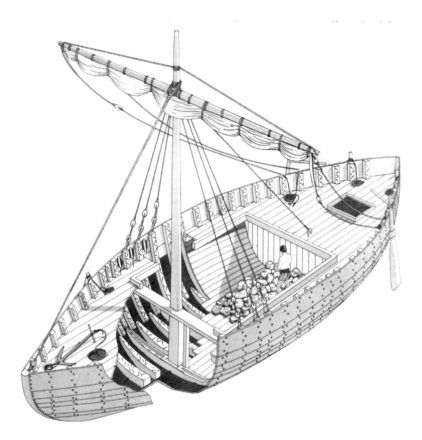

Classic image of the Blackfriars 1 merchant shipwreck as excavated with its load of
Kentish ragstone at the confluence of the rivers Thames and Fleet. (© Historic England)

Roman *codicaria* towed river barge with towing mast set forward. (Elizabeth Elliott)

Half-finished millstones or column bases from likely *Classis Britannica* wreck in the River Medway near East Farleigh, Maidstone. Baseball bat for scale! (Author's collection)

Port view of Roman bireme model made by the author. Note triple-pronged ram beak and forward-set balisata. (Author's collection)

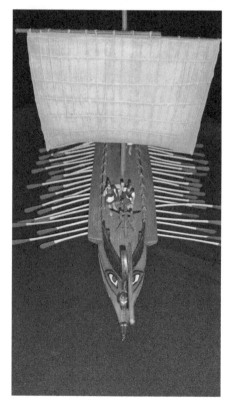

Roman bireme bow on, the business end in full view. Model made by the author. (Author's collection)

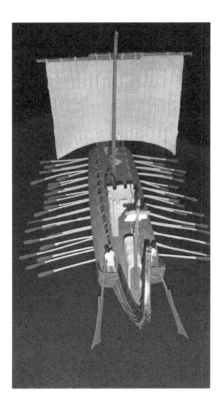

Stern view of Roman bireme model made by the author showing the control positions aft and two rudder men. (Author's collection)

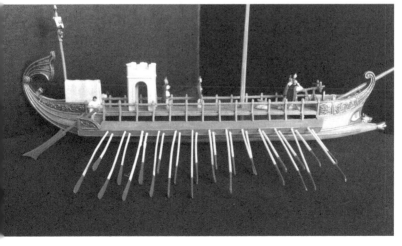

Starboard view of Roman bireme model made by the author. Note command team aft. (Author's collection)

Artist's impression of the legionary fortress at Caerleon in the second century, featuring the harbour used by the *Classis Britannica*. (Peter Guest, Cardiff University © 7reasons)

Plautius' view of the Medway battlefield as he crested Bluebell Hill on the North Downs before descending towards the river which flows left to right between the two industrial estates. At the time of the engagement the Britons would have been arrayed in battle order on the far bank and visible to the Romans. (Author's collection)

Plautius' approach route to the Medway from Bluebell Hill, river to the right of the image and behind photographer. (Author's collection)

Medway crossing battle site, river to left and behind photographer. (Author's collection)

The actual point where the river was forced during Plautius' river-crossing battle on the Medway. Snodland church is to the left. (Author's collection)

Modern monuments to Plautius' Medway-crossing battle. (Author's collection)

Cuxton on left bank, Borstal on right. This is the likely crossing point for Plautius' flanking Batavians in the Medway River-crossing battle. (John Lambshead)

Plautius' route to the Thames looking south from Church Street near Higham, less than 1km from the river. (Author's collection)

Thames crossing battle site; Church Street and Higham at centre right. Roman war galleys would have been prolific on the river during the engagement. Hector the Goldendoodle for scale! (Author's collection)

Thames River-crossing battle site from Church Street, north of Higham. (Author's collection)

Second phase of the Roman villa at Folkestone – a grand affair often linked with the commander of the *Classis Britannica*. (A Town Unearthed © Drew Smith and Mikko Kriek)

The 'Rocklands ship' image found in north Norfolk, a Roman war galley as graffiti on waste lead showing, unusually for northern waters, what appears to be a lateen sail. Possibly a votive offering for a sailor about to set out on a difficult voyage. (James Beckerleg)

7

THE CAMPAIGNS OF THE MATURE *CLASSIS BRITANNICA* (AD 101–AD 191)

This chapter will consider the campaigns of the *Classis Britannica* in the second century, including extensive activity in the reigns of Hadrian, Antonius Pius, Marcus Aurelius and Commodus. It will also look at how the *Classis Britannica* during this period interacted with the other regional fleets of the west when the Empire was at the height of its territorial expansion.

As the century began the overall mood in the province of Britannia was one of stability. The main island of Britain had been fully conquered and integrated into the Empire as far as the Solway Firth–Tyne line, with troops and *milites* remaining in some of the key forts and military harbours up to the Clyde–Forth line and perhaps beyond. This presence north of the border was not significant, however, as we know that key sites such as the major fortress at Newsteads remained unoccupied until nearer the middle of the century.

Economically the province had begun to take on the geographical appearance that was to dominate its structure for much of the rest of the occupation, with the south and east below a line drawn from the Severn to the Humber being a fully productive and economically integrated part of the Empire that provided a steady return to the Imperial *fiscus*. Above this line, however, the north and west remained a border territory where the regional economy was geared towards maintaining the exponentially large military presence deployed there. Thus we have a significant component of the *Classis Britannica* operating out of the military harbours at Chester on the west coast and South Shields on the east, and the three legionary headquarters now being located at the major legionary fortresses at Caerleon, Chester and York.

For the regional fleet, despite this significant northern deployment, we do know that its headquarters remained at Boulogne, this reflecting its responsibilities across the North Sea as well as around the British Isles. In fact, it was at the beginning of the second century that the substantial fortress detailed in Chapter 4 was built there, enclosing an area of 12.5ha and able to accommodate some 3,500 *milites* in substantial 49m × 8m barracks buildings. This would have been enough to man more than sixty *liburnae*. The lighthouse built at the time of Caligula's abortive invasion in AD 40 also remained in use (surviving until the sixteenth century, by which time it was known as the Tour d'Ordre), as did the extensive wharfing and storage facilities built in Boulogne at the same time.

Meanwhile, across the English Channel construction of the first *Classis Britannica* fort and harbour at Dover began in AD 116. For unknown reasons this structure was not completed, although one could reasonably speculate an association here with the AD 117 insurrections of the north. A second and bigger fortress was finally completed around AD 130, with this building also serving as the secondary headquarters for the regional fleet. Though smaller than its counterpart at Boulogne, that at Dover was still substantial, occupying a promontory to the west of the River Dour with a harbour front protected by a spit of shingle. This narrowed the river entrance to around 50m and provided a harbour basin protected from bad weather, ideal for the transport vessels that travelled to and from Boulogne. Thus, while Richborough remained the official Imperial gateway with its grand triumphal arch, Dover became the principal economic link with northern Gaul. The fort at Dover featured ten substantial barrack blocks and two granaries, being rebuilt in AD 160 and staying in use (save a brief period of inactivity in the AD 180s) until the early third century AD. With its substantial stone walls it was also protected by a large ditch on three sides, with the sea providing protection on the other. Each barrack building housed a full crew for a *liburnian* bireme and in total the fort would have housed up to 640 men. The fine quality of the facilities within the fort is indicated by the fact that the *principia* commanders' house had hypocausts to provide under-floor heating, with the floors themselves made from good quality *opus signinum*. The fort is associated with the two famous *pharos* lighthouses built on the high ground either side of the River Dour, one of which is still in existence today (it being reused as the tower of St Mary-in-Castro church within the grounds of Dover Castle).

Excavations in the nineteenth and twentieth centuries have also provided insight into the structure of the Roman port facilities at Dover. They have shown that at some stage in the second century AD a 30m-long mole or breakwater was built out from the eastern side of the *Classis Britannica* fort to further protect the anchorage. This ran transversely across the mouth of the inlet of the River Dour and was constructed of large-scale timber framing with a shingle infill. Meanwhile, on the western side of the inlet a huge chalk block harbour front was built, together with a timber jetty, these both being found during excavations in 1956. An extension to this, fronting out to the sea, was found in 1974. The official status of Dover is also indicated by the presence of the famous Painted House located in 1970 and excavated by Dr Brian Philp and the Kent Archaeological Rescue Unit over twenty-five years, which Mason (2003, 111) interprets as a *mansiones* lodgings for officials and the couriers of the *cursus publicus*. We know of at least one official who made use of its facilities, Olus Cordius Candidus, who while the governor's transport officer (*strator consularis*) erected an altar on the site to the mother goddesses of Italy. Given this level of activity by the regional navy in Dover it is probable that the likely *Classis Britannica* forts at Lympne and Pevensey (see Chapter 4) were also built at the same time, with similar designs and capacity.

Moving back to the chronological narrative of the campaigns of the *Classis Britannica*, we next come across the regional navy in the context of trouble in Britain at the beginning of Hadrian's reign in AD 117 (*Historia Augusta*, Hadrian, 5.1–2):

> When he took over the Empire, Hadrian reverted to an earlier policy, devoting his energies to keeping the peace throughout the world. The people subdued by Trajan had rebelled, the Moors were launching attacks, the Sarmatae making war, and the Britons could not be kept under control.

The only other near contemporary reference we have to this apparently traumatic event in Britain is from the Roman rhetorician and grammarian, Marcus Cornelius Fronto, who, writing in the AD 130s to his former pupil and now Emperor, Marcus Aurelius, says the casualties suffered by the latter in conflict with the Parthians in the east were comparable to those suffered at the beginning of Hadrian's reign in Britain (Birley, 2005, 118). Our primary sources give little further detail about the nature of this incident but it appears to be part of a pattern repeated later many times involving the native tribes of Scotland, still not the cohesive political entities they were later to become, taking advantage whenever the attention of Rome was diverted elsewhere. Any insurrection may also have involved the disgruntled Brigantes of the occupied north of the province, given the region was a militarised border zone. In this regard a key reference in one of the famous writing tablets from the *vexillation* fortress of Vindolanda dating from this period may be particularly important. Written on tablet number 164, this refers to 'nasty little Britons' (*Brittunculi*) and certainly shows there was no love lost between the armies of Rome and the natives. Meanwhile, a cavalry prefect called Titus Haterius Nepos also features in a contemporary inscription carrying out a census in Annandale in Dumfries and Galloway, this seemingly designed to put the stamp of Rome on an unimpressed local populace.

Whatever happened in AD 117, the situation was clearly serious as a tombstone from Ferentinum in Italy records one Titus Pontius Sabinus, a senior centurion (*primus pilus*) of the *legio* III *Augusta* who at this time commanded an '*expeditone Britannica*' deployed to the province comprising *vexillations* from the *legio* VII *Germina*, *legio* VIII *Augusta* and *legio* XXII *Primigenia*. These substantial legionary (not auxiliary) reinforcements, totalling more than 3,000 men from the *limes Germanicus* and Spain, give serious context to the events in Britain as the last time such replacements were required was in the wake of the Boudican revolt (see Chapter 6). These new troops were evidently transported by the *Classis Britannica* directly to South Shields on the Tyne, from where they deployed north. It is worth remembering that at this time Hadrian's Wall had yet to be constructed and the frontier was being held along the Solway–Tyne line by a number of *vexillation* and smaller fortresses that had been built along the Stanegate military road. These included Vindolanda as mentioned above, where a centurion of the 1st Auxiliary Cohort of Tungrians (from modern Belgium) was killed in the fighting in this campaign and is commemorated on a tombstone. One other contemporary piece of epigraphic evidence comes in the form of the tombstone of the auxiliary prefect of *cohors* II *Asturum*, who around this time was decorated *bello Britannico* (for out-standing service) before being transferred to serve with the *legio* III *Cyrenaica.*

Whatever the exact nature of this conflict in the north, the situation seems to have been stabilised by AD 119 when com-memorative coins were struck. These are noteworthy as for the first time ever they carried an image of Britannia, the now famous female warrior (more parallels with the Boudican revolt perhaps) armed with a shield and a spear. The incident was certainly serious enough to have a major impact on the new Emperor as, having very early in his reign decided to halt the outward expansion of the Empire, he chose Britain as the place where this policy would be physically embodied. This was, of course, in the form of Hadrian's Wall built along the Solway Firth–Tyne line running 117km from Bowness-on-Solway to Wallsend (Roman *Segedunum*). Construction of this most physical of borders began in AD 122 in the year Hadrian visited the province, most likely to see for himself the reconstruction taking place after the AD 117 insurrection and to satisfy himself order had been restored. The regional fleet would have been prominent at this time in its trans-port role given the size of the entourage that accompanied the Emperor. This included Sabrina, his wife, civil serv-ants and courtiers, detachments of his guard units including Praetorians, and the 5,500 men of the *legio* VI *Victrix*. The Emperor was clearly taking no chances given recent history; he headed north rapidly (except his wife, who toured the south of the province) where he tasked the new Governor Aulus Platorius Nepos with the task of sealing off the most northerly border of the Empire with the wall that today car-ries Hadrian's name.

In terms of the activities of the *Classis Britannica* in this sequence of events from AD 117 until the construction of the wall, we are obviously lacking specific detail given the scarcity of primary references (at least until the physical building of the fortification began). Given we are aware of the military roles of the regional fleet, however, we can be sure that while the insurrection lasted the *Classis Britannica* would have continued to operate along the western and eastern coasts up to and beyond the northern border, in the first instance maintaining control of the littoral zone. In this they seem to have been successful given there is no evidence of the use of naval forces by the Britons to bypass the border as did happen later during the occupation, for example in the Great Conspiracy of AD 367. We are also definitely aware that the fleet fulfilled its transport role, for example ferrying Sabinus' '*expeditone Britannica*' strategic reserve to the province at a key stage in the conflict. Finally, of course, it would have continued the patrolling and scouting of the littoral zone as it had since the middle of the previous century.

It is in the context of non-military activity that we next have visibility of the fleet. As Hadrian and Nepos headed north, passing through York with its legionary fortress, they began to put in place the logistics to build the wall. In the first instance a new and substantial bridge was built across the Tyne at Newcastle (Roman *Pons Aelius*) by the *legio* VI *Victrix* that carried a 5.5m-wide roadway. Hadrian and the army dedicated two altars here to Neptune and Oceanus before heading further north where construction of the wall began.

Threaded with milecastles and watchtowers (two of the latter between each of the former in the most complete stretches), the western half of the fortification was originally constructed of turf blocks, although these were later replaced with the stone construction of the eastern section. We may actually have insight into the AD 117 event here in that the turf-walled western section seems to have been built first and in haste, hinting at the direction of the principal threat. The line chosen for the wall was slightly to the north of the Stanegate, with the usual fore-ditch facing to the north. Additionally, however, a large vallum flat-bottomed ditch was also built to the immediate south that may have been designed to protect the wall's rear. Intriguingly this may indicate continuing concern at the time over the reliability of the Brigantes.

It is in the construction of the wall that we now have visibility of the regional fleet, by this time heavily in attendance at South Shields on the Tyne to support the presence of the Emperor and governor. This is because, at some stage during the five-year construction period, two inscriptions actually show the regional fleet building sections of the fortification. Fully detailed in Chapter 1, in the first instance we have the inscription on a stone block on Hadrian's Wall between Birdoswald and Castlesteads made by a detachment of *Pedites Classicorum Britanniorum* (marines of the British fleet) recording them building this section. Secondly, we have the similar inscription in the portico of the granary of the fort at Benwell, the third on Hadrian's Wall, this made by a *Vexillatio Classis Britannicae*.

It is around this time that we begin to see permanent defences set up along the north-west and north coasts for the first time, perhaps reflecting a growing awareness among the Roman occupiers of Britain that their presence along the northern frontier was beginning to have an impact on the unconquered Britons of the north. In this context it is a common result of the presence of a more 'developed' political entity alongside one less so to see over a period of time the steady osmosis of wealth, material culture and patronage from the former to the latter. A common result is a coalescence of wealth and power among an ever narrower group of elites in the less 'developed' region until truly political units appear.

This certainly happened in Scotland in the second century, and the building of these northern coastal defences shows the process in action in real-time. Previously there is no indication of any naval threat in the littoral zone around the frontier, where Rome had total control. This was clearly changing at this time or the substantial investment in the building of the defensive infrastructure would have been uneconomic and in that regard very un-Roman.

We have insight into these events in the form of two pieces of epigraphy. The first, as detailed in Chapter 1 and dating slightly later to AD 146, is in the form of a discharge diploma from the fort at Chester mentioning a *Cohors 1 Aelia Classica*, this being the same unit named in another diploma dated to AD 158 found near the Roman Fort at Ravenglass on the Cumbrian coast. We know from the archaeological record that the coastal defences along the Cumbrian coast around the promontory of the Lake District consisted of the same kind of network of mile-forts and watchtowers as were found along the length of Hadrian's Wall, all occupying prominent positions with views out into the Irish Sea. Clearly the threat of raiding from that direction was growing in importance too, with the natives of north-eastern Ireland becoming ever more aware of the wealth on offer from the successful plundering of the Roman province a short distance across the waterway. It seems likely in this context that the *Cohors 1 Aelia Classica* was actually based at Ravenglass, being a unit of *milites* of the regional fleet and thus suggesting that the military harbours built here during the campaigns of Cerialis remained in use and the fleet presence strong. Similarly we see around this time similar fortification on the north-eastern coast, with, for example, the fort at Newcastle overlooking the Hadrianic bridge being built by the middle of the century to protect docking facilities slightly further up the Tyne than Wallsend and South Shields.

It is as we approach this period that we again see the *Classis Britannica* involved in renewed campaigning in the north. Having made his everlasting mark on the Empire, Hadrian died in AD 138 and within a year his successor Antoninus Pius had ordered renewed campaigning in the north of Britain. Whether this was in response to further disturbances as in

AD 117 or a desire on the part of the new Emperor (as with
Claudius ninety-five years earlier) to make his Imperial mark
is unclear, but the decision marked a dramatic shift in Roman
policy with regard to its far northern frontier. Within a year
the Governor Quintus Lollius Urbicus was in the north and
overseeing a significant upgrading of the logistical infrastructure there to support a northern campaign. This included the
refurbishment of the key fort at Corbridge and those further north at Risingham and High Rochester. We have little
visibility of the ensuing campaign but it was clearly over by
AD 142 when coins were being minted to commemorate a
famous victory over the northerly Britons. We can track the
progress of the campaigning up to the old Clyde–Forth line
by the rebuilding of the old Flavian forts and the additional
building of new ones, with the advance clearly being rapid
and decisive. Any British opposition seems to have been easily
overcome, indicating that the reasoning behind this particular
venture was more Imperial aggrandisement than because of a
renewed existential threat.

This advance of the frontier northwards was once again
accompanied by the renovation of Flavian military harbours
and the construction of new ones, together with storage facilities. These were often quays at the site of the major coastal
forts. On the Clyde these included Dumbarton on the north
shore and Lurg Moor and Bishopton on the south, while on
the Forth they included Inveresk, Cramond and Carriden.
Inveresk, possibly the next port of call along the north-east
coast after South Shields during this campaign, is particularly important given it features two pieces of epigraphy in
the form of dedications (one to Apollo Grannus, the deity of
mineral and thermal springs who was associated with heal-
ing) by Quintus Lusius Sabinianus, the *procurator Augusti*. This
is a big deal in that here, in the farthest reaches of the Empire
and in the context of yet another campaign of conquest in
the north, we find the actual procurator of the province in

residence for a long enough period to have two dedications made in his name. Could it be that he was there to determine once and for all whether Scotland, at least in the south, was economically worthy of incorporation into the Empire (especially as the tribal entities had begun to consolidate following contact with Rome)? It would seem that on this occasion the answer was yes, because this rapid campaign was followed by the building of a new and significant frontier fortification along the Clyde–Forth line, namely the Antonine Wall. This sequence of events was significant enough to have warranted comment in the *Historia Augusta* (Antoninus Pius, 5.4), which says the Emperor:

> … defeated the Britons through his legate Lollius Urbanicus, and having driven back the barbarians, he built another wall, of turf.

As can be deduced from the quote, the Antonine was built with blocks of turf as had the western stretch of Hadrian's Wall originally. The construction technique involved the use of well-built stone foundations with the blocks of turf layered on top, and with culverts for drainage threaded throughout to maintain the integrity of the structure. Six main forts were originally integrated along the length of the wall in the initial planning phase, with the wall itself forming their northerly facing. These were located at Carriden, Mumrills, Auchendavy, Castlecary, Balmuildy and Old Kilpatrick. The latter three were built before the wall was constructed, with those at Castlecary and Balmuildy being the only ones actually built of stone. Many more forts were added later, however, as construction progressed, eventually totalling nineteen larger forts and twenty-nine smaller fortlets. Built either integral to the wall itself or standing slightly proud, these additional larger and smaller fort sites included locations such as Castlehill, Cadder, Barr Hill, Westerwood, Rough Castle, Bearsden, Croy Hill and

Duntocher. As with Hadrian's Wall, a defensive ditch was also constructed to the north of the wall, though no vallum to the rear, which indicates at the time of its construction no significant threat was expected from there.

The wall appears to have been constructed in haste (hence perhaps its turf construction), with the whole of the *legio* II *Augusta* and *vexillations* from the *legio* VI *Victrix* and *legio* XX *Valeria Victrix* involved. Up to 7,000 remained to garrison the frontier. Interestingly we have no inscriptions indicating the *Classis Britannica* was involved, even more surprising given the ease of access to the western and eastern stretches afforded by the Clyde and Forth. This may indicate the fleet was preoccupied to the north, where control of the littoral zone on both coasts was vital to prevent any hostile interventions that might destabilise the building process. It was also very probable that the lines of supply from the original occupied zone to the new border were stretched at this point given the huge undertaking of actually building the wall. In that regard the *Classis Britannica* would again have had its hands full facilitating the supply route up and down the two coasts, with Camelon and Carriden both being suggested as the principal port for the new wall.

Once constructed the border was officially moved up to the Antonine Wall, with Hadrian's Wall being abandoned for the most part (though interestingly the coastal defences along the Solway Firth and the River Tay and around the Cumbrian and Northumberland coasts more broadly remained in place). The occupying Romans were clearly intending to stay along the new frontier given the refurbishment of the northerly road up to the line of the River Tay, and the reoccupation of some of Agricola's most northerly forts. This presence in the far north was not on the scale of the late first century AD, however, given that some of the larger sites on the Tay such as the legionary fortress at Inchtuthil were not reoccupied.

We next come across the *Classis Britannica* in the mid-AD 140s when it was deployed to transport troops from Britain to

North Africa to campaign against the Moors, and then bring them back. This indicates the situation in the north was quiet following the building of the Antonine Wall, but this peaceful existence along the northern frontier was not to last. In the AD 150s trouble erupted again, with once more reserves being urgently redeployed from the legions and auxilia of Upper and Lower Germany (using the *Classis Britannica* once more). We know of this from dedications they erected to Antoninus Pius (which also mention *vexillations* of the three resident British legions) in a shrine next to the bridge over the Tyne, the location once again hinting that they disembarked in the north-east. The trouble in the north is also attested by the minting of base metal coins in Rome dating to AD 154–155 that show an image of Britannia in mourning. Finally, the Greek geographer and traveller Pausanias (*Description of Greece*, 8.43.4) mentions Antoninus Pius depriving the Brigantes of their territory. If this reference is from the later period of the Emperor's long reign then it may be that the trouble in the north at this time was from a threat at least partly to the rear of the Antonine Wall rather than purely from the north.

Other than these references, however, we have no further detail from the primary sources or from archaeology that detail the troubled events in Britain in the AD 150s. What we do know, however, is that by AD 158 the Antonine Wall was abandoned, only sixteen years after its construction had begun and seemingly acknowledging Pausanias' southern threat. The evacuation of the north above the Solway Firth–Tyne line was successfully carried out by the Governor Gnaeus Julius Verus, who re-established the northern border along the line of the newly renovated Hadrian's Wall and began the rebuilding of key sites in the north of occupied Britain, such as Brough-on-Noe in the Pennines and Corbridge, to re-establish the logistical network requirement to maintain the new frontier. Interestingly, during the governorship of Verus' next but one replacement, Sextus Calpurnius Agricola, the vallum to the rear of Hadrian's Wall was also filled in, clearly indicating the Roman occupiers of Britain felt the Brigantian threat had been removed once and for all. We can only imagine the traumatic and systematic way in which this was accomplished within a generation and one gets the distinct impression that the immediate north and south of Hadrian's Wall was now effectively barren of human settlement. To the north of the wall, as happened in the immediate period following the post-Agricolan Scottish withdrawal, some of the forts remained garrisoned as late as the AD 190s, when troops from the *legio* VI *Victrix* dedicated an altar to the god Mercury at the stone fortress at Castlecary on the line of the old Antonine Wall. Events at Dover around AD 160 may be tied in to these developments, where a rebuilding phase began at the *Classis Britannica* fort there. This may indicate that units from the regional fleet were deploying south once again with the border comparatively quiet.

Continuing our chronology of the century, in AD 169 at the time of the death of co-Emperor Lucius Verus, the *Historia Augusta* (Marcus Aurelius, 22.1), again references trouble brewing in Britain, although with no further details. Then around AD 175 the *Classis Britannica* comes into view again, this time in a transport role when 5,500 Sarmatian heavy cavalry were deployed from the Continent to Britain (eventually being based at Ribchester in Lancashire).

Late in the century trouble erupted along the northern border yet again. Dio (77.12) explains that by this time there were two main races of 'Britons', the Maeatae north of Hadrian's Wall and the Caledonians to the north of them. Both were confederations (official rather than general polities), which amalgamated the previously separate northern tribes that had by now fully coalesced following contact with their southern superpower neighbour. The Caledonians, and almost certainly the Maetae, breached Hadrian's Wall in AD 182 and, heading south along Dere Street, destroyed the forts at Halton

Chesters, Rudchester and Corbridge, a Roman general being killed in the process. The new Emperor, Commodus, responded decisively by ordering the British Governor, Ulpius Marcellus, to counter-attack, with the *Classis Britannica* again providing support in the littoral zone operating out of the harbours at Chester and Bowness on the west coast and South Shields, Wallsend and Newcastle on the east. Anecdotally, sea control still seems to have been in place given there is yet again no record of any attempts to carry out raiding south of the border by sea. The campaign seems to have been successful given three epigraphic inscriptions (one at Corbridge and two from Carlisle) that speak of successful action beyond Hadrian's Wall at this time (Southern, 2012, 229). Confirmation comes in AD 184 when Commodus received his seventh acclamation as Imperator and took the title *Britannicus*, with the *Classis Britannica* once again free enough of front-line military duties to transport two of the three British legions to Brittany to help defeat a rebellion, and then return them.

Events again gather apace in Britain and for the *Classis Britannica* less than a decade later following the assassination of the increasingly unpopular Commodus on New Year's Eve in AD 192, this ushering in the so-called Year of the Five Emperors. At this point I will look in depth at events in Rome surrounding this and subsequent events as they have a particular importance for later developments in Britain. The plot to kill the erratic Emperor was led by Praetorian Prefect Quintus Aemilius Laetus, the Imperial Chamberlain Eclectus and Commodus' mistress, Marcia. Laetus immediately cast around for a 'tame' successor for Commodus and alighted on the urban prefect Pertinax, who was rushed to the Praetorian camp on New Year's Day and proclaimed Emperor. The son of a freed slave and a former teacher, Pertinax had a particular resonance in Britain given he was governor from AD 185 through to AD 187. He seems to have struggled to gain the respect of the military during his time in the province, however, allegedly being injured in one confrontation (Dio, 74.4), and is best known for his time in Britain through the life-size bust of him found at the Roman villa at Lullingstone and now on display in the British Museum.

Pertinax decided to style himself on the highly regarded Marcus Aurelius and strove to be a worthy Emperor, instituting reforms of the welfare system for the poor and of the currency (the latter by increasing the silver purity of the *denarius*). This was not what Laetus had been expecting, however, and matters swiftly came to a head when Pertinax next tried to reform the Praetorian Guard itself. The relationship with his guard was already poor, the new Emperor having failed to pay them a generous *donativum*, and a plot to kill Pertinax was soon in the offing. An early attempt to replace him with *consul* Quintus Sosius Falco three months into his reign failed, but one at the end of the March succeeded when 300 disgruntled Praetorians forced the palace gates and, despite his attempts to reason with them, eventually killed him.

Next up a wealthy senator called Didius Julianus tried to bribe his way to power, but was quickly discarded by the ever powerful Praetorians. This left three serious contenders for power: Pannonia Superior Governor Septimius Severus, Syrian Governor Pescennius Niger, and British Governor Decimus Clodius Albinus. The first and last have important parts to play in the story of the Roman occupation of Britain and the *Classis Britannica*'s role in that regard.

It was Severus who was the first to make his move, sitting as he was on the Danube frontier, his proximity to Rome giving him an immediate strategic advantage. The first Emperor of North African descent, he was to become one of the great military leaders of the middle Empire and already had a long track record of civilian and military experience behind him (he was first made a senator by Marcus Aurelius). Severus had held the *limes* along the Danube since AD 191, when he had taken up his latest governorship, and in April AD 193 shortly after the death of Pertinax his troops proclaimed him Emperor in the provincial capital of Carnuntum. Knowing he had the backing of the sixteen legions along the Rhine and Danube, he displayed his ruthless nature immediately by marching directly on Rome. The lightning strike paid off and Severus was swiftly accepted by the Senate, the unfortunate Julianus being quickly put to death as the new Emperor began his eighteen-year reign.

His first priority was to deal with the remaining rivals for the Imperial throne, Niger in Syria and Albinus in Britain. The former, responding to the pleas of the mob in Rome, had by this time also proclaimed himself Emperor so Severus prioritised the eastern threat. Securing his western flank by proclaiming Albinus in Britain his *caeser* (Herodian, 2.15), he fought a year-long campaign against Niger, defeating him at the Battle of Issus in May AD 194 and capturing the would-be competitor as he attempted to flee to Parthia. A beheading ensued soon after, followed by campaigning against Niger's erstwhile eastern allies, including the Parthians. The region pacified, Severus then returned to Rome and two years of peace followed with his *caesar* in Britain, where for once the northern borders seem to have been quiet. It was not long, however, before trouble once again loomed at this most north-westerly of the Roman provinces. Herodian (2.15) is explicit that Severus' appointment of Albinus to the rank of his *caesar* was a ruse to buy him time, and it seems this was indeed the case. Albinus became increasingly suspicious of Severus' intentions, especially as the latter had begun to officially favour his sons, Caracalla and Geta, in public in Rome. By AD 196 matters had reached a head and Albinus began minting his own coins, on which he styled himself *augustus*. Proclaiming himself Emperor, he survived an assassination attempt by Severus (Herodian, 3.5) and then gathered the legions of Britain for the crossing to Gaul. The role of the *Classis Britannica* in Albinus' usurpation attempt is implicit here as such a crossing would have been impossible without their support. This was a sizeable force travelling across the English Channel given that by the time the crisis came to a head a year later Albinus had troops from three legions, 35,000 auxiliaries and up to 5,000 cavalry with him (Moorhead and Stuttart, 2012, 150). Even taking into account troops joining him on the Continent, and troops newly raised to support his cause, much of this army would have originated in Britain (only one Continental legion seems to have joined him, from Spain). Therefore the regional fleet would have played a key role in an oceanic zone sea control capacity to ensure a smooth crossing, in a littoral zone role controlling both ends of the sea crossing (these roles continuing throughout the usurpation), and finally – and perhaps most importantly – in a transport role using its own and indentured transport vessels.

Defeating the legate Virius Lupus, whom Severus had sent to stop Albinus' advance in Gaul, the usurper arrived in southern France and set himself up with Lyon (Colonia Copia Claudia Augusta Lugdunum) as his capital. Severus, ever decisive, decided to take matters into his own hands and advanced quickly on Albinus, engaging him at the Battle of Lugdunum in AD 197. Very bloody and a close-run thing, Severus was eventually victorious and Albinus committed suicide rather than let himself be captured. Severus sent his head to Rome, where it was displayed on a cross, with the *Historia Augusta* describing the now unchallenged Emperor riding over Albinus' body on his own horse to ritually trample it (Sev. 11.8). The fortunes of the usurper's British troops who survived the battle are not known, though given Severus' severe treatment of all who stood in his way, their prospects can be expected to have been limited. It is noteworthy that Albinus only took some of the troops from his British legions with him, not all, so some would still have been based in the province, together with his administration and that of the procurator. In this regard the Emperor still clearly viewed Britain as a threat on his western flank and his next move was to install Virius Lupus (who had survived his defeat at the hands of Albinus) as the new governor of the province, additionally sending military commissioners to help him restore Imperial order and suppress any surviving supporters of the usurper (and, on a practical note, to repair the northern frontier that had been damaged by increased raiding since Albinus' absence). He also took the drastic step of initiating the planning process which early in the next century would see the occupied part of the island divided into two provinces, *Britannia Superior* and *Britannia Inferior*. For the *Classis Britannica*, given my assertion above that common sense dictates it sided with Albinus, perhaps this was also the beginning of the end as we know it disappears from history in AD 249, as detailed in Chapter 3. In fact, for a short time, while the military commissioners went about their work, it may have been amalgamated with the *Classis Germanica*, *Classis Moesica* and *Classis Pannonica* given the reference to one of its admirals in Rome (see discussion in Chapter 1).

In concluding this chapter, one can reflect that the first century in Britain was effectively one long period of harrying for the peoples of the north above the Pennines, with the fate of the Brigantes in the AD 150s seemingly indicative of what those who resisted Rome in the sporadic outbreaks of rebellious violence could expect. In short, the sword. Things were about to get even worse, however, for Septimius Severus decided to finish what Agricola could not. He determined to settle the problems of the northern borders of Britain once and for all, in a dramatic classical world example of shock and awe at its most violent. And once again the *Classis Britannica*, cleansed of the supporters of Albinus, led the way.

8

THE LATER CAMPAIGNS OF THE *CLASSIS BRITANNICA* (AD 192–AD 249)

This chapter will examine the role played by the *Classis Britannica* in the major campaigns in Britain of Septimius Severus, how it was affected by the onset of the 'Crisis of the mid-third century', and additionally tell the story of the decline of the *Classis Britannica*'s fortresses and their replacement by the early forts of the Saxon Shore.

The narrative of Severus' campaign begins back in Rome where the Emperor returned after defeating Albinus. In the first instance he again turned his attention to Parthia, invading with his full strength and capturing (and, given his reputation, no doubt sacking) the capital Ctesiphon in late AD 197. He stayed in the east for five years before returning to Rome via Egypt, where he viewed the body of Alexander the Great. Now physically ailing and eager to get away from intrigue in Rome, Severus finally focused back on Britain and its troublesome northern borders.

Back in *Britannia*, despite the efforts of Lupus and the military commissioners, the Caledonians and Maeatae continued

The Campaigns of Septimius Severus, AD 209–211

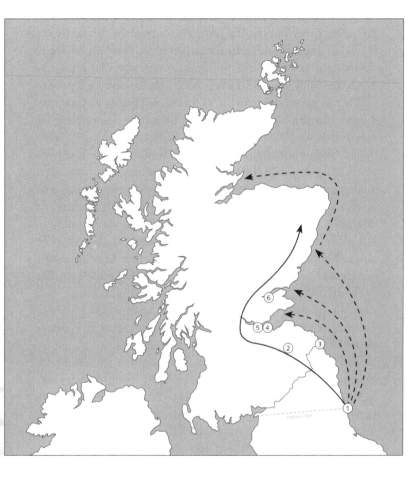

① South Shields   ——————▶   Army
② Newstead   – – – – – – ▶   *Classis Britannica*
③ Berwick
④ Cramond
⑤ Carriden
⑥ Carpow

to harass the frontier. Southern (2012, 237) says that when the new governor had arrived in AD 197 he had found a province in chaos following Albinus' departure. He quickly set about restoring order but the Caledonians, soon to be joined by the Maeatae, lost no time in causing even more trouble and began agitating along the border yet again. A new invasion across the Hadrian's Wall now in prospect, and with no reserve troops to call upon given the Emperor's focus on Parthia at this time, Lupus had few options and opted to secure peace along his northern borders with massive payments of money (Dio, 76.5). Such enormous injections of wealth to the northern elites of unconquered Britain, while buying peace for a short time, in the long run only further assisted the increasing coalescence of power among the leaders of the Caledonians and Maeatae, with their threat to occupied Britain continuing to hang over the island. Matters came to a head in AD 207 when the tribes began gathering once again before heading south, where they renewed their campaign of pillage and plunder. Herodian (III.14) describes the situation as so severe that Lupus requested a new injection of troops into the province, or indeed the attendance of the Emperor himself. Fortune smiled kindly on the governor and he got both.

The response of Severus to this request to attend his northern-most province and restore order would be very recognisable today in the context of the 2003 Iraq War and can only be described as shock and awe writ large. In short, the Emperor's intervention was massive in scale and ambition, and in terms of size and effort ranks above even the campaigns of Agricola. In early AD 208 he crossed the English Channel aiming to finally tame the north of the troublesome province, accompanied by the squabbling Caracalla and Geta and his wider Imperial family, key senators, courtiers and advisors, the Imperial *fiscus*, the Praetorian Guard and *vexillations* of some of his crack legions along the Rhine and Danubian frontiers. The whole were again transported by the *Classis Britannica*, landing at the Imperial gateway of Richborough, where the Emperor entered his troubled province through the monumental arch. This enormous civil and military entourage then travelled along Watling Street to the provincial capital of London before heading north along Ermine Street. Gathering troops from the regions of Britain passed through as they travelled, the Imperial procession arrived at York within a month, where the Emperor turned the principal town of northern Britain into his Imperial capital. He then called upon his remaining legionary troops in the province to join him (the *legio* VI *Victrix* already being based in York) and began planning the onslaught on the north. And at this point, before we go into detail regarding Severus' campaigns in Scotland and the role of the *Classis Britannica* therein, it is perhaps a timely moment to reflect on the nature of the relationship between Severus and his soldiers and *milites*, this lying at the core of both his civil and military leadership and providing insight into the campaign in the narrative that follows.

Severus was the first of the truly reforming Emperors with regard to the Roman military establishment. He initiated the process that, through the later reforms of the likes of Diocletian and Constantine, saw the frontier-based legions and auxilia of the earlier Empire transformed into the *comitatenses* field army troops and *limitanei* border troops of the later Empire. All his reforms were rooted in his experience of the path to power in AD 193. Noting their role in the fates of Commodus, Pertiniax and Didius Julius, he first turned his attention to the Praetorian Guard, disbanding the original force and restructuring it to allow battle-hardened troops from both the northern (particularly Dalmatia and Pannonia where he had held command) and eastern frontiers to join its ranks. This shrewd move, iconoclastic given membership had previously only been open to those of Italian birth, provided a solid mass of 10,000 battle-hardened troops in Rome to keep society high and low in order when the Emperor was away on campaign (and who as seen above later joined him on his last campaign in Britain). Next he recruited three new legions, *legios* I, II and III *Parthica*, the second being the most important historically given it was recruited through the conscription of 6,000 Italian natives (unlike the Praetorians, by this time few Italians joined the ranks of the ordinary legions) and was based at Albanum, 34km from Rome. This was yet more icono-clasm writ large given that until this moment it was extremely unusual to find a legion deep within the Empire, let alone so close to the capital. The message it sent, in addition to that of the reformed Praetorians actually embedded in Rome itself, was clear and succinct. Behave or else! Anecdotally, these two bodies of troops also provided Rome with its first mobile field army, setting a trend that would begin to dominate Roman military thinking as the army and navies began to adapt to the new threats and circumstances of the later Empire.

Next, Severus set to improving the lot of his troops across the Empire, both land-based and naval. First off he granted the soldiers the right to officially marry, this providing spouses and offspring with legal rights for the first time. Interestingly, the sailors and marines of the regional fleets appear to have got a jump on their land-based counterparts here as the dis-charge papers of individual sailors and marines from around AD 166 differ from those previously issued in indicating these particular *milites* had been allowed to marry during their term of service (Mason, 2003, 33). Most relevant to this work, how-ever, Severus also increased the annual salary of a legionary to 450 *denarii*, up from 300, at the same time raising the pay of the auxiliaries from 100 to 150 *denarii*. Similarly, the cavalry of the legions saw their pay rise from 400 to 600 *denarii*, while auxil-iary cavalry had a rise to 300 *denarii* from 200 if they belonged to a cohort, and from 333 to 500 *denarii* if they were based on the wing of a battle formation. There is no reason to believe that the *milites* of the regional fleet were treated any differently, with their pay being similarly increased. This was, of course, an emperor who valued above all the loyalty of the soldiers and sailors who kept him in power, with Dio (77.16) famously reporting him on his deathbed advising his sons, Caracalla and Geta, to enrich the soldiery and ignore the rest of society.

Indeed Caracalla, having later dispatched the unfortunate Geta, took this to heart and increased the pay of the military even further, such that by the end of his reign it was double what it had been under Commodus in the late second century. The implications of this economically destabialising though long overdue increase in the pay of the military is discussed in Chapter 9 in the context of the demise of the *Classis Britannica*, but needless to say the Imperial *fiscus* was hit hard, leading to the debasement of coinage across the Empire.

It is in this context that one can understand the loyalty of the Roman military establishment to Severus as he planned his campaign to bring the recalcitrant far north of Britain to heel, based in the *principia* of the legionary fortress in York over the freezing winter of AD 208. One of the keys to the success or otherwise of the forthcoming campaign would be the attention paid to logistics, and we know from archaeological data that in this the Emperor and his high command were faultless. Noting the largest army fielded by Agricola in the north during his last campaign was 30,000, Severus determined to take with him 50,000 and see the job finished. These included the Praetorian Guard, *legio* II *Augusta* (under new leadership given it had played a prominent role in the campaigns of Albinus), *legio* VI *Victrix*, *legio* XX *Valeria Victrix*, possibly the Italian-based *legio* II *Parthica*, the Rhine and Danubian legionary *vexillations* who had travelled to Britain with the Emperor, up to 35,000 auxiliaries and, of course, the *milites* of the regional fleet. The sheer size of this force shows why the Emperor had also travelled with his *fiscus* given the amount of coin and bullion needed to pay for the expedition.

To support this colossal army the fort and harbour at South Shields was chosen to be the main supply depot. Here the fortress itself was extended and then converted into a supply base with new immense granaries being built (twenty to add to the original two) that could hold 2,500 tonnes of grain, enough to feed the whole force for two months. From here the vessels of the *Classis Britannica* fulfilled their transport role, using the Tyne and well-trodden eastern coastal routes to keep the army supplied once the campaign began. The fort at Corbridge on Dere Street just short of Hadrian's Wall was similarly upgraded, with the granaries there rebuilt even before Severus had arrived (showing the degree of logistical fore planning). Then in the spring of AD 209 Severus began the first of his two assaults against the Maeatae and Caledonians to the north, leaving Geta behind in York to take charge of the Imperial administration together with the Empress Julia Domna (Herodian, 3.14).

The pattern of campaigning was an exact copy of the later examples of those of Agricola but on a larger scale, with the focus again being in the east rather than the west. Again the army ground its way up Dere Street and along the coast, the *Classis Britannica* once more sitting tightly on the eastern flank. As the Praetorians, legionaries and auxilia slowly cut their way through the Maeatae in the Scottish Borders, the *milites* of the regional fleet recommissioned the old military harbours along the east coast to ensure the advance could continue with secure lines of supply. Each step of the campaign was marked with a report back to the Senate and people of Rome, as usual painting the natives as savages and the terrain as unforgiving. Dio (77.12) goes to great lengths to emphasise the hardships endured by the troops of the army and *milites* of the fleet, noting the hostile weather and mountainous terrain in which the natives lived. While this commentary is typically dehumanising and purely from a Roman perspective, there is no doubting the difficulty of the campaign and the hard fighting, which was largely asymmetrical with the natives resorting to guerrilla warfare (understandable given the sheer scale of the onslaught they faced). In this regard Herodian (3.14) comments particularly on the advantage the Britons gained from their local knowledge of the terrain and environment.

The importance of the fleet during the campaign is signified by a number of interesting coin issues featuring a naval theme, unusual in normal circumstances. Some silver and bronze coins minted between AD 208 and AD 210 show a galley with its stern adorned with standards, as previously used on imagery dating to Trajan's Dacian campaigns where again they were used to show the importance of the regional fleets in that campaign. Meanwhile, one of AD 209 shows a bridge of boats under the term *Traiectus*, this referencing a 'crossing over', again an image previously associated with Trajan in Dacia, while some issues from AD 209 through to AD 211 show the gods Neptune and Oceanus. Mason (2003, 138) believes the role of the navy was actually crucial, not only in its logistical capacity but also in controlling the littoral as these latest legionary spearheads advanced, and additionally scouting far ahead to provide an alert in the event of any major gathering of the opposition. Just as with every campaign of conquest in Britain since Vespasian's lightning assault on the south-west in the mid-first century, Mason further details that the fleet's *milites* secured each natural harbour ahead of the advance to ensure supplies awaited the land forces as they arrived.

Both Dio (77.13.1) and Herodian (3.15) say that the principal target of the AD 209 campaign was the Caledonians, the more northerly of the two confederations and clearly viewed by Rome as the principal source of agitation north of the border. Thus, the territory of the Maeatae punched through, the Roman juggernaut headed into the far north. The two principal forts and harbours to anchor this advance above South Shields were again Cramond on the south shore of the Forth and Carpow further north on the Tay (the latter home to the *legio* II *Augusta* and *legio* VI *Victrix* in this campaign). Both were extensively refurbished (that at Carpow being totally rebuilt, with Mason arguing that the boat bridge on the above coin issue was located here, 2003, 138), they becoming the only permanent rather than temporary forts and military harbours in southern Scotland, though a series of very large marching camps of 65ha, 53ha and 25ha illustrate the progress up to the Tay in this first year of campaigning. The larger are to the south on the march up to the line of the Clyde–Forth, showing the force staying as one formation, though above that it split into two lines of smaller camps showing the force being divided before again uniting at Inverbervie, south of modern Aberdeen. This was deep in Caledonian territory, showing that while resistance was clearly fierce the size of the force was irresistible. However, the steady stream of casualties from guerrilla activity did begin to tell against the Romans and, unlike in Agricola's seventh campaign and its key engagement at Mons Graupius, Severus' first assault on the north appears to have fizzled out on the line of the Moray Firth. It may well be that by this time the ageing Emperor, suffering from severe gout and campaigning in a litter, was too exhausted to continue. Whatever the exact reason, the Emperor decided to agree terms with an equally exhausted enemy. This may have been unpopular with the military leadership and troops as Dio (76.14) next tells the famous tale of an attempted Imperial patricide. He says that at the exact moment Severus was riding out (on his horse rather than his usual litter) to meet the Caledonians to discuss a truce and the terms for peace (he specifically says the enemy army was arrayed in full for the event) his eldest son, Caracalla, drew his sword to strike him in the back. He was foiled, however, by members of the Roman negotiating party who alerted the Emperor, the latter continuing with the task at hand and no doubt later finding a way to severely rebuke his wayward son. Notwithstanding the above tale, the negotiations seem to have been favourable to Rome with the Maeatae and Caledonians ceding plentiful territory to the Empire (perhaps up to the Antonine Wall line once more though there is no definitive evidence for this). Severus next proclaimed a famous victory, with him and his two sons being given the title *Britannicus* and with celebratory coins being struck. Campaigning, at least for the short term, was over to apparent Imperial satisfaction. As always to date in this narrative with the north of Britain, however, such a state of comparative calm was not to last.

Clearly the terms that had so satisfied the Romans in AD 209 were not so agreeable to at least the Maeatae as a year later they revolted again. Severus (no doubt with his Imperial legacy in mind) once more determined to march north and this time finish the job, though it seems his ill health got the better of him and the ensuing campaign (of which we have fewer details than the previous incursion) was led by the evidently forgiven Caracalla. The Emperor was less forgiving to the natives, however, especially when the Caledonians predictably joined in, ordering his troops to kill all the Britons they came across (Southern, 2013, 248). This was apparently in response to the natives' rough treatment of the invading Romans, with Dio (77.14) emphasising the brutal nature of the campaign when he says that Roman troops likely to be left behind were dispatched by their comrades to prevent their capture and torture.

This new campaign seems to again have been successful from a Roman perspective as commemorative coins of Caracalla and his brother Geta celebrating victory in Britain were being minted in Rome in AD 212 (Mason, 2003, 139). Further, while occupation of the fort at Carpow on the Tay and further south at Newsteads ceased after this time, indicating a northern withdrawal once again, the region seems to have seen an unusual period of peace for around eighty years from this point, with Roman forces settling down along the frontier line of Hadrian's Wall again. Southern (2013, 251) reflects that this may indicate that the 'slash and burn' policy of the second advance north had led to severe depopulation in the region that took several generations of peaceful co-existence to overcome. An inscription to *Brittones dediticii* at the fort at Walldurn on the *limes Germanicus* dating to this period may also indicate that forced conscription as part of the peace deal may have been a factor here too (noting Caracalla actually campaigned in Germany in AD 213). Taking all of this into account, matters Severan in Scotland seem to have been concluded satisfactorily.

The price the Emperor paid for the settlement of the north was severe, however, as, already an ill man ravaged by the winters of the far north after his arrival in Britain AD 208, in AD 211 he passed away in York at the age of 65. Succeeded by his two sons, he was cremated in York and his ashes returned to Rome with the Royal Family to be interned in the mausoleum of Hadrian in the purple stone urn that had travelled to Britain with him. Clearly he did not expect to return home from his northern adventures.

While we have much insight into what happened in Rome next, with Caracalla murdering his brother to become sole Emperor, events in Britain are less clear and indeed for the rest of the first half of the century our primary written sources are few and far between. In this regard Dio's records end in AD 229 while Herodian finishes his imperial histories with Gordian III, his account concluding in AD 238 (and this with notable gaps). We do, of course, know about the main political fallout in Britain following first the failed Imperial bid of Albinus and then the campaigns of Severus, with the official division of the single province of Britain into two in AD 211–212 around the time of Severus' death (noting that planning had begun in AD 197). Thus, after this time we have two distinct provinces reflecting the previously unofficial division of southern- and northern-occupied Britain. These provinces were *Britannia Superior* with its capital in London and *Britannia Inferior* with its capital in York (*Superior* and *Inferior* in this context reflecting the distance from Rome). The former was

governed by a consular rank governor, who had charge of the
legio XX *Valeria Victrix* based at Chester and the *legio* II *Augusta*
based at Caerleon. Meanwhile, the latter was governed by an
equestrian rank governor who held command of the *legio* VI
Victrix, based as he was in York. Given the fact that for much of
the period of the existence of Britain as a two-province region
the north was relatively quiet, it is unclear whether in times of
trouble the governor of the north took control of the south-
erly legions as they headed towards the border. Certainly the
northerly deployment of legionary vexillations took place, for
example when troops of the *legio* XX *Valeria Victrix* and *legio* II
Augusta were sent to help building activity north of Hadrian's
Wall at Netherby in AD 219. What does seem likely though is
that the *Classis Britannica* continued to be headquartered in
Boulogne given its responsibilities in the North Sea (especially
in the context of increasing instability in the north-west of the
Continental Empire), with at the start of this period its south-
erly presence in Britain centred as always on Dover and with
regular northern deployments to Chester and Bowness on the
north-west coast and South Shields on the north-east.

This pattern of deployment for the regional fleet was to
change, however, as the first half of the century progressed. In
the first instance the *Classis Britannica* fort at Dover fell out of
use, with Mason (2013, 140) saying this occurred as early as
AD 215 and with Cleere (1977, 19) highlighting the fact it was
deliberately slighted. In this regard the later Saxon Shore fort
dating to AD 270 in Dover was built on a completely different
alignment to its earlier *Classis Britannica* counterpart, indicating the latter's complete destruction. This clearly illustrates
that in the last half-century or so of the *Classis Britannica*'s
existence in the post-Severan period things were beginning to
change radically for the regional fleet.

A key factor to consider here is a potential re-prioritisation
from this point onwards of the military roles for the *Classis
Britannica* and its successors as the third century progressed,

especially given the eight decades of peace in the north following the last campaign of Severus under Caracalla. While in the later first and second centuries the regional fleet had participated in major campaigning in Britain every thirty years or so, with a focus on littoral control, transport and intelligence gathering, by the first half of the third century the naval forces of Roman Britain were increasingly operating in the oceanic zone of the North Sea basin, interdicting newly arrived seaborne raiders originating from the Continent and protecting merchant traffic. This led to a dramatic change in the life experiences of the *milites* of the British fleet, used until this time to short bursts of intense campaigning largely in the littoral zone followed by long periods of peaceful routine. Now, increasingly, this was being replaced by continuous patrolling in all but the worst weathers in not only the littoral zone but now the oceanic zone, too. In this regard, instead of moving step by step supporting the legions as they headed north, now the *Classis Britannica* found itself participating in small-scale actions as it interdicted raiders on land or at sea, with the occasional punitive mission being mounted on the northern Continental coast. As Mason (2003, 142) argues, what had been a regional fleet on the offensive had suddenly, increasingly, found itself on the defensive.

The emergence of this new naval threat, not present for most of the existence of the *Classis Britannica*, is very evident in the advent of something else new to Britain and the northwest coast of Europe at this time, namely the forts of the Saxon Shore. The first three of this famous chain, which was to eventually fortify the coasts of the whole of the south-east of Britain and northern Gaul, were built between AD 220 and AD 230 at Brancaster on the north coast of Norfolk, Caister-on-Sea (some 80km further along the Norfolk coast) and Reculver (Roman *Regulbium*) on the north coast of Kent at the northern extremity of the Wantsum Channel. These forts are very different from the earlier *Classis Britannica* forts and clearly had a function leaning more towards military power projection than fulfilling a headquarters or harbouring role as with those of the regional fleet. At around 3ha in size, the three early forts were square in plan and featured a very substantial perimeter wall with internal towers and, based on epigraphic evidence, their own bespoke garrisons. Thus we know of the *Cohors* 1 *Aquitanorum* auxiliary unit based at Brancaster and the *Cohors* 1 *Baestasiorum* auxiliary unit at Reculver.

Interestingly, at the latter fort there is a clear association with the *Classis Britannica* for the last few years of the latter's existence, given the use in the fort of tiles made of the same material as those made regionally featuring the stamp of the regional fleet (though noting these could have been reused from earlier nearby structures).

The three new forts are all located at sites with sheltered natural harbours that would have been attractive to potential aggressors. This raises an important question, namely what actually was this new threat to Roman Britain? Here we have to rely on anecdote and analogy (for example the considerable investment in the building of the new forts, and their locations) in our period of interest given that the first official reference to these new maritime raiders dates to the later third century. Given the unusually long period of comparatively peaceful co-existence being enjoyed north of Hadrian's Wall they are most likely therefore to have originated from the coastal communities of north-eastern Germany and southern Scandinavia, and are later generically called Saxons. The specific tribes themselves, however, would also have included the Angles, Jutes (both later to join the Saxons in the context of the popular appreciation of their conquest of eastern Britain in the fifth century), Frisians, Rugians, Danes and Frankish Bructeri. All these populations to the north of the *limes Germanicus* would have been experiencing the same political and economic effects of contact with the Roman superpower to the south as had happened with the Maeatae and Caledonians, with the coalescence of power among fewer and fewer members of their elites and the introduction of improved political structures. At some stage in the early third century this obviously facilitated the degree of necessary economic critical mass to allow significant investment in speculative raiding across the North Sea. In this regard we have an insight into the maritime technology used thanks to Lyne's analysis of ship fittings at Richborough (detailed in Chapter 2), where the third most common type of vessel found were Germanic-style, clinker-built (overlapping-plank), fast-rowing designs. While these vessels date to either the late occupation period or indeed just after the occupation it is unlikely that such technology had changed in the previous 200 years.

Thus we have being used in the early third century what would appear to the casual observer to be the Saxon equivalent of the much later Viking longboat, though somewhat smaller and (as detailed in Chapter 4) with no mast, given we have no evidence that the 'Saxons' possessed sail technology. This latter issue raises the question of the route taken by the raiders. The common assumption is that given their lack of a sail they would have followed a coast-hugging route down the Continental coast until they arrived at the closest crossing points, for example the English Channel between Boulogne and Dover. However, given the complete control of the littoral zones of both sides of these crossing points by the *Classis Britannica* (and indeed, for much of the occupation, its naval successors), this seems unlikely in the extreme and it may well be that these hardy proto-Vikings actually crossed the North Sea directly from their homelands to East Anglia and northern Kent. Thus we have the initial locations for the first Saxon Shore forts and the change in the tasking of the regional fleet to counter this new (and admittedly at this time limited) threat to Roman control of the oceanic zone. It is also no coincidence that it is at this time we see the initial phases of wall building in the Romano-British towns most easily accessed by maritime raiders, for example London. Additionally, sites further up the east coast also began to receive defensive attention, with for example the fort and supply depot at Brough-on-Humber being rebuilt on a different alignment with significant stone-walls featuring bastions. Another example would be Wallsend on the Tyne, where the harbouring facilities for the fort at the eastern end of Hadrian's Wall were fortified. Meanwhile, as the century progressed, recognition of newly emerging naval raiding threats spread to others parts of Britain, for example at key sites in Wales and along the west coast of Britain. In this latter case the threat was from emboldened Irish raiders from across the Irish Sea, perhaps sensing a weakness in occupied Britain exposed by the raiding from the Continent.

One final point for consideration here is the role of the *Classis Britannica* in the context of its mission to protect the western flank of the *limes Germanicus* and the northern Continental coast as the 'Crisis of the third century' began to unfold (this being explored in more detail in Chapter 9). With its headquarters remaining at Boulogne, clearly the Continental responsibilities of the regional fleet were still an important aspect of its everyday activity. While we have no direct evidence of any specific deployments, we can use analogy and anecdote to determine that the *Classis Britannica* would have been busy in its more traditional roles of littoral zone control, transport and scouting as firstly new symmetrical threats from north of the Imperial border emerged, these then being compounded by political instability. In the case of the former, the Alemanni were the first of the major new tribal confederations to begin agitating along the *limes Germanicus* in the AD 230s, while in the case of the latter the assassination of Alexander Severus in AD 235 at Mainz while campaigning against this new German threat led to political destabilisation and frequent civil wars for much of the rest of the century. It is in the context of these events that I next consider the whys and wherefores of the end of the *Classis Britannica*.

9

THE END OF THE
CLASSIS BRITANNICA

This chapter will review the end of the *Classis Britannica*, examining the various theories regarding its decline. It will also look at the specific threats that were beginning to emerge for Roman-occupied Britain from the middle of the third century, and take a view about the impact these were to have on the naval capability that fulfilled the maritime role in Britain and across the North Sea after the demise of the regional fleet.

The *Classis Britannica* was one of the great institutions of Roman Britain, not only fulfilling the wide-ranging military roles detailed in the preceding three chapters but also operating in an equally wide number of civilian roles to ensure the smooth running of the province on behalf of the procurator. Its war galleys and transport ships were clearly common visitors to the coastlines of Britain given the frequency with which they appear on casual graffiti. Yet not only does it disappear without a bang, it vanishes without even a whimper. As detailed in Chapter 1, the last epigraphic reference to the existence of the *Classis Britannica* is from a testament in

Arles to the North African Saturninus, an ex-*trierarchus* in the British fleet. Dated to AD 244–249 (Russel, 2002), after this we have a silence among our literary and epigraphic sources fit to match that regarding the fate of the *legio* IX *Hispana* and its famous lost *aquila*. This silence also extends to the industries that I argue in Chapter 5 were run by the regional fleet, with the *metalla* of the iron industry in the Weald and the ragstone quarrying in the Medway Valley also ending at the same time the fleet disappears.

As can be seen in the conclusion to Chapter 8, the *Classis Britannica* did survive the initial military reforms of Septimius Severus, and indeed the separation of the original single province of Britannia into two. In fact, given its re-tasking to counter the advent of sea raiding from the Continent, one could argue that as the third century progressed, the regional fleet was in rude health. We therefore have to look elsewhere to find the catalyst behind the demise of the *Classis Britannica*, and in that regard I believe its disappearance has roots in much wider events taking place across the Roman Empire at this time rather than being a specifically British affair. This is because similar changes were taking place elsewhere, with for example the *Classis Britannica*'s sister regional fleet the *Classis Germanica* also disappearing from the historical record at roughly the same time, according to both Mason (2003, 140) and Pitassi (2012, 50). These 'wider events' are helpfully encapsulated in the famous phrase 'Crisis of the third century' when the golden age of the Roman Empire came to a juddering halt and for the first time the beginning of the decline that was to bring down the west of the Empire and transform the east 200 years later became apparent. Within this catch-all phrase for the turbulent period of Roman history between the murder of Alexander Severus detailed in Chapter 8 and the accession of Diocletian in AD 284 I believe there are three events that might be considered candidates to explain the disappearance of the *Classis Britannica*, one actually post-dating the beginning of Diocletian's rule but having its roots in the earlier troubles. These are the struggle for power between the newly arriviste military leadership and more traditional senatorial political stakeholders at the beginning of the 'Crisis', in the context of the Gallic Empire initiated by Postumus in AD 260 that lasted until AD 274, and finally with the dramatic story of the 'pirate king' Carausius and his breakaway Empire in Britain and northern Gaul from AD 286 through to AD 296.

The 'Crisis of the third century' is a catch-all phrase used to describe the woes of the Empire at this time, taking in a variety of troubles including external threats and invasion, civil war, economic depression and plague. The period began with the assassination of Alexander Severus in a military coup on the German frontier. Dubbed a 'mummy's boy' by the troops for being unduly influenced by his mother, Julia Mamaea, the 27-year-old Emperor and last of the Severan dynasty failed to heed the advice of its founder to his sons in keeping the troops happy above all else. His main failing seems to have been an inability to satisfy his legions' desire for military glory. An indecisive campaign against the newly emerging Sassanid Persian superpower to the east was followed by a similarly unsatisfactory expedition to the Rhine to counter endemic German raiding. When the Emperor tried to bribe the tribes of Alemanni threatening his borders the lack of respect he was increasingly suffering from his troops took a fatal turn and the latter offered the purple to one of the leading legates, Gaius Julius Verus Maximinius, who commanded the *legio* IV *Italica*. A giant of a man risen from the ranks and known to history as Maximinus Thrax because of his Thracian origins, he and his fellow conspirators lost no time in removing Alexander Severus and his mother permanently from the scene, a party of supportive centurions carrying out the coup de grâce in the Imperial tent.

A soldier to his very core, Thrax's first act was to double the rations of the soldiers, revoke any outstanding punishments and to promise the legions sizeable financial rewards. Never to set foot in Rome, the new Emperor was to last but three years during which he campaigned successfully against the Alemanni across the Rhine and the Sarmations across the Danube. His military success was also the root of his downfall, however, for to fund his military adventures he extorted money from the wealthy, confiscated private property from the aristocratic landowners in Italy and finally reduced the corn dole for the poor. Eventually senatorial level opposition to an Emperor they viewed as a commoner (they had only reluctantly recognised him in the first place) reached a tipping point, with the governor of the wealthy province of Africa Proconsularis being proclaimed a rival Emperor by his own nobles. Called Marcus Antonius Gordianus, he is better known to history as Gordian I and the Senate back in Rome lost no time in recognising the 80-year-old and his son (Gordian II) as joint Augusti, thus throwing the Imperial leadership into chaos. A cascade of failed Imperial candidates followed, with Gordian II being killed in fighting against the loyal governor of neighbouring Numidia and his father committing suicide, the Senate then elected two ageing former consuls as the new joint Emperors, these being Decius Caelius Calvinus Balbinus and Marcus Clodius Pupienus Maximus. To these the Senate then added the grandson of Gordian I, who became Gordian III, in a bid to placate the Roman mob, who were clearly worried about the retribution of Thrax when he chose to descend on the Imperial capital. These fears proved unfounded, however as, while on route to Rome, Thrax himself was assassinated by troops of the Praetorian Guard (evidently not as reformed as Septimius Severus may have hoped) and *legio* II *Parthica* while besieging the north Italian city of Aquileia. The Guard then killed Balbinus and Pupienus, elevating Gordian III to sole ruler.

While this young Emperor was to see some military success against the Persians, he was in turn assassinated by his troops to be succeeded by his regent, Philip the Arab. The latter lasted five years in the Imperial chair although he suffered numerous usurpation attempts, being defeated and killed while challenging the last of these in battle at Beroea in Macedonia in AD 249. The successful challenger was Quintus Decius Valerius, another of senatorial rank. Seemingly capable, he was then killed in battle against the Goths in AD 251. Next up was Trebonianus Gallus (again elevated by the troops, a now recurring pattern) whose two-year reign was dominated by plague in Rome and defeat to the Persians in the east, the latter including the unthinkable sacking of Antioch. When the Goths then began agitating along the northern frontier matters turned against Gallus, with the northern legions proclaiming Upper Moesian Governor Aemilius Aemilianus as Emperor in AD 253 after he led them to victory. Gallus gathered an army to challenge the new usurper but he in turn was murdered by his own troops. Recognised by the Senate, Aemilianus was to survive only four months before another candidate replaced him, Publius Licinius Valerianus, who as Governor of Raetia and Noricum had been summoned to Rome to support the unfortunate Gallus. When the latter was assassinated Valerian's troops in turn proclaimed him Emperor, with the unfortunate Aemilianus being deserted by his troops and murdered. Valerian then entered Rome as the sole Emperor and his recognition by the Senate (along with his son Gallienus as joint Augustus) ushered in a temporary respite to the chaos that had plagued the Imperial leadership since AD 235, with the father heading east to take charge there and his son staying in Rome to control the west.

This above power struggle between the military and Senate between AD 235 and the early AD 250s might seem somewhat irrelevant to the *Classis Britannica* in the faraway provinces of Britain given that it was played out along the Rhine and Danube frontiers, the Balkans, North Africa and the east. However, it is likely this was far from the case. We have already seen how support for the Imperial ambitions of Albinus in the late second century had seen the *Classis Britannica* suffer the unhelpful attentions of Septimius Severus, with perhaps for a time its command being combined with those of other neighbouring regional fleets. This illustrates how complicated Imperial succession was, and how unpredictable its impact on the various political and military stakeholders who would have had to make difficult choices regarding whether to side with an incumbent or a usurper. Further, in an age before the advent of modern communications such decision taking was even more problematic. One could side with one party, just to find them dead with the next communiqué. Therefore on the one hand the regional fleet could have met its end simply by being caught out thus, backing the wrong side and suffering the retribution of a (at least in the short term) victor. Further, given the increasing (and understandable) hostility of the Senate to all things military, the fleet may also have been caught in a wider senatorial policy of lobbying for the decentralisation of military power. In this regard significant-sized units of military capability such as that offered by both the *Classis Britannica* and *Classis Germanica* might have been 'watered down' into smaller-sized units that lacked the critical mass to challenge senatorial power (see discussion of post-*Classis Britannica* naval activity in Britain).

One further point for discussion in this first consideration of candidate events behind the demise of the regional fleet in Britain is with regard to the cost of its operation. We have already seen that both Septimius Severus and his eldest son, Caracalla, increased the pay of the military significantly enough to have an impact on the Roman economy. It would have been as one approached the middle of the third century that this impact would really have begun to bite, this being exacerbated as each Imperial contender (at least if they wanted to survive) strove to pile more and more wealth on the soldiery (noting for example Thrax's promise of financial betterment for the troops who supported him in replacing Alexander Severus). Each of these increases in pay, whether regularised or a one-off, placed a heavier and heavier burden on the Imperial *fiscus*, with the currency being continually debased. It may be that those military units within the Roman martial system that were not being used to capacity simply fell from favour through proving too costly in this climate. As we have seen, the *Classis Britannica* at this time may have been one such candidate given the lack of any requirement to campaign in its traditional roles of littoral control, transport and scouting north of the comparatively quiet northern border. A decision could therefore have been made to cut back on its activity, perhaps focusing purely on the interdiction of raiding from the Continent and Ireland, with the once great institution's name simply slipping away as its unneeded *milites* were let go and ships laid up. Any required capacity for maritime transport and similar needs would then have been taken up by private contractors. One could additionally argue that the cost of using the fleet to carry out civilian work on behalf of the state in the two provinces of Britain also became prohibitive, and perhaps it is this that links the disappearance of the regional fleet with the chronologically contemporary ending of the *metalla* industries of iron manufacturing and ragstone quarrying in Kent.

The next event for consideration in the context of the demise of the *Classis Britannica* is the advent of the Gallic Empire. This was initiated by the usurper Marcus Cassianus Latinius Postumus in AD 260, with Britain taking a leading role in this breakaway north-western corner of the Empire (Elliott, 2014, 121) that came into existence amid the renewed Imperial chaos that occurred at the end of the AD 250s. This was initiated in AD 258 by extensive Gothic raiding in Asia Minor, taking advantage of Valerian's attentions further east in recapturing Antioch from the Persians. The Alamanni then burst across the Rhine in AD 259 while matters were being settled with the Goths, managing to campaign as far south as northern Italy before being defeated near Milan by Gallienus. Finally, in AD 260 a calamity occurred when Valerian's campaigning against the Persians faltered at Edessa, his army hamstrung by an outbreak of plague. Trying to secure a peace settlement with the Persian King Shapur I, he was betrayed and captured while negotiating. Never to return to Rome, some sources point to a staggeringly desperate fate for him, being used as a footstool by the Persian King and later, after his death, his flayed skin being stuffed and displayed in a Persian temple. From that point onwards Gallienus ruled alone, though he proved incapable of keeping his Empire together given the external pressures on all fronts. Eventually the eastern frontier was stabilised by the Roman client state of Palmyra, whose King Odaenathus pushed the Persians out of Syria. In the west, however, the troops of the Rhine legions, lacking any faith in Gallienus to bring any sort of order to the northern border, elevated Postumus to the purple and thus was born the Gallic Empire (*Imperium Galliarum*).

The territory he carved out included all of Gaul (perhaps except Narbonensis in the south) and the various provinces of Britain, Germany and Spain. It may have even included parts of Raetia to the east. The scale of the administration set up by Postumus shows this was not the usual usurpation attempt, for he in effect replicated the entire Imperial court at his capital of Trier (Roman *Augusta Treverorum*) with a Senate, two annually elected consuls and a Praetorian Guard. Postumus set about rebuilding his ravaged frontier zone and certainly, at the beginning of his new Empire's existence, he could have descended on Italy where Gallienus lay fatally exposed. He chose not to, however, and consolidated his own position, his territory surviving two attempts by Gallienus to reconquer the north-west of the Empire in AD 261 and AD 265. In fact, he even outlived the Emperor with Gallienus being assassinated by his senior military leaders in AD 268. Postumus himself fell a year later when, after defeating one Laelianus (the commander of the *legio* XII *Primigenia* at Mainz who in turn was attempting to usurp him), his own troops killed him when he refused them permission to sack the German city. A succession of Imperial candidates then followed to parallel the experiences back in Rome, which the founders of the Gallic Empire had tried to escape. Thus sequentially we have Marius becoming the Gallic Emperor for no more than three months before he in turn was killed by Postumus' former Praetorian Prefect Victorinus, he lasting in the Imperial chair until AD 271 when he in turn was killed to be replaced by Tetricus I and his son Tetricus II, the latter as the former's *caesar*. Both these latter lasted until AD 274 when the great soldier Emperor Aurelian, having gained the purple and decisively secured the eastern frontier, defeated Tetricus and his son at the Battle of Chalon, thus bringing the territories of the Gallic Empire back into the Imperial fold.

Set against this whirl of changes to the leadership of the north-western provinces of the Empire one can certainly see opportunities continually arising for the *Classis Britannica* to find itself on the wrong side of a power struggle. In the first instance this could have been at the time of the creation of the Gallic Empire by Postumus, who Mason (2003, 148) says made frequent use of the images of war galleys on his coinage and so clearly valued his maritime military capability. The instability of the rapid turnover of the Gallic Emperors would similarly have provided an opportunity for the British regional fleet to back the wrong horse, as of course would the Aurelianic reconquest. In the latter regard, it is instructive that a coin hoard of Tetricus I, last of the Gallic Emperors, has been found at Allington Castle north of Maidstone on the site of a prospective Roman villa and quarry (particularly relevant given the discussion regarding the role of the *Classis Britannica* in the ragstone-quarrying industry of the upper Medway Valley in Chapter 5).

Next for consideration with regard to the end of the *Classis Britannica* we have the enigmatic story of Carausius the 'pirate king'. The background for his rise is set once more against a crisis on the northern frontiers, this time with the Alamanni again bursting through the northern frontier in AD 276 and penetrating deep into Gaul, where sixty towns were sacked. Though the Emperor Probus restored order (with a wave of fortification following for the major cities and towns), the region was destabilised once more, with another usurpation attempt following shortly after and trouble again erupting in Britain. Our source for the latter is the late Roman author Zosimus, who says (*New History*, 1.68.3) that around this time Probus sent some captured Vandals and Burgundians to Britain who helped put down a revolt, and that (*New History*, 1.66.2) he also sent the North African legate Victorinus to Britain to similarly put down a revolt (a usurper being specifically mentioned in the latter context). Assuming these are the same event, it seems likely that the issue here was one of internal revolt rather than trouble along the northern border, although it may not have been finally suppressed until the following reign of Carus, who celebrated some kind of victory in Britain by taking the title *Britannicus Maximus*. One point of interest here given our focus on Roman naval capability is that there appears to have been some kind of maritime component to these military endeavours given one reference refers to the use of the Pole star, a key nautical navigation aid in the classical world and a contemporary literary device to similarly indicate naval activity.

Next, in AD 285 the new Emperor Diocletian appointed Marcus Aurelius Valerius Maximianus to be his Caesar with responsibility for Italy and the provinces in the west (he being elevated to joint Emperor the following year). Maximianus' first task was to tackle the organised banditry in Gaul (known as the Bagaudae) who were plaguing the countryside following the earlier invasion by the Alamanni, and in this he was assisted successfully by Marcus Aurelius Mausaeus Carausius, our future 'pirate king'. This led to the appointment of the latter to head a special task force designed to tackle another significant threat that had emerged by this time and which is fundamental to our consideration of the demise of the *Classis Britannica*. This is because the new threat was naval in nature and involved intensive coastal and sea-based raiding from the estuary of the River Rhine down to Brittany (presumably also including Britain) by Saxon and Frankish pirates. One thought jumps out immediately here, namely that control seems to have been lost not only in the oceanic zone of the North Sea basin but, for the first time since the Roman conquest of Gaul and Britain, also in the littoral zone. For that to happen something dramatic must have already happened to the *Classis Britannica*, especially given Carausius' first task was to build a fleet (clearly not necessary if the regional fleet had still existed). This is an issue I will address once I have told the story of the 'pirate king'.

Carausius had grown up on the coast of Belgica and served as a river pilot before later joining the military and serving with evident distinction. Given the nature of the maritime threat that Maximianus had to address he clearly was the man of the hour best suited to rid the seas of the pirate nuisance. Basing himself at the old *Classis Britannica* headquarters fort at Boulogne, Carausius' naval campaign was a great success with order being restored to both the oceanic zone and along both littorals in Britain and the Continent. In fact, from Maximian's perspective he was too successful, with the Emperor accusing Carausius of complicity in the raiding by using foreknowledge to intercept the perpetrators after each raid and then pocketing the plunder. Carausius was sentenced to death but was tipped off before the sentence could be carried out, fleeing to Britain where in AD 287 he staged a usurpation attempt that in the short term was successful in recreating part of the Gallic Empire. At the outset this included north-eastern Gaul, including the crucial fortress of Boulogne, together with both provinces in Britain. He proved a charismatic and popular ruler given his local roots, with significant forces at his disposal to maintain him in power. These included his newly reconstituted fleet (he clearly recognised their value as early on he raised their pay to guarantee their loyalty, Mason, 2003, 33), the three legions of Britain, the l*egio* XXX *Ulpia Victrix* from the fort at Xanten in the modern Germany and a number of *vexillations* from the other Rhine legions.

His breakaway Empire set up, Carausius settled in for the long haul. He established Britain's first official mint in London with his coins being notably superior to those in circulation when he arrived, styling himself as a British saviour (*Restitutor Britanniae*). Some coins also show he clearly understood the old Severan maxim about keeping the troops happy, them bearing the legend 'Harmony with the Army' (*Concordia Militum*). A number of the major Saxon Shore forts such as those at Portchester and Pevensey also date to this period, leading to speculation that the holistic chain (incorporating the earlier ones) was designed to actually keep the Empire out rather than deterring Saxon raiding.

Maximian was clearly rattled by this development in Britain but, lacking a fleet, he was rather hamstrung until a new naval force could be created. This was ready for action by AD 289, when it sailed down the Rhine and into the North Sea to tackle the usurper. The expedition proved an epic failure, however, as an uneasy peace was soon agreed, with Carausius following the age-old plan of claiming legitimacy through association. In terms of his own public relations campaign, this was in the form of minting coins featuring himself as an equal with the western Emperor Maximian and the eastern Emperor Diocletian.

The latter two clearly did not recognise this picture of brotherly love, and before long the western Caesar Constantius Chlorus was dispatched westwards with orders to defeat

Carausius and return his usurping territories back into the Imperial fold. He proved far more capable than Maximian and by AD 293 had defeated Carausius' Frankish allies around the Rhine estuary, then recapturing Boulogne and the usurper's Gallic lands and so isolating him in Britain. Sadly for the 'pirate king' he was not to survive these reverses, being assassinated by one of his leading officers named Allectus. Confusion surrounds the actual identify of this far less charismatic leader, with some styling him as Carausius' procurator, others his Praetorian prefect and yet others a Frankish mercenary leader. Whatever his origins, he was to survive ruling in Britain only three more years (during which time he also minted his own patriotic coins to try to emulate his predecessor) before Chlorus was ready to invade Britain and claim the provinces back. Thus in AD 296 the final and fourth invasion of Britain took place, with Chlorus dividing his force into two. While his own smaller division aimed for the Thames Estuary, the larger half headed for the Solent under the Praetorian Prefect Asclepiodotus, slipping past Allectus' fleet in fog and disembarking safely. Heading inland, they quickly came to grips with Allectus' land forces, defeating them in short order and killing the usurper. Meanwhile Chlorus, making slower progress due to bad weather, finally reached London in time to save it from being sacked by some of Allectus' Frankish mercenaries. Britain was finally again part of the Empire, with Chlorus making a triumphal entry into London in an event commemorated in a gold medallion carrying the legend 'Restorer of the Eternal Light' (*Redditor Lucis Aeterna*).

It comes as no surprise that around this time Britain was politically reordered yet again, this time into a *diocese* as part of the Diocletianic Reformation, with the four provinces of *Maxima Caesariensis*, *Britannia Prima*, *Flavia Caesariensis* and *Britannia Secunda* coming into being. Diocletian was taking no chances of another successful usurpation, the aim here being to diminish the power base of any future would-be Emperor.

Having restored order (and improved the northern frontier defences) Chlorus left for the Continent the following year. As a footnote though he was to return in AD 306 when, as a full Augustus, he led a campaign to defeat the agitating tribes north of the border once more (with naval forces again at the forefront of activity). Like Septimius Severus before him he was to die in York later that summer to be succeeded by his very famous son, Constantine, who was proclaimed Emperor by the troops. Thus followed the next bout of civil war in the Empire and the beginning of the path whereby a century later Christianity was the official religion of Rome, though that takes us out of the narrative of our tale about the *Classis Britannica*.

We can now revisit the debate about whether the requirement for Carausius to be appointed to tackle rampant piracy in the North Sea in the first place is indicative that by the time his story begins the *Classis Britannica* had already disappeared. The answer to my mind is a resounding yes, given that prior to this time the Roman military had certainly not lost control of the littoral zones around the North Sea at all since the beginning of the first century AD, and had also beaten off raiders travelling through the oceanic zone of the North Sea basin (even noting the reprioritisation to tackle the latter in the early third century). Further, it should be noted that during Carausius' campaigns with and against the Empire, not one but three fleets had to be built – his own one to re-secure the North Sea oceanic and littoral zones, that of Maximian to challenge him in the first instance and finally that of Chlorus to defeat him. None of these would have been required at all if the regional fleet had still been in existence. To my mind one need only look to a variety of scenarios during the existence of the Gallic Empire of Postumus and his successors to find causational events that finished off the *Classis Britannica* and *Classis Germanica*, setting the scene for the maritime chaos across the North Sea in the late AD 270s and AD 280s (see fuller discussion in this regard in Chapter 10).

Finally in this chapter I consider official maritime activity around Britain after the disappearance of the regional fleet. Given the prominence of the *Classis Britannica* in regional maritime activities until its demise in the middle of the third century, it is likely that the frequency of regional maritime trade in both Morris' and Evans' models (see Chapter 1) would have become more problematic later in the occupation (with Evans' reference to the decline of east coast trade from the middle of the third century here noted, again see Chapter 1). What is clear, however, is that maritime trade did continue though, and with the involvement of the state in some form. In this regard Moody (2008, 154) points to the appearance in the later third century of imported black-burnished ware in Thanet of a type most often associated with the military. We can also look here again to a Roman villa at East Farleigh on the River Medway where a Folkestone greensand quern and another of millstone grit from Derbyshire or Yorkshire have been found in a fourth-century context, evidence of the continuance of the long-range trade.

In terms of military maritime activity, after the demise of the regional fleets Britain largely depended on resources specifically created to fulfil isolated regional requirements. Pitassi (2012, 15) says that by the reign of Diocletian (AD 285–305) the grand Imperial fleets had been replaced by smaller squadrons (probably reflecting changes in the army in the same period). In a British context, Russel (2002) agrees that the military and state functions of maritime activity in Britain after this time become more regional, perhaps linked to individual military units, although there is no epigraphic evidence for an official later British flotilla to parallel the likes of the *Classis Anderetianorum* based in Paris. An example of a maritime capability that did continue would be the fourth century *numerous barcariorum Tigrisiensum* detachment of Tigris boatmen from Arbeia (Finkle, 2014, 138), operating on the River Tyne from the fort at South Shields (Hodgson, 23, 2007). Additionally we can reference the later *limitanei/riparienses* units that policed border regions featuring a river (for example the Rhine or Danube) and which would certainly have maintained a riverine capability (Hughes, 2010). Peaks and troughs in maritime capability seem to have become the norm in this later period, with Cunliffe (2013, 424) saying that at certain times, in certain circumstances, the North Sea for example would still have been alive with shipping. Moorhead and Stuttard (2012, 174 and 207) believe that such highpoints would have been during the Carausian revolt, and later during Julian's period as Caesar when he ordered 600 ships to be built to convoy grain from Britannia to feed the Rhine armies. They go on to explain that this latter effort was only short-lived, and that by AD 367 the fleet was once again too small to prevent barbarians using the seas around the *diocese*. Finally, Pitassi (2012, 21) argues that by AD 395 any semblance of control in the North Sea had been lost, paralleling the chaos that had led to the appointment of Carausius.

10

Conclusion

In this short chapter I review the story of the *Classis Britannica*
as told in this narrative to pick up on the essential highlights,
using what we definitively know about the regional fleet or
what we can reasonably infer based on analogy and anecdote.

The *Classis Britannica* played a leading and often unher-
alded role in the story of occupied Roman Britain, reporting
to the procurator and thus directly in a chain of command
to the Emperor, while also being a military resource used
heavily by successive governors. In its military capacity it
fulfilled a variety of key roles, essential particularly in the
context of Britain being an island province (and later provinces). These included controlling the oceanic zone of the
North Sea basin and the Atlantic approaches, similarly controlling the littoral zone around the coasts of Britain and
the Continental North Sea coast, intelligence gathering and
patrol (in both the above zones, though principally the littoral), transport and amphibious operations, supply, and finally
communications. Meanwhile, the British regional navy was

also a resource used heavily by the state for a diverse variety of civilian tasks, including administration, construction and engineering, and finally to run industry on behalf of the state, such as those of the *metalla* (in this case iron manufacturing and quarrying).

In terms of its mission and utilisation, the *Classis Britannica* was one of the major regional fleets that emerged following the Augustan reforms of Roman military maritime capability. It had its roots in the Claudian invasion of Britain in AD 43 when a fleet of 900 ships was gathered together on the coast of north-eastern France to facilitate the transport of an astonishingly large army of conquest numbering 40,000 men although planning for this operation can be dated back to the abortive plans of Caligula or even those of Augustus.

Unlike the incursions to Britain of Caesar in 55 BC and 54 BC, that of Claudius was ultimately successful, with the campaigns over a fifty-year period of Plautius in the south-east, Vespasian in the south-west, Cerialis in the north, Frontinus in Wales and Agricola in the far north firmly cementing the province of Britannia into the Imperial fold. In all these campaigns the *Classis Britannica* played a crucial role, working in tandem with the land forces such that as each legionary spearhead penetrated deep into hostile territory the littoral zone was controlled to protect the exposed naval flank, supplies were transported ahead of the legionaries and auxiliaries to fortified harbours to keep the advance moving, and scouting vessels deployed to provide advance warning of any gathering opposition. The spectacular success of these campaigns of the conquest period, even taking into account the significant challenges of penetrating the hostile territories of Wales and the north (and indeed of course during the Boudican revolt), is testament to how effective was this combination of the legions and the *Classis Britannica*. The campaigns also saw a number of the fortified harbours expanded to become permanent large naval bases, such that by the end of the century those on the west coast at Chester and Bowness were home to squadrons of the *Classis Britannica*, while similarly those at South Shields, Camelon and Carpow housed the *liburnae, myoparo* and *scapha* of the regional fleet on the east coast up to the line of the Tay. By this time its headquarters had also been established, at a major fortress in Boulogne in north-eastern Gaul, this reflecting the regional navy's important role in also controlling the littoral zone of the Continental coast up to the line of the *limes Germanicus.*

The regional fleet then spent the second century on the front line of the perpetual friction along the northern border of occupied Britain as it bounced between Hadrian's Wall on the Solway–Tyne line and the Antonine Wall on the Clyde–Forth line. As the century closed it was to find itself on the wrong side of the Imperial bid for power by British Governor Albinus. Perhaps as a punishment, for a short while afterwards it may have been merged into a combined fleet with that of the *Classis Germanica*, the *Classis Moesica* and the *Classis Pannonica* by Septimius Severus, the winner of the Year of the Five Emperors. Severus then took the *Classis Britannica* on its biggest adventure as he attempted to finish what Agricola had tried more than a century earlier and conquer the whole island. Two campaigns and two peace treaties later the north was pacified (though not fully conquered), and this comparative calm along Hadrian's Wall was to last for another eighty years. From this point onwards the regional fleet found itself increasingly re-tasked to counter Saxon raiding across the oceanic zone of the North Sea, and later similar Irish raiding across the Irish Sea. However, the end was now in sight for the British regional fleet.

In terms of the causation of the end of the *Classis Britannica*, in Chapter 9 I explored a number of theories and hypotheses. That the regional fleet disappears from the historical record is not in doubt, and what replaced it seems to have been lesser in stature and capability. Emotively one is obviously drawn to the tale of Carausius the 'pirate king', though to my mind the fact he was needed in the first instance to tackle what was clearly a major issue with North Sea piracy indicates that the *Classis Britannica* had already disappeared by the time of his ascension. Meanwhile, an association with its demise in the context of the onset of the 'Crisis of the third century' after the assassination of Alexander Severus in AD 235, the accession of Maximinus Thrax and the subsequent senatorial push back seems too early given our last epigraphic reference to Saturninus and the *Classis Britannica* dates to AD 249 at the latest. This leaves us with the whirlwind of changes to the political leadership of the north-west of the Empire in the context of the Gallic Empire between AD 260 and AD 274, and here I think we have the most likely candidate for the catalyst that finished off the regional fleet in Britain, at least in an official capacity (and indeed its sister fleet in Germany). Perhaps in this context the leadership of the *Classis Britannica* found itself on the wrong side of a regional or Empire-wide Imperial succession, the case for its survival being further undermined by the cost of its operation in an age of economic crisis when its roles were being re-prioritised away from supporting *en masse* the outward expansion of the Empire and towards surgically interdicting raiders in the North Sea and Irish Sea.

One final reflection in my book concerns historiography and agency, given there are things that we know about the past, things that we may infer, and things that are unknowable. In this context we know the *Classis Britannica*'s official name, the name of a very few of its specific war galleys (see Chapter 3) and the name of some of its *praefectus*, *navarchus*, *trierarchus* and *milites* (see Chapter 1). What we do not know, however, is how these brave sailors of antiquity viewed themselves in terms of their own sense of self-identity, at a macro level this being in the same context as the British Expeditionary Force in 1914 calling themselves the 'Old Contemptibles' or the US 1st Armoured Division in the Second World War the 'Old Ironsides'. To me, though, the fleet of Roman-occupied Britain will always be the 'Sea Eagles', their *aquila* emblazoned across the bulging sails of *liburnae* as they cut through the chill waters of the dark far north of the classical world.

TIMELINE

The below timeline is designed to act as a guide to the key events described in this book on the *Classis Britannica*, including those taking place after the regional fleet's demise given the light they can shed through analogy and anecdote. Events detailed mainly focus on the province, later two provinces and finally (following the Diocletianic reformation) four or even five provinces within the later *diocese* of *Britannia*, though key events in Roman history are also included given their impact on this north-western tip of the Empire.

57 BC	Veneti submit to Caesar.
56 BC	Rebellion of the Veneti, Battle of Morbihan.
55 BC	First Caesarian incursion to Britain (first Roman invasion of Britain).
54 BC	Second Caesarian incursion to Britain (second Roman invasion of Britain).
AD 40	Aborted Caligulan invasion of Britain.

AD 43	Claudian invasion, with troops led by Aulus Plautius (third invasion of Roman Britain). Likely landing place north-east Kent coast near Richborough followed by river-crossing battle, likely on the River Medway. Thames then crossed and Catuvellauni tribal capital at Colchester (Camulodunum) captured. Arrival of Claudius to proclaim victory. Aulus Plautius appointed first governor of new province.
AD 44	Vespasian successfully campaigns in south and south-west.
AD 47	Aulus Plautius returns to Rome and is granted an *ovatio* (lesser triumph). Vespasian returns also. New Governor Publius Ostorius Scapula campaigns in north Wales, then subdues the first revolt by Iceni tribe.
AD 48	First revolt of the Brigantes.
AD 49	*Coloniae* for veterans founded at Colchester after the *legio* XX *Valeria Victrix* moves to Gloucester. Scapula campaigns in southern and central Wales.
AD 50	Building begins of first forum in London (Londinium). Establishment of ragstone quarrying industry in Medway Valley, run by the *Classis Britannica.*
AD 51	British resistance leader Caratacus captured after being handed over by Brigantian Queen Cartimandua.
AD 52	Silures in south Wales pacified by Governor Didius Gallus.
AD 57	Quintus Veranius Nepos is governor, dies in office. Intervention of Rome in favour of Cartimandua.
AD 58	Gaius Suetonius Paulinus is governor.

AD 59–60	Initial subjugation of Druids in far west, and initial invasion of Anglesey by Gaius Suetonius Paulinus. Campaign cut short by Boudican revolt.
AD 60–61	Boudican revolt, destruction of Colchester, London and St Albans. Defeat of Boudican revolt, suicide of Boudica.
AD 61–63	Publius Petronius Turpilianus is governor, followed by Marcus Trebellius Maximus.
AD 69	Death of Nero, Year of the Four Emperors. Cartimandua, Queen of the Brigantes and ally of Rome, overthrown by former husband Venutius. Marcus Vettius Bolanus is governor.
AD 70	*Classis Britannica* named for the first time, by Tacitus in the context of the Batavian Revolt of Civilis.
AD 71	Emperor Vespasian orders new British Governor Quintus Petilius Cerialis to campaign in the north. Brigantes defeated, Venutius captured and killed.
AD 74	Last in the series of northern garrison forts built at Carlisle.
AD 74	Sextus Julius Frontinus appointed governor in Britain. Further campaigning in Wales. Chester founded.
AD 77	Gnaeus Julius Agricola becomes governor. Wales and western Britain finally conquered by Agricola following final definitive attack on Anglesey.
AD 78	Agricola consolidates Roman control of Brigantian territory.
AD 79	Agricola attends grand opening of civic centre of St Albans and mounts 'hearts and minds' campaign to encourage British elites to

embrace *Romanitas* by learning Latin, wearing togas, and investing in public buildings. Beginning of campaign to subdue the whole of northern Britain including Scotland.

AD 80   Continued campaigning in Scotland.

AD 81   Agricola contemplates invasion of Ireland, leading to speculation today that the provincial capital would have moved to Chester from where the whole of the British Isles would have been ruled. Invasion cancelled.

AD 82   Continued campaigning in Scotland.

AD 83   Agricola defeats combined Caledonian tribes at Battle of Mons Graupius in Scottish highlands. *Classis Britannica* circumnavigates northern Scotland, proving that Britain is an island, reaching the Orkney Islands. Conquest of Britain 'complete'. Construction begins of monumental arch at Richborough to commemorate the event.

AD 87   Roman troops withdrawn from the far north of Britain due to pressures elsewhere in the Empire, with the major legionary fortress of Inchtuthil on Tayside being abandoned and systematically dismantled.

AD 90   Gloucester and Lincoln become *coloniae*.

AD 98   Publius Metilius Nepos is governor, followed by Titus Avidius Quietus.

AD 100   Emperor Trajan orders full withdrawal of Roman troops from Scotland and establishes a new frontier along the Firth–Tyne line.

AD 103   Lucius Neratius Marcellus is governor.

AD 115   Marcus Atilius Bradua is governor.

AD 117   Major disturbances in the north of the province.

AD 122   Emperor Hadrian visits Britain and initiates construction of Hadrian's Wall. Aulus Platorius Nepos is governor.

AD 126   Lucius Trebius Germanus is governor.

AD 131   Sextus Julius Severus is governor.

AD 133   Publius Mummius Sisenna is governor.

AD 138   Quintus Lollius Urbicus is governor. Major fire in London.

AD 142   Renewal of military engagement north of Hadrian's Wall by Quintus Lollius Urbicus on orders of new Emperor Antonius Pius to subdue tribes of northern Britain and southern Scotland, the latter geographical region being conquered again. Construction of Antonine Wall along Clyde–Forth line.

AD 145   Gnaeus Papirius Aelianus is governor.

AD 155   Central St Albans destroyed by fire.

AD 157   Gnaeus Julius Verus is governor.

AD 158   Antonine Wall evacuated, renewal of northern border along Hadrian's Wall.

AD 162   Marcus Statius Priscus is the Governor of Britain, followed by Sextus Calpurnius Agricola.

AD 169   More trouble in northern Britain.

AD 174   Caerellius is governor.

AD 175   5,500 Sarmatian cavalry sent to Britain.

AD 178   Ulpius Marcellus is governor.

AD 182   The tribes either side of Hadrian's Wall begin agitating and raiding along and across the frontier, with Roman-occupied Britain responding with counter-raids. Towns far south of the wall begin constructing the first earth-and-timber defence circuits, indicating that tribal raiding penetrated far into the province. This state of affairs continues for some time.

AD 184   Commodus receives his seventh acclamation as Imperator and takes the title *Britannicus*. *Classis Britannica* transports two of the three British legions to Brittany to help defeat a rebellion.

AD 185	1,500 picked British troops travel to Rome with a petition for the Emperor Commodus to dismiss Praetorian Prefect Perennis (Dio, 72.9). New governor in *Britannia*, future Emperor Publius Helveius Pertinax.
AD 191	Decimus Clodius Albinus becomes Governor of Britain.
AD 192	Albinus sides with Septimius Severus in the latter's bid to be Emperor.
AD 193	Year of the Five Emperors.
AD 196	Albinus invades Gaul and is proclaimed Emperor by the legions of Britain and Spain.
AD 197	Albinus defeated by Septimius Severus at Battle of Lugdunum (Lyons) in close-run engagement and is killed. Plans begin to divide the province of Britain into two, *Britannia Superior* and *Britannia Inferior*. Virius Lupus is the governor in Britain.
AD 197–198	Severus sends military commissioners to Britain to suppress the supporters of Albinus. Troops rebuild parts of Hadrian's Wall (some of which may have been destroyed and the northern defences damaged by increased tribal raiding after Albinus had travelled to Gaul with his troops). Beginning of Severan reforms of the military.
AD 202	Gaius Valerius Pudens is governor.
AD 205	Lucius Alfenus Senecio is governor.
AD 208	Prompted by ongoing raiding along the northern frontier, Severus arrives in Britain and plans a major campaign against the Maeatae and Caledonian tribal confederations north of Hadrian's Wall.
AD 209	First Severan campaign in Scotland.
AD 210	Second Severan campaign in Scotland, under Caracalla.

AD 211	Severus dies at York. His sons Caracalla and Geta become joint Emperors. The northern campaign is suspended and the brothers return to Rome. Britain officially divided into two provinces, *Britannia Superior* and *Britannia Inferior*.
AD 212	Caracalla gives citizenship to all freemen in Europe.
AD 213	*Brittones dediticii* recorded at the fort at Walldurn on the *limes Germanicus*.
AD 215	Roman land wall around London built.
AD 216	Marcus Antonius Gordianus Governor of *Britannia Inferior*.
AD 222	Tiberius Julius Pollienus Auspex Governor of *Britannia Superior*.
AD 223	Claudius Xenephon Governor of *Britannia Inferior*.
AD 225	Maximus Governor of *Britannia Inferior*.
AD 226	Calvisius Rufus becomes Governor of *Britannias Inferior*, followed by Valerius Crescens and then Claudius Apellinus.
AD 237	Tuccianus becomes Governor of *Britannia Inferior*. York becomes a *colonia*.
AD 238	Marcus Martiannius Pulcher becomes Governor of *Britannia Superior*. Maecilius Fuscus becomes Governor of *Britannia Inferior*, quickly followed by Egnatius Lucilianus.
AD 242	Nonius Philippus becomes Governor of *Britannia Inferior*.
AD 244	Aemilianus becomes Governor of *Britannia Inferior*.
AD 249	Last potential mention of *Classis Britannica*, on epigraphy commemorating *Saturninus*, ex-captain in the British fleet.
AD 250	Irish raiding along the west coast, and Germanic raiding along the east coast. First use

of the term Pict to describe confederation of
tribes in northern Scotland.

AD 253   Desticius Juba becomes Governor of *Britannia
Superior.*

AD 255   London wall circuit completed with building of
river wall and bastions.

AD 260   'Gallic Empire' declared by Postumus, splitting
Britain, Gaul and Spain away from the Empire.

AD 262   Octavius Sabinus becomes Governor of
Britannia Inferior.

AD 268   Postumus murdered by his own troops.

AD 274   Emperor Aurelian defeats 'Gallic Empire',
Britain, Gaul and Spain rejoin the Empire.

AD 277   Vandals and Burgundians settled in Britain,
Victorinus defeats British usurpation.

AD 284   Diocletian becomes Emperor, beginning of
Diocletianic reforms of military.

AD 287   Usurpation of Carausius, splitting Britain and
northern Gaul away from the Empire.

AD 293   Western *caesares* Constantius Chlorus recaptures
northern Gaul from Carausius, who is assassinated by Allectus, the latter taking over from his
former master.

AD 296   Constantius Chlorus invades Britain and
defeats Allectus, returning the two provinces
to the Empire (fourth Roman invasion of
Britain). Britain declared a *diocese* as part of the
Diocletianic Reformation, with the four provinces of *Maxima Caesariensis*, *Britannia Prima*,
Flavia Caesariensis and *Britannia Secunda*.

AD 306   Constantius Chlorus campaigns in the north
and dies at York. His son, Constantine, is proclaimed Emperor by his troops.

AD 312   Constantine becomes sole Emperor in the west.
Beginning of military reforms of Constantine.

AD 314	Constantine's Edict of Milan ends persecution of Christians. Three British bishops attend Council of Bishops at Arles.
AD 324	Constantine becomes sole Emperor of whole Empire.
AD 343	Emperor Constans makes winter crossing of the English Channel to Britain following the defeat of his brother, Constantine II, three years earlier, possibly because of a military emergency in the north.
AD 350	Military leader Magnentius (born in Britain) usurps power in Gaul, with Britain and Spain quickly supporting him and ultimately the whole of the Western Empire.
AD 351	Mangnentius defeated by Eastern Emperor Constantius II at Battle of Mursa Major, retreats to Gaul. Mangnentius defeated again at Battle of Mons Seleucus and commits suicide. Constantius II sends Paul 'the chain' to purge the British aristocracy after the revolt of Mangnentius. *Vicarius* of the *diocese* Martinus commits suicide rather than face trial.
AD 358	Alypius becomes *vicarius* of *diocese*.
AD 359	British bishops attend Council of Rimini. Emperor Julian builds 600 ships to transport grain from Britain to feed Rhine army.
AD 367	Civilis becomes *vicarius* of *diocese*. 'Great Conspiracy' of Picts from Scotland, Atteacotti from Western Isles, Irish and Germanic raiders attack Britain, overwhelming frontier defences.
AD 369	Count Theodosius arrives in Britain and suppresses the revolt, restoring order. Magnus Maximus serves under him. Northern frontier rebuilt again.

AD 383	Magnus Maximus (now British military commander and possibly *vicarius*) campaigns against Pictish and Irish raiders. He is then proclaimed Emperor by his troops, invading Gaul, which declares its support for him along with Spain.
AD 387	Magnus Maximus invades Italy and ousts Emperor Valentinian II.
AD 388	Magnus Maximus defeated and executed by Theodosius I, Emperor of the East.
AD 391	Theodosius I bans pagan worship, though it continues in Britain.
AD 395	Chrysanthus becomes *vicarius* of *diocese*.
AD 400	Western Empire *Magister Militum* (overall commander) Stilicho campaigns in Britain and defeats Pictish, Irish and Germanic raiders. He then withdraws many troops to help defend Italy against the Goths. The *diocese* is left dangerously exposed to further attack. Victorinus becomes *vicarius* of *diocese*.
AD 402	Last import of base coins into Britain.
AD 405	Heavy Irish raiding on south-western coast of Britain, possible date for capture of St Patrick.
AD 406	Vandals, Burgundians, Alans, Franks and Suevi overrun *limes Germanicus* near Mainz and invade Gaul.
AD 407	In swift succession the troops in Britain declare Marcus, then Gratian and finally Constantine III Emperor. The latter crosses to Gaul with the remaining *comitatenses* field army troops from the *diocese*, setting up his capital at Arles after stabilising the region.
AD 409	British aristocracy throw out Roman administrators, and the *diocese* is cut adrift from the remaining parts of the Western Empire.

AD 410	Western Emperor Honorius tells Britons to look to their own defences.
AD 411	Constantine III captured and executed on the orders of western Emperor Honorius.
AD 429	Visit to Britain by St Germanus to debate with Pelagian Christians. Conflict with Picts and Irish.
AD 430	Last Roman coin use in Britain.
AD 454	Britons appeal to *Magister Miletum* Flavius Aetius by letter in 'the groans of the Britons' for military assistance but no troops are available to help.
AD 476	Last western Emperor, Romulus Augustulus, deposed. End of the Empire in the west.

BIBLIOGRAPHY

Ancient Sources

Appian, *The Civil Wars* (1996, Carter. J., London: Penguin).

Decimus Magnus Ausonius, *The Mosella* (1933, Blakeney, E.H., London: Unknown Binding).

Julius Caesar, *The Conquest of Gaul* (1951, Handford, S.A., London: Penguin).

Marcus Cato, *De Agri Cultura* (1934, Ash, H.B. and Hooper, W.D., Harvard: Loeb Classical Library).

Cicero, *Phillipicae* (2010, Shackleton Bailey, D.R., Harvard: Loeb Classical Library).

Cassius Dio, *Roman History* (1925, Cary, E., Harvard: Loeb Classical Library).

Quintus Horatius Flaccus (Horace), *The Complete 'Odes' and 'Epodes'* (2008, West, D., Oxford: Oxford Paperbacks).

Herodian, *History of the Empire* (1989, Whittaker, C.R., Harvard: Loeb Classical Library).

Historia Augusta (1921, Maggie, D., Harvard: Loeb Classical Library)

Horace, *Odes and Epodes* (2004, Rudd, N., Harvard: Loeb Classical Library).

Pliny the Elder, *Natural History* (1940, Rackham, H., Harvard: Harvard University Press).

Pliny the Younger, *Epistularum Libri Decum* (1963, Mynors, R.A.B.,
    Oxford: Oxford Classical Texts – Clarendon Press).
Polybius, *The Rise of the Roman Empire* (1979, Scott-Kilvert, I.,
    London: Penguin).
Ptolemy, *Geographia* (1843, Nobbe, K.F.A., Charleston: Nabu Press).
Statius, *Silvae* (2004, Nagle, B.R., Bloomington: Indiana University Press).
Strabo, *The Geography* (2014, Roler, D.W., Cambridge: Cambridge
    University Press).
Suetonius, *The Twelve Caesars* (1057, Graves, R., London: Penguin).
Cornelius Tacitus, *The Agricola* (1970, Mattingly, H., London: Penguin).
Cornelius Tacitus, *The Histories* (2008, Fyfe, W.H., Oxford: Oxford
    Paperbacks).
Marcus Terentius Varro, *Rerum Rusticarum* (1932, Ash, H.B. and
    Hooper, W.D., Harvard: Loeb Classical Library).
Zosimus, *New History* (1967, Buchanan, J. and Davis, H.T., San Antonio:
    Trinity University Press).

Modern Sources

Ackroyd, P. (2012). *London Under.* London: Chatto & Windus.
Alexander, M. (2011). *Introduction to English Heritage Assets – Mills.*
    Swindon: English Heritage.
Allen, J.R. (2010). The Alkali-Metal Ratio in Romano-British Bloomery
    Slags, Severn Estuary Levels, South-West Britain: Values and
    Implications. *Archaeology in the Severn Estuary 2009. Annual Report of the
    Severn Estuary Levels Research Committee.* V.20, 41–5.
Allen, J.R. and Fulford, M.G. (1999). Fort Building and Military Supply
    along Britain's Eastern Channel and North Sea Coasts: The Later
    Second and Third Centuries. *Britannia,* V.30, 163–84.
Allen, J.R. and Fulford, M.G. (2004). Early Roman Mosaic Materials in
    Southern Britain, with Particular Reference to Silchester: A Regional
    Geological Perspective. *Britannia,* V.35, 9–38.
Allen, Prof. J.R. Emeritus Professor, University of Reading (pers. comm.
    12 November 2013).
Allen, Martyn, Post Doctorate Research Fellow, University of Reading
    (Presentation at Society of Antiquaries of London at the Roman Rural
    Settlement in the South-East Conference, 30 October 2013).
Anderson, J.D. (1992). *Roman Military Supply in North-East England.*
    Oxford: BAR/Archaeological & Historical Associates Ltd.
Andrews, C. (2001). Romanisation: A Kentish Perspective. *Archaeologia
    Cantiana,* V.121, 25–43.

Andrews, P. Biddulph, E. Hardy, A. and Brown, R. (2011). *Settling the Ebbsfleet Valley, Sites V.1.* Oxford: Oxford Wessex Archaeology.

Applebaum, S. (1972). Roman Britain. In: Finberg, H.P.R. ed. *The Agrarian History of England and Wales.* Cambridge: Cambridge University Press.

Ashbee, P. (2005). *Kent in Prehistoric Times.* Stroud: The History Press.

Ayears, Terence former Managing Director of Courage Brewery Maidstone Ltd (pers. comm. 4 May 2013).

Bang, P. (2008). *The Roman Bazaar: A Comparative Study of Trade and Markets in Tributary Empire.* Cambridge: Cambridge University Press.

Barker, G., Webley, D. (1997). An integrated economy for Gatcombe. In: Branigan, K. ed. *Gatcombe Roman Villa.* Oxford: BAR/Archaeological & Historical Associates Ltd.

Bateman, N. (2011), *Roman London's Amphitheatre.* London: Museum of London Archaeology.

Bell, M. (1981). Valley Sediments and Environmental Change. In: Jones, M.K. and Dimbleby, G.W. ed. *The Environment of Man: The Iron Age to the Anglo-Saxon Period.* Oxford: BAR/Archaeological & Historical Associates Ltd, 75–91.

Bell, T. (1999). Churches on Roman Buildings: Christian Associations and Roman Masonry in Anglo-Saxon England. *Medieval Archaeology,* Issue 42, 1–18.

Bennett, P., Ridler, I. and Sparey-Green, C. (2010). *The Roman Watermills and Settlement at Ickham, Kent.* Canterbury: Canterbury Archaeology Trust.

Betts, Ian Building Materials Specialist, Museum of London Archaeology (pers. comm. 24 October 2012).

Betts, Ian Building Materials Specialist, Museum of London Archaeology (pers. comm. 6 May 2014).

Biddulph, E. (2013). Salt of the Earth: Roman Industry at Stanford Wharf. *Current Archaeology,* Issue 276, 16–22.

Bidwell, P. (1980). *Roman Exeter: Fortress and Town.* Exeter: Exeter City Council.

Bidwell, P. (1995). Review of Anderson 1992. *Britannia,* V.26, 395–6.

Biot, T. (2011). *A Town Unearthed* (Online.) Available from: www. atownunearthed.co.uk/research/talks/talk-quern-stones/ [Accessed 10 January 2013].

Birley, A.R. (2005). *The Roman Government of Britain.* Oxford: Oxford University Press.

Black, E.W. (1982). The Roman Villa at Darenth. *Archaeologia Cantiana,* V.97, 159–83.

Black, E.W. (1987). *The Roman Villas of South-East England.* Oxford: BAR/ Archaeological & Historical Associates Ltd.

Black, E.W. (2013). Roman Relief: Patterned Tiles At Dover and Elsewhere in Kent. *Kent Archaeological Review*, V.191, 40–2.

Blagg, T. (1980). The Sculptured Stones. In: Dyson, T. ed. *The Roman Riverside Wall and Monumental Arch in London – Special Paper No 3*. London: London and Middlesex Archaeological Society, 125–93.

Blagg, T. (2002). Roman Architectural Ornament in Britain. Oxford: BAR/Archaeological & Historical Associates Ltd.

Blanning, E. (2013). *Towards an Interpretation of the Detached and 'Isolated' Bath Houses of Roman Kent – MA Dissertation*. Unpublished: University of Kent.

Blanning, E. (2014). *Landscape, Settlement and Materiality: Aspects of Rural Life in Kent during the Roman Period. Doctor of Philosophy (PhD) Thesis*. Unpublished: University of Kent.

Blanning, E. PhD Research Student, University of Kent (pers. comm. 9 June 2014).

Blockley, K., Blockley, M., Blockley, P., Frere, S.S. and Stowe, S. (1995). Excavations in the Marlowe Car Park and Surrounding Area, *The Archaeology of Canterbury*, V.5. Canterbury: Canterbury Archaeological Trust.

Blows, J. (2011). *Strategic Stone Study – A Building Stone Atlas of Kent*. Swindon: English Heritage.

Bonifay, M. (2014). Africa: Patterns of Consumption in Coastal Regions Versus Inland Regions. The Ceramic Evidence. *Late Antique Archaeology*, V.10 (1), 529–66.

Booth, P. (2012). Roman Britain in 2011 – Southern Counties. *Britannia* V.43, 271–421.

Borsos, E., Makra, L., Beczi, R., Vitanyi, B. and Szentpeter, M. (2003). Anthropogenic Air Pollution in the Ancient Times. *ACTA Climatologica Et Chorologica, Universitatis Szegediensis*, V. 36–7, 5.15.

Boyce, K. (2007). The Implications of Isolated Bath Houses in the Roman Cray Valley. *London Archaeologist*, V.11 Number 10, 260–64.

Bradley, P. (2013). Death Pits at Cliffs End. *British Archaeology*, Issue 131, 16–20.

Branigan, K. (1982). Celtic Farm to Roman Villa. In: Miles, D. ed. *Romano-British Countryside*. Oxford: BAR/Archaeological & Historical Associates Ltd.

Breeze, David, former Chief Inspector of Ancient Monuments at Historic Scotland and Honorary Professor of Classics at Edinburgh University (pers. comm. 29 April 2010).

Breeze, D.J. and Dobson, B. (2000). *Hadrian's Wall*. London: Penguin.

Briggs, A. (1994). *A Social History of Britain*. London: Weidenfeld & Nicolson.

Brigham, T., Goodburn, D., Tyers, I. and Dillon, J. (1995). A Roman Timbered Building on the Southwark Waterfront. *The Archaeological Journal*, V.152, 1–72.

Briquet, A. (1930). *Le Littoral du nord de la France et son evolution morphologique*. Paris: A.Colin.

Briscoe, J. (1989). The Second Punic War. In: Astin, A.E. ed. *The Cambridge Ancient History – Volume 8*. Cambridge: Cambridge University Press, 44–80.

Brodribb, G. (1970). Stamped Tiles of the Classis Britannica. *Kent Archaeological Review*, V.21, 25.

Brodribb, G. (1979). A Survey of Tile at the Roman Bath House at Beauport Park, Battle, East Sussex. *Britannia*, V.10, 139–56.

Brodribb, G., Cleere, H., Henig, M., MacKreth, D.F. and Greep, S.J. (1988). The 'Classis Britannica' Bath-House at Beauport Park, East Sussex. *Britannia*, V.19, 217–74.

Bromwich, J. (2009). *The Roman Remains of Northern and Eastern France: A Guidebook*. London: Routledge.

Brookes, S. and Harrington, S. (2010). *The Kingdom and People of Kent, AD 400–1066*. Stroud: The History Press.

Brooks, N.P. (1994). Rochester Bridge *AD* 43 to 1381. In: Yates, N. and Gibson, J.H. ed. *Traffic and Politics – The Construction and Management of Rochester Bridge* AD *42–1993*. Woodbridge: The Boydell Press, 1–35.

Brown, A.G., Meadows, I., Turner, S.D. and Mattingly, D. (2001). Roman Vineyards in Britain: stratigraphic and palynological data from Wollaston in the Nene Valley, England. *Antiquity*, V.75, 745–57.

Brown, J. (2013). Enshrined by Conservation: A Romano-British Shrine in Rutland Water. *Current Archaeology*, Issue 285, 20–4.

Brown, P. (2012). *Through the Eye of a Needle*. Princeton: Princeton University Press.

Burnham, B.C. and Davies, J.L. (2010). *Roman Frontiers in Wales and the Marches*. Aberystwyth: Royal Commission on the Ancient and Historical Monuments of Wales.

Burnham, B.C., Wacher, J. (1990). *The Small Towns of Roman Britain*. London: Batsford.

Campbell, B. (2011). *Rivers and the Power of Ancient Rome*. Chapel Hill: University of North Carolina Press.

Carroll, M. (2009). Cologne. In: Gagarin, M. ed. *The Oxford Encyclopaedia of Greece and Rome*. Oxford: Oxford University Press, 251–60.

Carruthers, W.J. (2014). The Charred and Mineralised Plant Remains. In: O'Shea, L. and Weeks, J. ed. Evidence of a Distinct Focus of Romano-British Settlement at Maidstone? Excavations at Church Street 2011–12. *Archaeologia Cantiana*, V.135, 143–47.

Castle, S.A. (1978). Amphorae from Brockley Hill, 1975. *Britannia*, V.9, 383–92.

Catling, C. (2013). Chedworth Roman Villa: Life in the Cotswolds Then and Now. *Current Archaeology*, Issue 284, 43.

Catling, C. (2014). Excavating Earth: Was the Roman Fenland an Imperial Estate. *Current Archaeology*, Issue 295, 20–5.

Champion, T. (2007). Prehistoric Kent. In: Williams, J.H. ed. *The Archaeology of Kent to AD 800*. Woodbridge: The Boyden Press and Kent County Council.

Chaplin, R.E. (1962). Excavations in Rochester, Winter 1961–2. *Archaeologia Cantiana*, Vol. 77, 1-li.

Chitty, R. Secretary, Medway River Users Association (pers. comm. 4 October 2012).

Chitty, R. Secretary, Medway River Users Association (pers. comm. 7 October 2012).

Cleere, H. (1977). *The Classis Britannica*. In: Johnston, D.E. ed. *The Saxon Shore*, York: CBA Research Report No. 18, 16–19.

Cleere, H. and Crossley, D. (1995). *The Iron Industry of the Weald*. Cardiff: Merton Priory Press.

Coles (15 June 1630). *Mr Coles Observation of Nuisances on the Medway. An Account of the Proceedings of the Commissioners of Sewers Towards Making the River Medway Navigable between Maidstone and Penshurst 1627–1630*. ms. Strood: Medway Archives and Local Studies Centre. AZ1 (a late eighteenth-century reproduction of the original, within the Medway Navigation Company's papers for the year 1800).

Connolly, P. (1981). *Greece and Rome at War*. London: Macdonald Pheobus Ltd.

Cool, H.E.M and Mason, D.J.P. (2008). *Roman Piercebridge, Excavations by D.W. Harding and Peter Scott 1969–1981*. Durham: The Architectural and Archaeological Society of Durham and Northumberland.

Cooper, C. (2008). *Maidstone – A History*. Bognor Regis: Phillimore & Co. Ltd.

Cornwell, K. and Cornwell. L (2013). Footlands Farm, Seddlescombe: A geophysical survey of the iron-production complex and its transport links. *Hastings Area Archaeological Research Group*, No. 33, 1–22.

Cowan, R. (2015). *Roman Legionary AD 284–337*. Oxford: Osprey Publishing.

Creighton, Dr. J. (30 October 2013). Director of Information and Communications Technology and Associate Professor in Archaeology, University of Reading (responding to questions. Society of Antiquaries of London, Roman Rural Settlement in the South-East Conference).

Crew, P. (1998). Laxton Revisited. *Historical Metallurgy*, V.32, 49–53.

Croft, A., Munby, J. and Ridley, M. (2001). *Kent Historic Landscape Characterisation*. Maidstone: Oxford Archaeology.

Crowley, L. (2011). The role of mortuary ritual in the construction of social boundaries by privileged social groups within villa landscapes. In: Roymans, N. and Derks, T. ed. *Villa Landscapes in the Roman North*. Amsterdam: Amsterdam University Press.

Croxford, B. HER Record Officer, Kent County Council (pers. comm. 13 December 2010).

Croxford, B. HER Record Officer, Kent County Council (pers. comm. 3 January 2014).

Crummy, P. (2008). The Roman Circus at Colchester. *Britannia*, V. 39, 15–31.

Cunliffe, B. (1969). Roman Kent. In: Newman, J. ed. *The Buildings of England, West Sussex and the Weald*. London: Penguin, 22–4.

Cunliffe, B. (1980). The Evolution of Romney Marsh: A Preliminary Romney Statemen. In: Thompson, F.H. ed. *Archaeology and Coastal Change*. London: The Society of Antiquities, 37–55.

Cunliffe, B. (1988). Romney Marsh in the Roman Period. In: Edisson, J. and Green, C. ed. *Romney Marsh: Evolution, Occupation, Reclamation*. Oxford: OUCA Monograph 24, 83–3.

Cunliffe, B. (2009). *Iron Age Communities in Britain – An Account of England, Scotland and Wales from the 7th century BC Until the Roman Conquest*. London: Routledge.

Cunliffe, B. (2013). *Britain Begins*. Oxford: Oxford University Press.

Cunliffe CBE, Sir Barry, Emeritus Professor of European Archaeology, School of Archaeology, Oxford (pers. comm. 16 April 2014).

D'Amato, R. (2009). *Imperial Roman Naval Forces 31 BC–AD 500*. Oxford: Osprey Publishing.

Daniels, A. (2008). *An Archaeological Investigation Using Trial Pits into the Car Park and Cemetery Extension of St Margaret's Church, Barming*. Unpublished: Maidstone Area Archaeological Group.

Daniels, A. (2010). *East Farleigh Roman Buildings*. Kent Archaeological Society Newsletter. Issue 86, 12–13.

Daniels, A. (2015). *Excavations at Oaklands, Lower Road, East Farleigh, Maidstone, 2014*. Kent Archaeological Society, Issue 101 – 6.

Daniels, A. Chairman, MAAG (pers. comm. 31 July 2011).

Daniels, A. Chairman, MAAG (pers. comm. 17 January 2013).

Dark, K. and Dark, P. (1997). *The Landscape of Roman Britain*. Stroud: Sutton Publishing.

Darvill, T. and McWhirr, A. (1982). Roman Brick Production and the Environment. In: Miles, D. ed. *Romano-British Countryside*. Oxford: BAR/Archaeological & Historical Associates Ltd, 137–50.

Davies, H. Formerly of the Kent Archaeological Rescue Unit (pers. comm. 19 May 2010).

Davies, H. Formerly of the Kent Archaeological Rescue Unit (pers. comm. 28 March 2012).

Davies, M. (2009). The Evidence of Settlement at Plaxtol in the Late Iron Age and Romano-British Periods. *Archaeologia Cantiana*, V.129, 257–78.

Davies, M. Plaxtol and Springhead Archaeologist (pers. comm. 17 April 2012).

Davies, N. (2011). *Vanished Kingdoms*. London: Penguin.

Dawkes, G. (2009). *A Post Excavation Assessment Report and Updated Project Design on Archaeological Excavations at High Street, Snodland, Kent*. Portslade: ASE.

de la Bédoyère, G. (1992). *Roman Towns in Britain*. London: Batsford.

de la Bédoyère, G. (1999) *The Golden Age of Britain*. Stroud: Tempus.

de la Bédoyère, G. (2000). *Pottery in Roman Britain*. Princes Risborough: Shire Publications.

de la Bédoyère, G. (2015). Face to Face with the Past: Uncovering the Real Lives of Roman Britain. *Current Archaeology*, Issue 304, 26–33.

Devoy, R.J.N. (1990). Controls on Coastal and Sea-Level Changes and the Application of Archaeological Historical Records to Understanding Recent Patterns of Sea-Level Movement. In: McGrail, S. ed. *Maritime Celts, Frisians and Saxons*. York: CBA Research Group, 17–26.

Dumayne-Peaty, L. (1998). Forest Clearance in Northern Britain during Romano-British Times: Re-addressing the Palynological Evidence. *Britannia*, V.29, 315–22.

Durham, A. and Goormachtigh, M. (2015). Greenwich and the Early Emporia of Kent. *Archaeologia Cantiana*, V.1036, 163–76.

Dworakowska, A. (1983). *Quarries in Roman Provinces*. Wroclaw: Zaklad Narodowy im. Ossolinskich.

Elliott, P. (2014). *Legions in Crisis*. Stroud: Fonthill Media Ltd.

Elliott, S. (2014). The Mystery of the Medway Stones. *Current Archaeology*, Issue 298, 11.

Ellis Jones, J. (2012). *The Maritime Landscape of Roman Britain*. Oxford: BAR/Archaeological & Historical Associates Ltd.

English Heritage (2011). *Strategic Stone Study – A building Stone Atlas of Kent*. Swindon: English Heritage.

Esmonde Cleary, A.S. (1989). *The Ending of Roman Britain*. London: Batsford.

Esmonde Cleary, A.S. (2013). *Chedworth: Life in a Roman Villa*. Stroud: The History Press.

Esmonde Cleary, A.S. (2013). *The Roman West AD 200–500*. Cambridge: Cambridge University Press.

Evans, C. and Newman, R. (2014). *North West Cambridge: University of Cambridge. Archaeological Evaluation Fieldwork*. Cambridge: Cambridge Archaeological Unit.

Evans, J. (2014). Balancing the Scales: Romano-British Pottery in Early Late Antiquity. *Late Antique Archaeology*, V. 10 (1), 1–11.

Evans, J. Archaeological Horizons in the North Kent Marshes. *Archaeologia Cantiana*, V.66, 103–46.

Everitt, A. (1986). *Continuity and Colonisation*. Leicester: Leicester University Press.

Faulkner, N. (2001). *The Decline and Fall of Roman Britain*. Stroud: Tempus.

Fernando-Lozano, J., Gutierrez-Alonso, G. and Fernandez-Moran, M.A. (2015). Using Airborne LIDAR Sensing Technology and Aerial Orthoimages to Unravel Roman Water Supply Systems and Gold Works in NW Spain. *Journal of Archaeological Science*, V. 53, 356–373.

Fields, N. (2006). *Rome's Saxon Shore*. Oxford: Osprey Publishing.

Finkel, I. (2014). *The Ark Before Noah*. London: Hodder and Stoughton.

Fleming, R. (2010). *Britain After Rome*. London: Penguin.

Fulford, Prof. M. (30 October 2013). Presentation at Society of Antiquaries of London at the Roman Rural Settlement in the South-East Conference.

Furhmann, C.J. (2011). *Policing the Roman Empire: Soldiers, Administration and Public Order*. Oxford: Oxford University Press.

Gardiner, M. (1996). *An Archaeological Evaluation of Land Adjacent to Pested Bars Road, Boughton Monchelsea, Maidstone, Kent*. Unpublished: South-Eastern Archaeological Service.

Gardner, A. (2007). *An Archaeology of Identity*. California: Left Coast Press.

Gardner, A. (2013). Thinking about Roman Imperialism: Postcolonialism, Globalisation and Beyond? *Britannia*, V.44, 1–25.

Goacher, D. (2012). Kentish Ragstone from the Maidstone Area. *Kent Archaeological Society Newsletter*, Issue 94, 12–13.

Goldsworthy, A. (2003). *The Complete Roman Army*. London: Thames & Hudson.

Goldsworthy, A. (2014). *Augustus: From Revolutionary to Emperor*. London: Weidenfeld & Nicolson.

Goodburn, D. (1991). A Roman Timber Framed Building Tradition. *The Archaeological Journal*, V.148, 182–204.

Goodburn, D. Ancient Woodwork Specialist, AMTeC Co-Op Ltd (pers. comm. 17 December 2013).

Goodburn, D. Ancient Woodwork Specialist, AMTeC Co-Op Ltd (pers. comm. 28 February 2014).

Goodburn, D. Ancient Woodwork Specialist, AMTeC Co-Op Ltd (pers. comm. 13 November 2014).

Gough, Meyrick Water Strategy Planning Manager and Hydrologist, Southern Water (pers. comm. 6 November 2011).

Grainge, G. (2005). *The Roman Invasions of Britain*. Stroud: Tempus.

Gray, H. (1915). *English Field Systems*. Harvard University Press: Harvard.

Green, C. (2010). Forest Ports of the Severn. *Archaeology in the Severn Estuary 2009*. V.20, 47–63.

Green, C. Consultant, Canterbury Archaeological Trust (pers. comm. 29 August 2013).

Green, C. and Peacock, D. (4 December 2011). *The Puddingstone Industries in France and Britain*. (Online.) Available from: www.sal.org.uk/fundraising/research/puddingstone/ [Accessed 12 November 2012].

Green, C. and Peacock, D. (2012). Worms Heath Puddingstone Querns: Crawford Vindicated. *Surrey Archaeological Society Bulletin*, Issue 436, 1–3.

Greene, K. (1986). *The Archaeology of the Roman Economy*. Berkeley and Los Angeles: University of Chicago Press.

Griffin, E. (2010). *A Short History of the British Industrial Revolution*. Basingstoke: Palgrave Macmillan.

Grover, J.W. (1873). Notes on the Foundations of a Roman Villa at Teston, Kent. *The Journal of the British Archaeological Association*, V.29, 45–7.

Guest, P. and Young, T. (2009). Mapping Isca: Geophysical Investigation of School Field and Priory Field, Caerleon. *Archaeologia Cambrensis*, Issue 158, 97–111.

Hall, J. and Merrifield, R. (1986). *Roman London*. London: HMSO Publications for the Museum of London.

Halsall, G. (2013). *Worlds of Arthur*. Oxford: Oxford University Press.

Hann, Dr A. (2008). The Lower Medway Valley. Local History and Community Involvement Presentation for Victoria County History's 'England's Past for Everyone', sponsored by English Heritage. (Online.) Available from: www.english-heritage.org.uk/content/imported-docs/power-point-presentations/lower-medway-valley-local-history [Accessed 18 July 2013].

Hanson, W.S. (1996). Forest Clearance and the Roman Army. *Britannia*, V.27, 354–358.

Harrington, S. and Welch, M. (2014). *The Early Anglo-Saxon Kingdoms of Southern Britain*. Oxford: Oxbow Books.

Harrison, A.C. and Flight, C. (1968). The Roman and Medieval Defences of Rochester in Light of Recent Excavations. *Archaeologia Cantiana*, V.83, 55–104.

Haselgrove, C. (1997). Iron Age Broach Deposition and Chronology. In: Gwilt, A. and Haselgrove, C. ed. *Reconstructing Iron Age Society*. Oxford: Oxbow Monograph 71, 51–72.

Haselgrove, C. (2005). A New Approach to Analysing the Circulation of Iron Age Coinage. *The Numanistic Chronicle*, V.165, 129–174.

Haslam, J. (2010). *Early Medieval Towns in Britain*. Princes Risborough: Shire Archaeology.

Hasted, E. (1798). *The History of Topographical Survey of the County of Kent – Vol. IV, East and West Farleigh*. Ashford: 2008 reprint by Old Towns Books & Maps.

Hasted, E. (1798). *The History of Topographical Survey of the County of Kent – Vol. IV, East Barming, Teston and West Barming*. Ashford: 2008 reprint by Old Towns Books & Maps.

Hasted, E. (1798). *The History of Topographical Survey of the County of Kent – Vol. VIII, The Town and Parish of Rye*. Ashford: 2008 reprint by Old Towns Books & Maps.

Hastings, P. (2000). *Upon the Quarry Hills – A History of Boughton Monchelsea*. Maidstone: Boughton Monchelsea Parish Council.

Hayward, Dr K. Building Material Specialist, Pre-Construct Archaeology Ltd (pers. comm. 15 June 2014).

Hayward, Dr K. Building Material Specialist, Pre-Construct Archaeology Ltd (pers. comm. 2 July 2014).

Hayward, K.M.J. (2009). *Roman Quarrying and Stone Supply on the Periphery – Southern England*. Oxford: BAR/Archaeological & Historical Associates Ltd.

Heather, Peter. (2005). *The Fall of the Roman Empire*. London: Macmillan.

Heather, Peter. (2013). *The Restoration of Rome*. London: Macmillan.

Helm, R. and Carruthers, W. (2011). Early Roman Evidence Fort Intensive Cultivation and Malting of Spelt Wheat at Nonington. *Archaeologia Cantiana*, V.131, 353–72.

Henry Cleere, Honorary Professor, Archaeological Heritage Management, Institute of Archaeology, UCL (pers. comm. 6 May 2014).

Henson, D. (2006). *The Origins of the Anglo-Saxons*. Ely: Anglo-Saxon Books.

Hewitt, E.M. (1932). Industries. In: Page, W. ed. *The Victoria History of the Counties of England – Kent*. London: St Catherine Press, 371–431.

Higgins, C. (2013). *Under Another Sky: Journey's in Roman Britain*. London: Jonathan Cape.

Hill, J.D. (1997). The End of One Kind of Body and the Beginning of Another King of Body. In: Gwilt, A. and Haselgrove, C. ed. *Reconstructing Iron Age Society*. Oxford: Oxbow Monograph 71, 96–107.

Hill, P.R. and David, J.C.E. (1995). *Practical Stone Masonry*. Shaftsbury: Donhead Publishing.

Hingley, R. (1989). *Rural Settlement in Roman Britain*. London: Seaby.

Hingley, R. (2005). *Globalizing Roman Culture – Unity, Diversity and Empire*. London: Routledge.

Hirt, A.M. (2010). *Imperial Mines and Quarries in the Roman World*. Oxford: Oxford University Press.

Hodges, R. (2014). Roman Goldmines in Transylvania. *Current World Archaeology*, Issue 68, 54–7.

Hodgkinson, J. (1999). Romano-British Iron Production in the Sussex and Kent Weald: a review of current data. *The Journal of the Historical Metallurgy Society*, V.33, 68–72.

Hodgkinson, J. (2004). Field Notes. *Wealden Iron Research Group Bulletin*, Issue 24, 2–6.

Hodgkinson, J. (2008). *Waste as a Potential Indicator of Regional Iron Production and Organisation: An example from South-east Roman Britain*. Unpublished: Wealden Iron Research Group.

Hodgkinson, J. (2009). *The Wealden Iron Industry*. Stroud: The History Press.

Hodgkinson, J. Vice Chairman, Wealden Iron Research Group (pers. comm. 28 August 2013).

Hodgkinson, J. Vice Chairman, Wealden Iron Research Group (pers. comm. 4 September 2013).

Hodgkinson, J. Vice Chairman, Wealden Iron Research Group (pers. comm. 16 September 2013).

Hodgkinson, J. (16 November 2013). The Landscape of Iron Production in the Roman Weald – Presentation at CBA South-East Conference on Landscapes of South-Eastern Britain During the Roman Period.

Hodgkinson, J. Vice Chairman, Wealden Iron Research Group (pers. comm. 3 March 2014).

Hodgkinson, J. Vice Chairman, Wealden Iron Research Group (pers. comm. 15 April 2015).

Hodgson, Dr N. (2007). Arbeia Roman Fort – South Shields *Current Archaeology*, Issue 133, 24–42.

Hoggarth, C. University of Kent PhD Student and Roman Bridge Specialist (pers. comm. 9 June 2015).

Holman, D. (2000). Iron Age Coinage in Kent. *Archaeologia Cantiana*, V.120, 205–33.

Holman, D. (2005). Iron Age Coinage and Settlement in East Kent. *Britannia*, V.36, 1–54.

Holman, D. Dover Archaeological Group (pers. comm. 2 June 2013).

Holman, D. Dover Archaeological Group (pers. comm. 19 January 2013).

Hopkins, K. (1985). *Death and Renewal*. Cambridge: Cambridge University Press.

Houliston, M. (1999). Excavations at the Mount Villa, Maidstone. *Archaeologia Cantiana*.

Howell, I. (2014). Continuity and Change in the late Iron Age-Roman Transition Within the Environs of Quarry Wood Oppidum: Excavations at Furfield Quarry, Boughton Monchelsea. *Archaeologia Cantiana*, V.134, 37–66.

Hughes, I. (2010). *Stilicho: The Vandal Who Saved Rome*. Barnsley: Pen and Sword Books.

Hughes, J. (1850/51). On the pneumatic method adopted in constructing the foundations of the new bridge across the Medway – Minutes of the Proceedings of the Institution of Civil Engineers. In: Yates, N. and Gibson, J.M. ed. *Traffic and Politics – The Construction and Management of Rochester Bridge AD 43–1993*. Woodbridge: The Boydell Press, 9.

Hutchinson, J.N., Poole, C., Lambert, N. and Bromhead, E.N. (1985). Combined Archaeological and Geotechnical Investigations of the Roman Fort at Lympne, Kent. *Britannia*, V.16, 88–9.

Ingleton, R. (2012). Fortress Kent, the Guardian of England. Barnsley: Pen and Sword Books.

Jackson, R. (2012). *Ariconium, Herefordshire: An Iron Age Settlement and Romano-British Small Town*. Oxford: Oxbow Books.

James, S. (2011). *Rome and the Sword*. London: Thames & Hudson.

James, Simon. (1999). The community of the soldiers: a major identity and centre of power in Roman Britain. In: Baker, P., Jundi, S., and Witcher, R. eds *TRAC 98: Proceedings of the Eighth Annual Theoretical Roman Archaeology Conference, Leicester 1998*. Oxford: Oxbow, 14–25.

Jamieson, D. (2008). *PB Site, Horsewash Lane, Rochester*. Unpublished: Archaeology South-East.

Jeater, M. Curator, Museum of London (pers. comm. 10 February 2013).

Jessup, R.F. (1932). Romano-British Remains – Industries. In: Page, W. ed. *The Victoria History of the Counties of England – Kent*. London: St Catherine Press, 127–33.

Jessup, R.F. (1956). The 'Temple of Mithras' at Burham. *Archaeologia Cantiana*, V.70, 168–72.

Johnston, D.E. (2004). *Roman Villas*. Princes Risborough: Shire Archaeology.

Jones, A.H.M. (1952). Inflation Under the Roman Empire. *Economic History Review*, Issue 5, 293–318.

Jones, B. and Mattingly, D. (1990). *An Atlas of Roman Britain*. Oxford: Oxbow Books.

Jones, G.D.B. (1980). The Roman Mines at Rio Tinto. *The Journal of Roman Studies*, V.70, 146–64.

Jones, H.A. (1992). A Survey of Roman Fragments in Churches in S.E. Kent. *Kent Archaeological Review*, Issue 110, 230.

Jones, M. (1982). Crop Production in Roman Britain. In: Miles, D. ed. *Romano-British Countryside*. Oxford: BAR/Archaeological & Historical Associates Ltd.

Jones, M. (1986). Towards a Model of the Villa Estate. In: Miles, D. ed. *Archaeology at Barton Court Farm, Abingdon, Oxon. Council for British Archaeology Research Report*, V.50, 38–42.

Kaye, S. (2015). The Roman Invasion of Britain AD 43. Riverine, Wading and Tidal Studies Place Limits on the Location of the Two-Day River Battle and Beachhead. *Archaeologia Cantiana*, V.136, 227–40.

Keller, P.T. (1988). The Evidence for Ancient Quern Production at Folkeston. *Kent Archaeological Review*, Issue 99, 206–09.

Keller, P.T. (1989). Quern Production at Folkestone, South-East Kent. An Interim Note. *Britannia*, V.20, 193–200.

Kissick, E. (1990). Roman Building on Bluebell Hill: Where Is It? *Kent Archaeological Review*, Issue 102, 10–14.

Krier, J. and Heinrich, P. (2011). Monumental funerary structures of the 1st to the 3rd Centuries associated with Roman villas in the area of the Treveri. In: Toymans, N. and Derks, T. eds *Villa Landscapes in the Roman North*. Amsterdam: Amsterdam University Press, 211–34.

Lambert, M. (2010). *Christians and Pagans*. Yale: Yale University Press.

Laurence, R. (2013). Road To Success – How Money, Mules and Milestones Led to Roman Globalisation. *Current World Archaeology*, Issue 59, 42–6.

Lavan, L. (2014). Local Economies in Late Antiquity? Some Thoughts. *Late Antique Archaeology*, V. 10 (1), 1–11.

Lawrence, M. Author of *For All The Saints. St Michael's Church East Peckham. Parish and People*. (pers. comm. 26 March 2015).

Lawson, T. and Killingray, D. (2004). *An Historical Atlas of Kent*. Chichester: Phillimore & Co. Ltd for the Kent Archaeological Society.

Le Bohec, Y. (2000). *The Imperial Roman Army*. London: Routledge.

Legg, R. (1986). *Exploring the Heartland of Purbeck*. Sherborne: Dorset Publishing Company.

Lendering, J. (2002, Revision 4 October 2014). *Laurum*. (Online.) Available from: www.livius.org/place/laurum-woerden/ [Accessed 11 January 2015].

Ling, R. (1985). The Mechanics of the Building Trade. In: Grew, F. and Hobley, B. ed. *Roman Urban Topography in Britain and the Western Empire*. York: CBA Research Report No. 59, 14–27.

Locker, A. (2007). In piscibus diversis: the Bone Evidence for Fish Consumption in Roman Britain. *Britannia*, V.38, 141–80.

Locker, A. (2014). The Fish Remains. In: O'Shea, L. and Weeks, J. ed. Evidence of a Distinct Focus of Romano-British Settlement at

Maidstone? Excavations at Church Street 2011–12. *Archaeologia Cantiana,* V.135, 141–42.

Loe, L., Boyle, A., Webb, H. and Score, D. (2014). *Given to the Ground: A Viking Age Mass Grave on Ridgeway Hill, Weymouth.* Oxford: Oxford Archaeology.

Lott, G. and Cameron, D. (2005). *The Building Stones of South-East England; Minerology and Provenance.* Nottingham: British Geological Survey.

Lyne, Dr M. (pers. comm. 22 May 2013).

Lyne, Dr M. (pers. comm. 12 July 2013).

Lyne, Dr M. (pers. comm. 31 March 2014).

Lyne, Dr M. (September 1996). Roman Ship Fittings From Richborough: Speech at ROMEC X, Montpelier. (Online.) Available from: www.classis-britannica.co.uk/menu/shipping/shipping.htm [Accessed 10 October 2011].

Magness, J. (2011). A Reconsideration of Josephus' Testimony About Masada. In: Popovi, M. ed. *The Jewish Revolt Against Rome: Interdisciplinary Perspectives.* Leiden: Brill, 343–61.

Malim, T. (2005). *Stonea and the Roman Fenlands.* Stroud: Tempus.

Manley, J. (2002). *AD 43: The Roman Invasion of Britain.* Stroud: Tempus.

Margary, I.D. (1967). *Roman Roads in Britain.* London: John Baker Publishers Ltd.

Marsden, P. (1994). *Ships of the Port of London, 1st to 11th Centuries.* Swindon: English Heritage.

Mason, D.J.P. (2003). *Roman Britain and the Roman Navy.* Stroud: The History Press.

Mason, S. (1998). *Land Adjacent to Pested Bars Road, Boughton Monchelsea, Maidstone, Kent – An Archaeological Evaluation.* Unpublished: Museum of London Archaeology Service.

Matthews, J.D. (1989). Silvicultural Systems. Wotton-under-Edge: Clarendon Press.

Mattingly, D. (2006). *An Imperial Possession, Britain in the Roman Empire.* London: Penguin.

Mattingly, D. (2011). *Imperialism, Power and Identity – Experiencing the Roman Empire.* Princeton: Princeton University Press.

McGrail, S. (2014). *Early Ships and Seafaring: European Water Transport.* Barnsley: Pen and Sword Archaeology.

McOmish, D. (2011). *Introduction to History Assets – Oppida.* Swindon: English Heritage, 359–77.

McRae, S.G. and Burnham, C.P. (1973). *The Rural Landscape of Kent.* London: Wye College.

McWhirr, A. and Viner, D. (1978). The Production and Distribution of Tiles in Roman Britain with Particular Reference to the Cirencester Region. *Britannia*, V.9.

Merrifield, R. (1965). *The Roman City of London*. London: Ernest Benn Ltd.

Millett, M. (1990). Introduction: London as a Capital. In: Watson, B. ed. *Roman London: Recent Archaeological Work*. Portsmouth: Journal of Roman Archaeology Supplementary Series Number 24, 7–12.

Millett, M. (1990). *The Romanization of Britain*. Cambridge: Cambridge University Press.

Millett, M. (2007). Roman Kent. In: Williams, H. ed. *The Archaeology of Kent to 800AD*. Woodbridge: The Boyden Press and Kent County Council, 135–86.

Millett, Prof. M. Laurence Professor of Classical Archaeology, Faculty of Classics, University of Cambridge (pers. comm. 17 April 2014).

Millett, Prof. M. Laurence Professor of Classical Archaeology, Faculty of Classics, University of Cambridge (pers. comm. 4 May 2014).

Millett, Prof. M. Laurence Professor of Classical Archaeology, Faculty of Classics, University of Cambridge (pers. comm. 3 June 2014).

Millett, Prof. M. Laurence Professor of Classical Archaeology, Faculty of Classics, University of Cambridge (pers. comm. 5 June 2014).

Mills, P.J.E., 2013. The Supply and Distribution of Ceramic Building Material In Roman Britain. In: Levan, L. and Mulryan, M. eds. *Field Methods and Techniques in Late Antique Archaeology 10*. Leiden: Brill, 451–70.

Milne, G. (2000). A Roman Provincial Fleet; The Classis Britannica reconsidered. In: Oliver G., Brock, R., Cornell, T. and Hodgkinson, S. eds *The Sea in Antiquity*. Oxford: BAR/Archaeological & Historical Associates Ltd, 127–31.

Milne, G. Honorary Senior Research Associate UCL (pers. comm. 8 March 2011).

Milne, G. Honorary Senior Research Associate UCL (pers. comm. 31 May 2011).

Money, J.H., Fulford, M.G., and Eade, C. (1977). The Iron-Age Hill-Fort and Romano-British Iron-Working Settlement at Garden Hill, Sussex: Interim Report on Excavations, 1968–76. *Britannia*, V.8, 339–50.

Moody, G. (2008). *The Isle of Thanet. From Prehistory to the Norman Conquest*. Stroud: Tempus.

Moore, F.G. (1950). Three Canal Projects, Roman and Byzantine. *American Journal of Archaeology*, 54, 97–111.

Moorhead, S. (2014). *A History of Roman Coinage in Britain*. Witham: Greenlight Publishing.

Moorhead, S. National Finds Adviser for Iron Age and Roman Coins, Department of Portable Antiquities and Treasure, British Museum (pers. comm. 21 January 2013).

Moorhead, S. National Finds Adviser for Iron Age and Roman Coins, Department of Portable Antiquities and Treasure, British Museum (pers. comm. 26 February 2013).

Moorhead, S., Anderson, I. and Walton, P. (2012). *The Roman Coins from the Excavation at Whitefriars, Canterbury.* Unpublished: British Museum.

Moorhead, S. and Stuttard, D. (2012). *The Romans Who Shaped Britain.* London: Thames & Hudson.

Morris, F.M. (2010). *North Sea and Channel Connectivity during the Late Iron Age and Roman Period (175–150 BC– AD 409).* Oxford: BAR/ Archaeological & Historical Associates Ltd.

Morris, P. (1979). *Agricultural Buildings in Roman Britain.* Oxford: BAR/ Archaeological & Historical Associates Ltd.

Mynott, E. (1978). A Roman Stone Coffin at Keston. (Online.) Available from: cka.moon-demon.co.uk/KAR054/KAR054_Keston.htm [Accessed 15 July 2013].

Neilson, R. (2000). *Land Adjacent to Pested Bars Road, Boughton Monchelsea, Maidstone, Kent – A Post-Excavation Assessment and updated Project Design.* Unpublished: Museum of London Archaeology Service.

Newman, J. (1969). West Kent and the Weald. In: Pevsner, N. ed. *The Buildings of England Series.* London: Penguin.

Newton, G. Stone Mason and Proprietor of The Stone Shop in East Farleigh (pers. comm. 5 June 2014).

Nightingale, M.D. (1952). A Roman Land Settlement Near Rochester. *Archaeologia Cantiana,* V.65, 150–59.

Oldham, P. Founder of the Maidstone Area Archaeological Group, Archaeologist and Historian (pers. comm. 4 May 2010).

Papworth, M. (2015). Chedworth Roman Villa. *Current Archaeology,* Issue 305, 12–8.

Parfitt, K. Dover Field Officer, CAT, *The Roman Building at Harp Wood, Saltwood, Near Hythe. Kent Archaeological Review,* Winter 2004.

Parfitt, K. (2011). The Rocky Road to the Iron Age: Excavations at Folkestone Roman Villa, 2011. *Kent Archaeological Society Newsletter,* Issue 92, 2–4.

Parfitt, K. (2013). Folkestone During the Roman Period. In: Coulson, I. ed. *Folkestone to 1500, A Town Unearthed.* Canterbury: Canterbury Archaeological Trust, 31–54.

Parfitt, K. Dover Field Officer, CAT (pers. comm. 21 June 2013).

Parfitt, K. Dover Field Officer, CAT (pers. comm. 5 July 2013).

Parfitt, K. Dover Field Officer, CAT (pers. comm. 24 January 2014).

Parfitt, K. Dover Field Officer, CAT (pers. comm. 3 March 2014).

Parker, P. (2009). *The Empire Stops Here.* London: Jonathan Cape.

Payne, G. (1880). Roman Remains Found at Chatham and at Barming. *Archaeologia Cantiana*, V.13, 168–72.

Peacock, D.P.S. (1977). Bricks and Tiles of the Classis Britannica: Petrology and Origin. *Britannia*, V.8, 235–48.

Peacock, D.P.S. (1982). *Pottery in the Roman World: An Ethnoarchaeological Approach.* Harlow: Longman.

Peacock, D.P.S. (1987). Iron Age and Roman Quern Production at Lodsworth, West Sussex. *The Antiquaries Journal*, V.67, 61–85.

Peacock, D.P.S. (2013). *The Stone of Life.* Southampton: The Highfield Press.

Pearson, A.F. (1999). Building Anderita: Late Roman Coastal Defences and the Construction of the Saxon Shore Fort at Pevensey. *Oxford Journal of Archaeology*, V.18 (1), 95–117.

Pearson, A.F. (2002). Stone Supply to the Saxon Shore Forts at Reculver, Richborough, Dover and Lympne. *Archaeologia Cantiana*, V.122, 197–222.

Pearson, A.F. (2003). *The Roman Shore Forts.* Stroud: Tempus Publishing. Oxford: BAR/Archaeological & Historical Associates Ltd.

Pearson, A.F. (2003). The Construction of the Saxon Shore Forts. British Archaeological Report No. 349. Oxford.

Pearson, A.F. (2006). *The Work of Giants. Stone Quarrying in Roman Britain.* Stroud: Tempus Publishing.

Perring, D. (1991). *Roman London.* London: Routledge.

Perring, D. (2009). *The Roman House in Britain.* London: Routledge.

Petrikovits, H von. (1975). *Die Innenbauten römischen Legionslager während der Prinzipatszeit.* Warsaw: Westdeutscher Verlag.

Pettitt, P. and White, M. (2012). *The British Palaeolithic.* London: Routledge.

Philp, B. (1968). The Roman Cemetery at Keston. *Kent Archaeological Review*, Issue 11, 10.

Philp, B. (1972). The Discovery and Preservation of the Roman Villa at Horton Kirby. (Online.) Available from: cka.moon-demon.co.uk/KAR030/KAR030_Horton.htm [Accessed 5 June 2015].

Philp, B. (1980). *The Excavations of the Roman Forts of the Classis Britannica in Dover 1970–1977.* Dover: Kent Archaeological Rescue Unit.

Philp, B. (1982). Romney Marsh and the Roman Fort at Lympne. *Kent Archaeological Review*, Issue 68, 175–91.

Philp, B. (1984). *Excavations in the Darent Valley, Kent.* Dover: Kent Archaeological Rescue Unit.

Philp, B. (1989). *The Roman House with Bacchic Murals at Dover.* Dover: Kent Archaeological Rescue Unit.

Philp, B. (1990). Excavations on the Roman Villa at Folkestone 1989. (Online.) Available from: www.cka.moon-demon.co.uk/KAR099/ KAR099_Folkestone.htm [Accessed 14 June 2014].

Pitassi, M. (2012). *The Roman Navy.* Barnsley: Seaforth.

Pitts, M. (2014). London Eagle Watched Over Roman Tomb. *British Archaeology*, January/February 2014, Issue 134, 8.

Plouviez, J. (1995). A Hole in the Distribution Map: The Characteristic of Small Towns in Suffolk. In: Brown, A.E. ed. *Roman Small Towns in Eastern England and Beyond.* Oxford: Oxbow Books, 69–80.

Pope, M. Senior Research Fellow, Archaeology South-East Boxgrove Projects, Institute of Archaeology, UCL (pers. comm. 21 May 2010).

Pratt, S. Canterbury Project Manager, Canterbury Archaeological Trust (pers. comm. 1 February 2014).

Pritchard, F.A. (1986). Ornamental Stonework from Roman London. *Britannia*, V.17, 169–89.

Proctor, J. (2012). Roman Faverdale, A Frontier Trading Settlement. *Current Archaeology*, Issue 273, 20–5.

Pryor, F. (2004). *Britain AD: : A Quest for Arthur, England and the Anglo-Saxons.* Glasgow: Harper Collins.

Rackham, O. (1997). *The Illustrated History of the Countryside.* London: Orion Publishing.

Rady, J. (1992). *Archaeological Investigation at Teston, Maidstone, Kent.* Unpublished: Canterbury Archaeological Trust.

Rady, J., and Shand, G. (2004). *An Archaeological Evaluation of the Former ADT Building Site, Florence Road, Maidstone.* Unpublished: Canterbury Archaeological Trust.

Reece, R. (1980). Town and Country: The End of Roman Britain. *World Archaeology*, V.12/1, 77–92.

Reece, R. (1981). The Third Century, Crisis or Change? In: King, A. and Hennig, M. eds *The Roman West in the Third Century.* Oxford: BAR/ Archaeological & Historical Associates Ltd.

Richardson, A. Outreach and Archives Manager, CAT (pers. comm. 21 June 2013).

Rigold, S.E. (1969). The Roman Haven of Dover. *The Archaeological Journal*, Issue 126, 79–100.

Robertson, A.S. (1974). Romano-British Coin Hordes: Their Numismatic, Archaeological and Historical Significance. In: Casey, J. and Reece, R. eds *Coins and the Archaeologist.* Oxford: BAR/Archaeological & Historical Associates Ltd, 12–36.

Robertson, Reverend Canon S. (1876). Medieval Folkestone. *Archaeologia Cantiana*, V.10, civ.

Robertson, Reverend Canon S. (1883). Traces of Roman Occupation in and Near Maidstone. *Archaeologia Cantiana*, V.15, 68–88.

Rowsome, P. (1996). The Billingsgate Roman House and Bath – Conservation and Assessment. *London Archaeologist*, V.7/16, 421–22.

Rowsome, P. (1999). The Huggin Hill Baths and Bathing in London: Barometer of the Town's Changing Circumstances? In: DeLaine, J. and Johnston, D. eds *Roman Baths and Bathing*. Portsmouth: Journal of Roman Archaeology Supplementary Series Number 37, 263–77.

Rubel, R.C. (2012). Command of the Sea. *Naval War College Review*, V.65, 1–14.

Rudling, D. (16 November 2013). Roman Period Settlement and Land-use in the Sussex Ouse – Presentation at CBA South-East Conference on Landscapes of South-Eastern Britain During the Roman Period.

Rudling, D. Academic Director, The Sussex School of Archaeology (pers. comm. 19 November 2013).

Rudling, D. Academic Director, The Sussex School of Archaeology (pers. comm. 3 March 2014).

Rudling, D., Cartwright, C., Swift, G., Foster, S., Shepherd, J., Hinton, P. and Tebbutt, F. (1986). The Excavation of a Roman Tilery on Great Cansiron Farm, East Sussex. *Britannia*, V.17, 191–230.

Rule, M. and Monaghan, J. (1993). *A Gallo-Roman Trading Vessel from Guernsey: The Excavation and Recovery of a Third Century Shipwreck.* St Peter Port: Guernsey Museum Monograph 5.

Russel, Dr A. (5 October 2002). Archaeology Unit Manager, Southampton City Council Archaeology Unit (Speech at Museum of London Conference on *Classis Britannica*, accessed at www.classis-britannica. co.uk/sml/index.htm).

Russel, Dr A. Archaeology Unit Manager, Southampton City Council Archaeology Unit (pers. comm. 21 May 2010).

Russel, Dr A. and Elliott, G.L. (2013). Survey of Roman Structures in the River Itchen between Clausentum and St Denys, Southampton. Unpublished: Southampton Archaeology Unit.

Russell, B. (2013). Gazetteer of Stone Quarries in the Roman World. (Online.) Available from: www.romaneconomy.ox.ac.uk [Accessed 12 January 2015].

Russell, B. (2013). *The Economics of the Roman Stone Trade*. Oxford: Oxford University Press.

Russell, Dr C. and Staveley, D. (2012). A Geophysical Survey at Great
    Cansiron Farm, Butcherfield Lane, Hartfield, East Sussex. Unpublished:
    Chris Butler Archaeological Services Ltd.
Rye, S. Collections Officer, The Guildhall Museum Rochester (pers.
    comm. 17 March 2014).
Salway, P. (1981). *Roman Britain*. Oxford: Oxford University Press.
Saynor, J. (1974). Roman Cremation Group From East Farleigh. (Online.)
    Available from: cka.moon-demon.co.uk/KAR035/KAR035_Farleigh.
    htm [Accessed 15 July 2013].
Scarre, C. (1995). *Chronicle of the Roman Emperors*. London: Thames and
    Hudson Ltd.
Schäfer, A. and Trier, M. (2013). Cologne – Revealing a Roman Gateway
    to the Rhine. *Current World Archaeology*, Issue 59, 32–6.
Scott, E. (1993). *A Gazetteer of Roman Villas in Britain*. Leicester: Leicester
    University Archaeological Research Centre.
Sealey, Dr. P. Curator of Archaeology, Colchester Museum (pers. comm.
    10 January 2014).
Selkirk, R. (1983). *The Piercebridge Formula*. Cambridge: Patrick
    Stephens Ltd.
Selkirk, R. (1995). *On the Trail of the Legions*. Ipswich: Anglia Publishing.
Selkirk, R. (2001). *Chester-le-Street & Its Place in History*. Durham:
    CASDEC Ltd.
Severn, J. (1975). *The Teston Story*. Teston: Rufus Fay Publications.
Shaffrey, R. (2006). *Grinding and Milling. A Study of Romano-British Rotary
    Querns and Millstones Made From Old Red Sandstone*. Oxford: BAR/
    Archaeological & Historical Associates Ltd.
Shaffrey, R. and Allen, J.R.L. (2014). A Complete Whetstone of Wealden
    Lithology from the Roman Site at Tackley, Oxfordshire. *Britannia*,
    45 (November 2014), 288–93.
Sheldon, H. (27 November 2010). Enclosing Londinium: The Roman
    Landward and Riverside Walls – Presentation to the London and
    Middlesex Archaeological Society Local History Conference.
Skelton, S. (2010). *UK Vineyards Guide*. London: Stephen Skelton.
Skelton, S. Author, UK Vineyards Guide 2010 (pers. comm. 1
    October 2012).
Smart, J.G.O., Bisson, G. and Worssam, B.C. (1975). *Geology of the Country
    around Canterbury and Folkestone – British Geological Survey Memoir*.
    Nottingham: British Geological Survey.
Smith, A. (2013). Roman Britain … As You've Never Seen It Before.
    British Archaeology, Issue 132, 20–3.
Smith, J. (1839). *The Topography of Maidstone and its Environs*. Maidstone:
    J. Smith Publisher.

Southern, P. (2012). *Roman Britain – A New History 55 BC–AD 450.* Stroud: Amberley Publishing.

Sowan, P.W. (1977). Reigate Stone in Kent. *Kent Archaeological Review.* (Online.) Available from: cka.moon-demon.co.uk/KAR048/KAR048_Reigate.htm [Accessed 10 February 2014].

Spain, R.J. (1984). Romano-British Watermills. *Archaeologia Cantiana,* V.100, 101–28.

Spencer, D. (2013). *The Dean Street Quarry – BA Dissertation.* Unpublished: University of Kent.

Spencer, D. Chairperson, Farleigh's History Society (pers. comm. 17 May 2013).

Starr, C.G. (1941). *The Roman Imperial Navy 31 BC–AD 324.* New York: Cornell University Press.

Staveley, D. Geophysical Survey Consultant, Chris Butler Archaeological Services Ltd (pers. comm. 28 December 2012).

Staveley, D. (16 November 2013). The Sussex Roman Road Network – Presentation at CBA South-East Conference on Landscapes of South-Eastern Britain During the Roman Period.

Stevens, S. (2014). Archaeological Investigations at Maidstone Hospital. Hermitage Lane, Barming. *Archaeologia Cantiana,* V.134, 141–52.

Strong, D.E. (1968). The Monument. In: Cunliffe, B. ed. *5th Report on the Excavations on the Roman Fort at Richborough, Kent.* Oxford: Oxford University Press, 40–73.

Stuart-Hutcheson, A. (2012). *The High Weald Roman Coin Hoard.* (Online.) Available from: brightonmuseums.org.uk/discover/2012/07/13/the-high-weald-roman-coin-hoard/ [Accessed 12 August 2013].

Symonds, M. (2013). Roman Track and Ore. *Current Archaeology,* Issue 279, 6–7.

Symonds, M. (2014). Emerson's Green: Live and Let Dye. *Current Archaeology,* Issue 287, 8.

Symonds, R.P. and Wade, S.M. (1989). A Remarkable Jar Found Inside an Amphora Cremation Chamber at Colchester. *Journal of Roman Pottery Studies,* V.2, 85.

Tatton-Brown, T. (2014). Gossenstein: Discovering An Unexpected Source of English Cathedral Columns. *Current Archaeology,* Issue 289, 38–41.

Taylor, C.C. (1982). 'The Nature of Romano-British Settlement', In: Miles, D. ed. *Romano-British Countryside.* Oxford: BAR/Archaeological & Historical Associates Ltd, 1–15.

Taylor, J. (1994). The idea of the villa. Reassessing Villa Development in South-East Britain. In: Toymans, N. and Derks, T. ed. *Villa Landscapes in the Roman North.* Amsterdam: Amsterdam University Press, 179–194.

Taylor, J. (2007). *An Atlas of Roman Rural Settlement in England*. York: CBA Research Report No. 151.

Taylor, J. (2013). Encountering Romanitas: Characterising the Role of Agricultural Communities in Roman Britain. *Britannia*, V.44, 171–90.

Taylor, M.V. (1932). Country Houses and Other Buildings. In: Page, W. ed. *The Victoria History of the Counties of England – Kent*, London: St Catherine Press, 102–27.

Taylor, M.V., Jessup, R.F., and Hawkes, C.F.C. (1932). Topographical Index. In: Page, W. ed. *The Victoria History of the Counties of England – Kent*. London: St Catherine Press, 144–77.

The Proposed Site of the A228 Roundabout and Services Bridge, (New Medway Works and Quarry, Holborough, Kent). Unpublished: Archaeology South-East, 2004).

Tomlin, R.S.O. (1996). A Five-Acre Wood in Kent. In: Bird, J., Hassall, M.W.C. and Sheldon, H. eds *Interpreting Roman London: Papers in Memory of Hugh Chapman*. Oxford: Oxbow Books, 209.

Trinder, B. (2013). *Britain's Industrial Revolution*. Lancaster: Carnegie Publishing.

Veen, van der M., Livarda, A., and Alistair Hill (2008). New Foods in Roman Britain – Dispersal and Social Access. *Environmental Archaeology*. V.13, 11–36.

Vego, M. (2014). On Littoral Warfare. *Naval War College Bulletin*, V.68, 30–67.

Vincent, A. (2007). *Roman Roads of Kent*. Midhurst: Middleton Press.

Visser, R.M. (2009). Growing and Felling Romans: Theory and Evidence Related to Silvicultural Systems. In: Moore, A., Taylor, G., Girdwood, P., Harris, E. and Shipley, L. eds *TRAC 09: Proceedings of the 19th Annual Theoretical Roman Archaeology Conference, Ann Arbor and Southampton*. Oxford: Oxbow, 11–22.

Waddlegrove, A.C. and Waddlegrove, E. (1990). Archaeology and Research into Sea-Level During the Roman Era: Towards a Methodology Based on Highest Astronomical Tide. *Britannia*, V.21, 253–66.

Wainright, G.J. (1991). Exploring Our Past: Strategies for the Archaeology of England. London: Historic Buildings and Monuments Commission for Britain, 1991.

Wallace, Dr L. (16 November 2013). A Newly Discovered Roman Villa in Bourne Park, Canterbury – Presentation at CBA South-East Conference on Landscapes of South-Eastern Britain During the Roman Period.

Walters, B. (1998). Huge Roman Quarry Found in North Wiltshire. *The Bulletin for the Association of Roman Archaeology*, Issue 6, 8–9.

Walton, P. (2008). The Finds from the River. In: Cool, H.E.M. and Mason, D.J.P. eds *Roman Piercebridge, Excavations by D.W. Harding and Peter Scott 1969–1981*. Durham: The Architectural and Archaeological Society of Durham and Northumberland, 286–93.

Ward, A. (1999). *An Archaeological Watching Brief at Tovil Mill, Tovil Hill, Maidstone*. Unpublished: Canterbury Archaeological Trust.

Ward, A. (2013). More Confusing Bits of the Archaeology of Rochester. *Kent Archaeological Review*, Issue 191, 49–57.

Ward, A. (2014). More Archaeological Problems at Rochester Cathedral. *Kent Archaeological Review*, Issue 196, 204–15.

Ward Perkins, J.B. (1971). Quarrying in Antiquity: Technology, Tradition and Social Change, *Proceedings of the British Academy*, V.57. Oxford: Oxford University Press.

Warry, P. (2010). Legionary Tile Production in Britain. *Britannia*, V.41, 127–47.

Watson, S. (8 March 2015). Excavations at Bloomberg London: New Discoveries Along the Wallbrook. Presentation at the Royal Archaeological Institute.

Webster, D., Webster, H. and Perch, D.F. (1967). A Possible Vineyard of the Romano-British Period at North Thoresby, Lincolnshire. *Lincolnshire History and Archaeology*, Issue 2, 55–61.

Weekes, J. (2014). Interpretation of the Site. In: O'Shea, L. and Weeks, J. eds *Evidence of a Distinct Focus of Romano-British Settlement at Maidstone? Excavations at Church Street 2011–12. Archaeologia Cantiana*, V.135, 147–50.

Weekes, R. (2012). MAAG Lead Scroll. Kent Archaeological Society Newsletter, Issue 94, 4.

Welch, M. (2007). Anglo-Saxon Kent to AD 800. In: Williams, H. ed. *The Archaeology of Kent to 800AD*. Woodbridge: The Boyden Press and Kent County Council, 187–250.

Wenban-Smith, F. (2007). The Paleolithic Archaeology of Kent. In: Williams, H. ed. *The Archaeology of Kent to 800AD*. Woodbridge: The Boyden Press and Kent County Council, 25–66.

Wheeler, R.E.M. (1932). Romano-British Remains – Towns. In: Page, W. ed. *The Victoria History of the Counties of England – Kent*. London: St Catherine Press, 60–101.

Whitby, M. (2002). *Rome at War AD 293–696*. Oxford: Osprey Publishing.

White, R. (2007). *Britannia Prima – Britain's Last Roman Province*. Stroud: Tempus.

Wild, J.P. (2002). The Textile Industry of Roman Britain. *Britannia*, V.33, 1–42.

Wilkinson, P. (2005). *An Archaeological Investigation of the Roman Aisled Stone Building at Hog Brook, Deerton Street, Faversham, Kent.* Unpublished: Kent Archaeological Field School.

Wilkinson, P. (2006). *The Historical Development of the Port of Faversham, Kent 1580–1780.* Oxford: BAR/Archaeological & Historical Associates Ltd.

Wilkinson, P. Director of the Kent Archaeological Field School (pers. comm. 30 April 2010).

Wilkinson, P. Director of the Kent Archaeological Field School (pers. comm. 20 May 2011).

Wilkinson, P. Director of the Kent Archaeological Field School (pers. comm. 4 June 2011).

Wilkinson, P. Director of the Kent Archaeological Field School (pers. comm. 11 June 2011).

Wilkinson, P. Director of the Kent Archaeological Field School (pers. comm. 26 October 2012).

Wilkinson, P. Director of the Kent Archaeological Field School (pers. comm. 6 April 2013).

Wilkinson, P. Director of the Kent Archaeological Field School (pers. comm. 29 April 2012).

Wilkinson, P. Director of the Kent Archaeological Field School (pers. comm. 21 January 2014).

Wilkinson, P. Director of the Kent Archaeological Field School (pers. comm. 31 March 2014).

Willis, S. (2007). Roman Towns, Roman Landscapes: The Cultural Terrain of Town and Country in the Roman Period. In: Fleming, A. and Hingley, R. eds *Prehistoric and Roman Landscapes.* Oxford: Windgather Press.

Willis, Dr S. (2010). *Brief Interim Report on Ongoing Archaeological Works and Observation at Harp Wood, Pedlinge, 2010.* Unpublished: University of Kent.

Wilmott, T. Senior Archaeologist of English Heritage (pers. comm. 20 May 2011).

Wilson, P. (2002). *Roman Catterick and its Hinterland Volume 1.* York: CBA.

Woodcock, A. (1998). *A Gazetteer of Prehistoric, Roman and Saxon Sites in Romney Marsh and the Surrounding Area.* (Online.) Available from: rmrt. org.uk/gazetter-of-prehistoric-roman-and-saxon-sites-in-romney-marsh-and-the-surrounding-area/ [Accessed 10 January 2012].

Worcester, Sir R. (2010). *History of Allington Castle, Kent* (Unpublished: Allington Castle).

Worcester, Sir R. Owner of Allington Castle and former Chancellor, University of Kent (pers. comm. 25 March 2012).

Worcester, Sir R. (17 April 2013). *Rochester's Pivotal Role in the XII Century and Why it Matters Today - Speech at Business Guild Dinner, Rochester Cathedral.* (Online.) Available from: magnacarta800th.com/wp-content/uploads/2013/04/MC-Rochester-Cathedral-speech-17.4.13-website1. pdf [Accessed 15 August 2014].

Worssam, B. (1995). The Geology of Wealden Iron. In: Cleere, H. and Crossley, H. eds *The Iron Industry of The Weald.* Cardiff: Merton Priory Press, 1–30.

Worssam, B. and Tatton-Brown, T. (1993). Kentish Rag and Other Kent Building Stone. *Archaeologia Cantiana,* V.112, 93–126.

Worssam, B.C. (1963). *Geology of the Country Around Maidstone.* Nottingham: British Geological Survey.

Yates, D. (2004). Kent in the Bronze Age: Land, Power and Prestige c.1500–c.700 BC. In: Lawson, T. and Killingray, D. eds *An Historical Atlas of Kent.* Chichester: Phillimore, 13–15.

Yates, N. and Gibson, J.M. (1994). *Traffic and Politics – The Construction and Management of Rochester Bridge AD 43–1993.* Woodbridge: The Boydell Press.

Yorke, B. (1995). *Wessex in the Early Middle Ages.* Leicester: Leicester University Press.

Young, C.J. (1981). The Late Roman Water-Mill at Ickham, Kent, and the Saxon Shore. In: Detsicas, A. ed. *Collectanea Historica: Essays in Memory of Stuart Rigold.* Maidstone: Kent Archaeological Society, 32–9.

Zerbini, A. (2014). The Late Antique Economy: Regional Surveys. *Late Antique Archaeology,* V.10 (1), 41–60.

INDEX